The Great
American
Baking Book

The Great American Baking Book

Breads, Cakes and Cookies

Judi Olstein

Exeter Books

NEW YORK

ISBN 0-671-07611
Typeset by CST, Eastbourne, East Sussex, UK
Food photography pages by Judd Pilossof,
food styling by Susan Culver and Paul Perry.
Color origination by Hong Kong Scannercraft Company Ltd.
Printed by Lee Fung-Asco Printers Ltd.
Printed in Hong Kong
Book design by Mixed Media
This book was produced by Footnote Productions Ltd.
6 Blundell Street
London N7 9BH

CONTENTS

INTRODUCTION

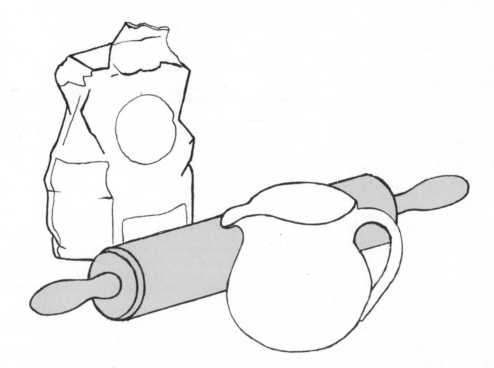

Nothing can compare to the aroma of fresh-baked bread as the oven door is opened, except perhaps for a plateful of delicate little cookies or a perfectly decorated torte or cake. Herein, you will find hundreds of recipes for tried and tested breads, cakes and cookies. They have been collected from every region of the country, from home bakers and professional patissiers, to create one of the most complete collections ever of American regional baking recipes.

Part of the difficulty with presenting a book of baked goods is the current trend toward lighter and more healthful eating. At the same time, however, Americans are rediscovering their food heritage, and baking looms large as a nostalgic reminder of the good things to eat from our past. With a sense of proportion, even cakes can be part of a reasonable diet, especially if they are reserved for a special occasion or a separate experience. After the average American dinner, no self-respecting person conscious of their figure would dare indulge in a portion of Devil's Food cake or New York cheesecake!

Further, the simple fact is that

something baked from scratch at home with the best ingredients will be far, far better than what can be bought at any bakery (with a few rare exceptions). This doesn't mean that you can bake from a mix and call it "homemade." I know a number of churches that have discontinued their traditional fund-raising bake sales simply because cakes from mixes have replaced real home-baked cakes. After all, if churches can't subscribe to truth in advertising, who can?

The effort expended in starting with flour, butter, sugar, eggs and natural flavorings is very little greater than opening a box, and the results will win many more compliments. With modern electric mixers, blenders and food processors, and an accurate oven, anyone who can follow a recipe can produce baked goods of savor and satisfaction. And follow you must! Unlike all the other courses in a meal, baking demands precise measurement. Chemical reactions between yeasts, sugar, fats and heat demand that you take care in sifting, leveling and apportioning your ingredients. If a recipe says to let the dough rise for two hours, don't think you can get by with one hour at a higher heat. It won't work!

Of course, at the end of the day, you will have some splendid food. All of it filling, fattening, loaded with carbohydrates and deeply satisfying. Serve the cakes and cookies by themselves, with first-class tea or coffee. Serve the plain breads with the best butter — sweet by preference — money can buy, the fancy breads and fruit loaves as light desserts or breakfast treats.

Above all, avoid that school of cake decoration that dictates that everything should look as if a bride and groom are about to parachute on top. Be restrained, let the simple beauty of a browned surface be shown off to its fullest. Don't get carried away with spun sugar clouds and icing rosettes. Firstly, they aren't very good for you; secondly, there is no way you will make them look as if they were done by a professional. Which doesn't mean you can't try, just that this sort of work takes a great deal of practice and expensive ingredients. Also, I beg of you, do not use food coloring. Nothing makes a cake or cookie look as artificial as food dyes, and most of them have a synthetic flavor and strange aftertaste.

Almost every baked product can be frozen. But, be warned, the flavor will diminish and the texture will change upon defrosting. The moister breads are the easiest to freeze, and respond best to reheating. Most of the breads in this book can be toasted with excellent results.

America, with its tradition of multi-ethnic diversity, has adapted many foreign recipes to American ingredients and native tastes. From the Scandinavians in the Midwest to the English in New England, from the Spanish in the Southwest to the French in New Orleans, the Germans in Milwaukee and the Irish everywhere . . . the diverse strains have both retained the original recipes and modified them to appeal to a broader range of tastes. THE GREAT AMERICAN BAKING BOOK is one attempt to make more readily available the scrumptious heritage of American regional baking.

BREADS

—YEAST BREADS—

ALMOND BREAD

makes 2 loaves

2 packages active dry yeast
1½ cups very warm water
1 teaspoon sugar
1½ teaspoons salt
2 cups or more flour
½ cup firmly packed light brown sugar
¼ cup sweet butter
½ cup boiling water
4 cups or more whole wheat flour
1½ cups coarsely broken almonds

Sprinkle the yeast into the very warm water in a bowl. Let stand for 2 minutes and then stir until yeast is dissolved. Add the sugar and proof. Let stand for 5 minutes more.

Transfer the yeast to a large mixing bowl. Add the salt and flour and beat until well combined. Let the mixture rise in a warm place until light and bubbly, about 30 minutes.

In a small bowl combine the brown sugar, butter and boiling water. Stir to dissolve. When the mixture has cooled to lukewarm, add it to the yeast and flour mixture. Add the whole wheat flour and nuts. Mix well.

Turn the dough out onto a lightly floured surface. Knead for approximately 10 minutes or until dough is smooth and elastic.

Place the dough in a bowl and cover with a damp towel. Let the dough rise in a warm place until doubled in bulk, about 1½ hours.

Turn the dough out onto a lightly floured surface. Divide in half. Cover the halves and let rest for 10 minutes.

Butter two 8 × 4 × 2-inch loaf pans.

Shape each dough half into a loaf and place in the pans. Cover and let rise until doubled in bulk, about 50 minutes.

Preheat the oven to 350°F.

Bake the loaves for 50 minutes or until done. Remove from oven and cool in pans for 5 minutes. Turn out onto cooling racks and cool completely.

ANADAMA BREAD

makes 1 loaf

½ cup corn meal
3 tablespoons sweet butter
¼ cup dark molasses
2 teaspoons salt
¾ cup boiling water
1 package active dry yeast
¼ cup warm water
1 egg, beaten
3 cups flour

In a large bowl combine the corn meal, butter, molasses, salt and boiling water. Mix well and allow to stand at room temperature until lukewarm.

Dissolve the yeast in the warm water. Stir it into the corn meal mixture. Stir in the egg and 1½ cups of flour. Beat well. Stir in the remaining 1½ cups flour and mix until the dough forms a soft ball.

Place the dough in a greased 9 × 5 × 3-inch loaf pan. Cover with a clean cloth and set in a warm place until dough doubles in bulk, approximately 1 to 1½ hours. Sprinkle the top with a little corn meal and salt. Bake in a 350°F oven for 50 to 55 minutes. Cool completely before slicing.

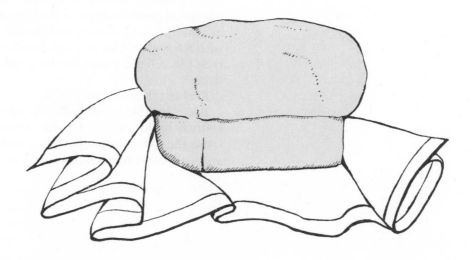

Basil Cheese Bread

makes 1 loaf

¼ cup warm water
1 package active dry yeast
1 tablespoon sugar
¾ cup milk
1 cup grated Parmesan cheese
½ teaspoon salt
¼ cup sweet butter
2 large eggs, lightly beaten
3½ to 4 cups flour
1 medium-sized onion, very finely chopped
2 teaspoons finely chopped garlic
4 cups packed, chopped, fresh basil leaves
black pepper to taste

Combine the warm water, yeast and ½ teaspoon of the sugar together in a small bowl. Stir until yeast and sugar dissolve. Let stand for 15 minutes or until foamy.

Heat the milk in a saucepan along with the Parmesan cheese, salt, half the butter and the remaining sugar. Stir, cooking over low heat, until the butter melts. Remove from the heat and cool mixture to lukewarm.

In a large bowl combine the yeast mixture and the cooled milk mixture. Stir to blend. Add the eggs and the flour. Use only enough flour to form a soft nonsticky dough.

Turn dough out onto a lightly floured board and knead for 10 minutes or until dough is smooth. Shape dough into a ball.

Generously butter a large bowl. Place the dough in the bowl and turn until well coated. Cover the bowl with plastic wrap and let rise in a warm draft-free place for 1½ to 2 hours or until doubled in size.

Melt the remaining butter in a skillet. Add the onion and cooking over a moderately low heat, stir constantly until soft, approximately five minutes. Add the chopped garlic and cook 2 minutes longer. Remove from the heat. Add the chopped basil and black pepper. Stir well and let the mixture cool.

Punch the dough down. Turn dough out onto a floured surface and gently knead in the basil mixture. Shape the dough into a loaf.

Generously butter a 9 × 5 × 3-inch loaf pan. Transfer dough, seam-side down, to the prepared pan. Carefully turn dough around in pan until well coated with butter. Cover pan with a towel and let rise again in a warm draft-free place for 30 minutes or until doubled in size.

Preheat the oven to 350°F.

Bake for 50 to 60 minutes or until bread sounds hollow when lightly tapped. Remove from the oven. Turn bread out onto wire rack and cool completely before slicing.

BLACK BREAD

makes 2 loaves

¾ cup cold water
⅜ cup corn meal
¾ cup boiling water
1 tablespoon sweet butter
1 tablespoon salt
2 tablespoons and 1 teaspoon brown sugar
1½ teaspoons caraway seeds
1 tablespoon unsweetened cocoa
1 tablespoon instant espresso powder
2 packages active dry yeast
¼ cup warm water
2 cups dark rye flour
1 cup whole wheat flour
2 cups flour
flour for kneading
1 egg white beaten with 2 tablespoons water

In a large bowl combine the cold water and the corn meal. Stir until well mixed. Add the boiling water and stir until the mixture has thickened. Then add the butter, salt, sugar, caraway seeds, cocoa and instant espresso. Mix very well and set aside.

In a small bowl dissolve the yeast in the warm water. Let it stand for 2 minutes. Add to the corn meal mixture and stir very well. Gradually blend in all the flours, adding more water if necessary. Stir until a fairly sticky dough forms.

Turn the dough out onto a floured surface and knead, adding more flour as needed to form a firm elastic dough. Shape the dough into a ball.

Generously butter a bowl. Put the dough in the bowl and turn until well coated. Cover the bowl with a towel and let rise in a warm draft-free place for 1 hour or until doubled in size.

Punch down the dough. Knead on a lightly floured surface for 3 minutes.

Butter two 8 × 4 × 2-inch loaf pans. Divide the dough in half and shape into two loaves. Place the loaves in the pans and cover with a towel. Let rise again in a warm draft-free place for 35 minutes or until almost doubled in size.

Prehead the oven to 375°F. Brush the loaves with the egg white mixture and bake in the oven for 50 to 60 minutes or until bread sounds hollow when lightly tapped.

Remove from the oven. Cool in pans on wire racks for 5 minutes. Turn breads out onto racks and cool completely.

BLACK PEPPER BREAD

makes 2 loaves

1 pound fatty thick-cut bacon
½ cup minced shallots
1 teaspoon minced garlic
1 tablespoon active dry yeast
1 teaspoon sugar
½ cup warm water
3 large eggs
1 egg yolk
1 cup warm water
5 to 5½ cups flour
2 teaspoons freshly ground black pepper
6 tablespoons softened sweet butter
1 egg beaten with 1 tablespoon milk

Cut the bacon into ½-inch pieces. In a skillet, cook the bacon over a low heat for 20 minutes or until crisp and golden. Remove pieces with a slotted spoon and drain on paper towels. Coarsely chop the bacon and set aside. Remove all but 2 tablespoons of fat from the skillet.

Cook the shallots in the remaining fat, stirring frequently until lightly golden, approximately 5 minutes. Add the minced garlic and stir. Remove from the heat and cool to room temperature.

In a small bowl combine the yeast, sugar and ½ cup warm water. Stir to blend. Cover and let stand for 5 minutes or until foamy.

Add the eggs and yolk to the yeast mixture and combine until smooth. Pour in the remaining warm water and stir. Add 1½ cups of the flour, the shallot mixture and the pepper. Blend well. Stir in the remainder of the flour, adding 1 cup at a time, alternately with the soft butter. Add enough of the remaining flour to form a soft, sticky dough.

Turn the dough out onto a floured board and gradually knead in the bacon pieces. Knead the dough for 5 minutes or until it is elastic and smooth. Add only as much additional flour as necessary.

Generously butter a bowl. Transfer dough to bowl and turn it until well coated. Cover the bowl with a towel and let rise in a warm draft-free place for 1 hour or until doubled in size.

Punch dough down. Transfer to a lightly floured board and knead for 2 minutes. Divide the dough in half. Cover with a towel and let stand for 10 minutes.

Line two baking sheets with aluminum foil. Shape each piece of dough into an oval measuring approximately 8 × 5 inches. Place ovals on sheets and cover with a towel. Let rise again in a warm draft-free place for 1 hour or until doubled in size.

Preheat the oven to 375°F.

Brush each loaf with the beaten egg and milk combination. Using a sharp knife, make a slash in the top of each loaf. Bake in the oven for 40 minutes or until golden and hollow sounding when lightly tapped. Remove from the oven. Transfer to wire racks and cool completely.

BUTTERMILK BREAD

makes 2 loaves

6 cups flour
1½ cups buttermilk
3 tablespoons sweet butter
4 tablespoons honey
1 teaspoon salt
1 package active dry yeast
¼ cup warm water
melted butter

Place the flour in a large bowl.

In a saucepan heat the buttermilk, butter, honey and salt until the mixture registers 110°F on a cooking thermometer. Remove from the heat.

In a small bowl, dissolve the yeast in the warm water.

Add the yeast, then the heated liquid to the flour. Mix well. It may be necessary to add a little more flour in order to form a dough.

Turn the dough out on a lightly floured surface and knead until smooth and elastic; approximately 10 minutes.

Generously butter a bowl. Place the dough in the bowl and turn dough to coat with the butter. Cover with a warm towel and let rise in a warm draft-free place for 1 hour or until doubled in bulk.

Turn the dough out and punch it down. Cut the dough in half.

Generously butter two 9 × 5 × 3-inch loaf pans. Fit the dough into the pans. Cover the pans with a clean towel and let dough rise in a warm draft-free place for 30 to 35 minutes or until doubled in bulk.

Preheat the oven to 400°F. Bake for 30 to 40 minutes or until the breads sound hollow when lightly tapped. Remove to wire racks. Brush the tops of the breads with melted butter. Cool in the pans on wire racks for 30 minutes. Turn out onto racks and cool completely before slicing.

The honey in this bread makes it a good keeper.

CRUNCHY CORN MEAL BREAD

makes 2 loaves

1 cup water
1 teaspoon salt
½ cup corn meal
2 packages active dry yeast
1 cup warm water
1 tablespoon sugar
1 cup warm milk
2 to 3 teaspoons salt
¼ cup firmly packed dark brown sugar
4 to 4½ cups flour

In a saucepan, heat the 1 cup of water together with the salt to the boiling point. Add the corn meal and stir vigorously, cooking for 4 minutes or until it is thick. Pour mixture into a large bowl and cool.

Combine the sugar and warm water together in a bowl. Add the yeast and stir. Let stand until bubbly, then add to the cooled corn meal mixture. Mix well.

To the corn meal mixture add the warm milk, salt and brown sugar. Mix well. Add the flour, 1 cup at a time, stirring very well after each addition.

Turn the dough out on a lightly floured surface and knead for 10 to 12 minutes or until the dough is smooth and elastic. Add more flour while kneading if necessary.

Generously butter a bowl. Transfer the dough to the bowl and turn it to coat all sides. Cover with a clean towel and let rise in a warm draft-free place for 1 hour or until doubled in bulk.

Using your fist, punch the dough down in the center. Turn dough out on a floured surface. Cut the dough in half and shape into two loaves.

Generously butter two 9 × 5 × 3-inch loaf pans. Place the loaves in the pans and cover with a clean towel. Let rise in a warm draft-free place for 35 minutes or until just level with the tops of the pans.

Preheat the oven to 425°F.

Bake for 10 minutes. Reduce the heat to 350°F and bake 20 to 25 minutes longer or until the bread is golden and sounds hollow when tapped.

Remove the loaves from the pans. Return to the oven for 2 to 3 minutes for a crisp crust. Transfer the loaves to wire racks and cool completely.

CRUNCHY CRACKED WHEAT BREAD

makes 2 loaves

1½ cups boiling water
½ cup fine-grain cracked wheat
1 package active dry yeast
⅓ cup warm water
¼ cup softened sweet butter
1½ tablespoons salt
2 tablespoons molasses
2 tablespoons honey
1 cup milk
1 cup whole wheat flour
4 cups flour

To the boiling water in a saucepan add the cracked wheat. Cook, stirring frequently, for 10 minutes or until the wheat has absorbed all the water. Remove from the heat.

In a large bowl, dissolve the yeast in the warm water. Stir and allow the yeast to proof.

To the cooked wheat mixture add the butter, salt, molasses, honey and milk. Stir well. Allow the mixture to cool to lukewarm and then stir it into the yeast mixture.

With a large spoon stir in the flours, 1 cup at a time. When the dough is stiff turn it out onto a floured surface and knead for at least 10 minutes, working in as much remaining flour as necessary. Continue kneading until the dough is smooth and elastic.

Shape the dough into a ball and place it in a well-buttered bowl. Turn the dough until it is well coated. Cover the bowl with a clean towel and place in a warm draft-free place for 1½ hours or until doubled in size.

Generously butter two 9 × 5 × 3-inch loaf pans.

Punch the dough down and shape into two loaves. Transfer the loaves to the prepared pans and cover with a clean towel. Let rise again in a warm draft-free place for 50 minutes or until the dough reaches the tops of the pans.

Preheat the oven to 375°F.

Bake the breads in the oven for 30 to 35 minutes or until the loaves sound hollow when tapped lightly.

Cool in the pans on wire racks for 10 minutes. Turn out onto racks and cool completely before slicing.

DILL BREAD

makes 1 loaf

¼ cup warm water
1 package active dry yeast
1 cup cottage cheese
2 tablespoons sweet butter, melted and cooled
1 large egg
1 tablespoon sugar
1 teaspoon salt
4 teaspoons dried dill seeds
2 to 3 cups flour

In a large bowl combine the warm water and yeast. Let mixture stand for 5 minutes.

In a medium-sized bowl, combine the cottage cheese, butter, egg, sugar and salt. Stir until well mixed. Add the dill and mix well. Add cottage cheese mixture to yeast mixture and stir until very well blended. Add 2 cups of the flour and stir until well combined. Add enough additional flour to form a soft dough.

Transfer dough to a lightly floured board and knead for 2 to 3 minutes. Add more flour as needed in order to keep the dough from sticking.

Butter a large bowl. Transfer dough to bowl, turning until well coated. Cover with a towel and let rise in a warm draft-free area for 1 hour or until doubled in size.

Punch the dough down. Transfer to a floured surface and cover with a towel. Let dough rest for 5 minutes.

Butter a 9 × 5 × 3-inch loaf pan.

Flatten the dough with your hand and shape into a loaf. Place dough in the prepared pan and cover. Let rise again in a warm draft-free area for 45 minutes or until doubled in size.

Preheat the oven to 375°F.

Bake for 50 minutes or until top is golden and bread sounds hollow when tapped lightly. Remove from the oven. Cool in pan on wire rack for 5 minutes. Turn bread out onto rack and cool completely before slicing.

HOLIDAY BREAD

makes 2 loaves

½ cup warm water
1 package active dry yeast
1 cup softened sweet butter
¼ cup sugar
1 teaspoon grated lemon peel
1 teaspoon salt
4½ cups flour
6 large eggs

FILLING:
⅔ cup firmly packed light brown sugar
2 egg yolks, beaten
½ cup melted sweet butter
2 tablespoons milk
¼ teaspoon pure vanilla extract
2 cups chopped walnuts

In a bowl combine the warm water and yeast. Stir well and let stand.

In a large bowl beat together the butter and sugar until light and fluffy. Add the lemon peel, salt, 1 cup flour, the eggs and the yeast mixture. Beat very well. Add the remaining flour, stirring until smooth.

Butter a large bowl. Turn dough into the bowl and cover with a towel. Let rise in a warm draft-free place for 1 hour or until doubled in size. Cover bowl and refrigerate overnight.

Remove dough from refrigerator and stir down with a large wooden spoon. Let dough stand at room temperature while you prepare the filling.

In a small bowl combine the brown sugar, egg yolks and 3 tablespoons of the melted butter. Mix well. Add the milk and vanilla extract; stir well. Stir in the walnuts.

Punch down the dough in the center. Divide in half and return one half wrapped in foil to the refrigerator. Roll out the remaining half on a floured board to form a 14 × 9-inch rectangle.

Brush the top of the dough with 1 tablespoon of the melted butter, then spread with half of the filling. Roll the dough up, beginning at the short ends, until the ends meet in the center. Transfer the dough, rolled side-up, to a buttered 9 × 5 × 3-inch loaf pan. Brush the top with some melted butter.

Repeat the above process with the remaining dough, filling and melted butter. Cover both pans with clean towels and let rise in a warm draft-free area for 40 to 50 minutes or until doubled in size.

Preheat the oven to 350°F.

Bake for 35 to 40 minutes or until golden. Remove from the oven and cool in pans on wire racks for 10 minutes. Turn bread out onto racks and cool completely.

HONEY BREAD

makes 2 loaves

1¼ cups milk
2 teaspoons salt
4 tablespoons sweet butter
¼ cup light honey
¼ cup sugar
2 packages active dry yeast
1½ cup lukewarm water
¼ teaspoon sugar
1 large egg
5 cups flour

In a large saucepan combine the milk, salt, butter, honey and ¼ cup sugar. Cook over low heat until the butter is melted.

Dissolve the yeast in the water with ¼ teaspoon sugar. Add to the heated milk mixture. Add the egg and flour. Combine thoroughly.

Knead the dough for 10 minutes. Place the dough in a large greased bowl. Cover with a clean cloth or a piece of plastic wrap. Place the bowl in the oven (do not heat the oven) with a bowl of hot water underneath. Let the dough rise until doubled in bulk, approximately 1 hour.

Remove the dough from the oven and divide in half. Knead each half for 1 minute. Place the halves in greased 9 × 5 × 3-inch loaf pans. Place the pans in the oven with a bowl of hot water underneath until the dough rises above the edge of the pans. This should take about 1 hour.

Bake at 350°F for 30 minutes or until the bread is lightly browned, firm to the touch, and sounds hollow when tapped. Cool thoroughly before slicing.

HUTZEL BROD FRUIT BREAD

makes 4 to 5 small loaves

3 cups dried pears
2 cups pear juice
1 package active dry yeast
3 cups flour
½ teaspoon salt
⅓ teaspoon baking soda
¼ cup lard
½ cup sweet butter
2 eggs
1 cup firmly packed dark brown sugar
1 pound dark seedless raisins, plumped
2 teaspoons cinnamon

Stew the dried pears gently in the juice for 30 minutes in a saucepan. Drain the juice from the pears into a large bowl. Dissolve the yeast in a ¼ cup warm water and add it to the juice. Set the pears aside.

Combine the flour and salt in a bowl. Add to the yeast-juice mixture. Cover and let stand overnight.

In the morning add to this mixture the baking soda dissolved in 1 tablespoon warm water. Mix the lard, butter, eggs and sugar in a large bowl. Dice the pears, sift flour over them, and add to bowl. Add the raisins and cinnamon. Add additional flour as needed and knead.

Set the dough aside in a greased bowl. Cover and let rise for 1 hour or until nearly doubled in bulk.

Preheat the oven to 350°F.

When the dough has risen, punch it down and knead for 1 minute. Shape the dough into 4 to 5 small loaves. Brush the tops with melted butter. Place the loaves on a greased baking sheet and bake 1¼ hours. Remove from oven when done and cool completely before serving.

LIMPA (SWEDISH RYE BREAD)

makes 2 round loaves

2 packages active dry yeast
½ cup warm water
½ cup firmly packed dark brown sugar
⅓ cup molasses
2 tablespoons sweet butter
1 tablespoon salt
3 tablespoons grated orange rind
¾ teaspoon anise seeds
1½ cups hot water
2½ cups medium rye flour
3 to 3½ cups flour
corn meal
milk

Add the yeast to the warm water and allow it to soften for 2 minutes. Stir to dissolve. Set aside.

In a large bowl combine the brown sugar, molasses, butter, salt, orange rind and anise seeds. Add the hot water and mix well. Let the mixture cool to lukewarm.

Add 1 cup rye flour to the mixture and beat until smooth. Add the yeast and stir. Slowly add the rest of the rye flour. Beat well. Add enough unbleached flour to make a soft dough, about 2½ to 3 cups. Beat until the dough starts to come away from the side of the bowl.

Turn the dough out onto a lightly floured surface and let rest for 8 to 10 minutes.

Knead in enough additional unbleached flour to make a smooth dough that does not stick. Shape the dough into a ball and place in a well-oiled deep bowl. Turn the dough to coat it. Cover with a clean towel and let rise in a warm place until doubled in bulk, about 2 hours.

Punch down the dough and remold it into a ball. Turn completely over in the bowl. Cover and let rise again until almost doubled in bulk, about 1 hour.

Punch down the dough and turn out onto a lightly floured surface. Divide the dough into halves and shape each half into a well-rounded smooth ball.

Grease a baking sheet and sprinkle it with cornmeal. Place the loaves on the sheet and cover with a clean towel. Let the dough rise again until doubled in bulk, about 30 minutes.

Preheat the oven to 375°F.

Bake the loaves for 25 to 30 minutes. Transfer to cooling racks and brush immediately with milk. Cool completely.

NO-KNEAD BROWN BREAD

makes 1 loaf

**3¾ cups whole wheat flour
1½ packages active dry yeast
2 cups warm water
2 tablespoons molasses
1 tablespoon salt**

Place the flour in a large ovenproof bowl. Put the bowl in the oven on the lowest possible setting. Leave in the oven for 30 minutes or until both the bowl and the flour are warm.

In a small bowl, dissolve the yeast in ½ cup of the warm water. Stir and then blend in the molasses. Allow the mixture to stand to proof the yeast.

Add another ½ cup of the water to the yeast mixture. Add the yeast mixture and the salt to the flour. Mix well. Add enough of the remaining water to form a wet, sticky dough.

Generously butter a 9 × 5 × 3-inch loaf pan. Turn the dough directly into the pan. Cover the pan with a clean towel and place in a warm draft-free place until the dough has risen by one-third its original size, approximately 50 minutes.

Preheat the oven to 450°F.

Bake the bread in the oven for 50 minutes or until it is golden and sounds hollow when lightly tapped. Remove the bread from the pan and turn off the oven. Return the bread to the cooling oven for 20 minutes. Remove from the oven and cool on a wire rack.

NO-KNEAD WHITE BREAD

makes 2 loaves

**1 cup milk
3 tablespoons sugar
1 tablespoon salt
2 tablespoons sweet butter
1 cup very warm water
2 packages active dry yeast
4¼ cups flour**

In a saucepan, scald the milk. Add the sugar, salt and butter and stir until the sugar is dissolved and the butter is melted. Remove the mixture from the heat and cool it to lukewarm.

Into a very large bowl, pour the warm water. Sprinkle in the yeast and stir until it dissolves. Add the cooled milk mixture and stir.

Add the flour and stir until blended. Beat for 1 to 2 minutes.

Cover the bowl with a clean towel and let the dough rise in a warm draft-free place for 40 minutes, or until it is doubled in bulk.

Preheat the oven to 375°F. Butter two 9 × 5 × 3-inch loaf pans.

With a wooden spoon, stir down the batter. Beat for 30 seconds.

Evenly divide the dough between the two pans. Bake for 50 minutes or until the breads are golden and hollow-sounding when tapped.

Remove the loaves from the oven. Cool in the pans on a wire rack for 15 minutes. Turn the loaves out of the pans onto racks and cool completely before slicing.

NO-SALT WHITE BREAD

makes 1 loaf

½ cup milk
1½ tablespoons sugar
4 teaspoons sweet butter
½ cup very warm water
1 package active dry yeast
3 cups sifted flour
melted butter

In a saucepan, scald the milk. Add the sugar and butter and stir until the sugar is dissolved and the butter is melted. Remove from the heat and cool to lukewarm.

Pour the warm water into a large bowl. Sprinkle in the yeast and stir until it dissolves. Add the cooled milk mixture and stir.

Add the flour to the mixture and stir until blended. Turn the dough out onto a lightly floured surface. Knead quickly but lightly until the dough is smooth and elastic, approximately 5 to 8 minutes. Transfer the dough to a generously buttered bowl. Brush the top of the dough with melted butter. Cover the bowl with a clean towel and let the dough rise in a warm draft-free place for 35 minutes or until doubled in bulk.

Remove the dough from the bowl. Punch the dough down with your fist and shape it into one loaf.

Generously butter a 9 × 5 × 3-inch loaf pan. Transfer the dough to the loaf pan and cover with a clean towel. Allow the dough to rise in a warm draft-free place for 45 minutes or until doubled in bulk.

Preheat the oven to 400°F.

Place the pan in the oven and bake for 50 minutes or until the bread is golden and sounds hollow when lightly tapped.

Cool the bread in the pan on a wire rack for 15 minutes. Turn the bread out onto the rack and cool completely before slicing.

Old-Fashioned Oatmeal Bread

makes 2 loaves

¾ cup milk
1 package active dry yeast
1 cup quick-cooking oatmeal
1¼ cups boiling water
1½ teaspoons salt
½ cup molasses
1 tablespoon sweet butter
5 cups flour
melted butter

Heat the milk in a saucepan until a thick skin forms on top. Remove the saucepan from the heat and skim.

When the milk has cooled to lukewarm, stir in the yeast.

In a large mixing bowl combine the oatmeal, boiling water, salt, molasses and sweet butter. Stir in the flour and the milk and yeast mixture. Mix thoroughly with your hands.

Cover the bowl with a clean towel and let stand in a warm place until doubled in bulk, about 1½ hours.

Turn the dough out onto a lightly floured surface and knead gently for 3 minutes. Divide dough into halves and shape each half into a loaf. Place into two buttered 9 × 5 × 3-inch loaf pans and cover with clean towels. Let dough rise until doubled in bulk, about 50 to 60 minutes.

Preheat the oven to 350°F.

Bake the loaves for 1 hour or until well browned. Remove from oven and brush tops with melted butter. Cool in the pans for 15 minutes. Turn out onto cooling racks and cool completely.

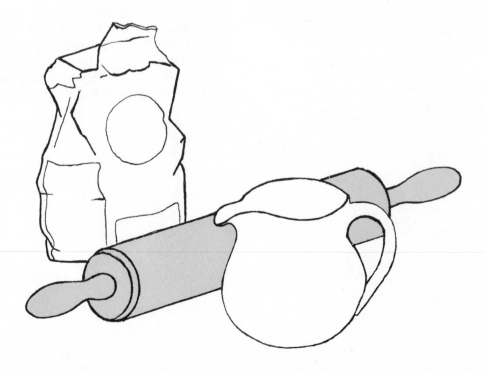

OLD-FASHIONED WHITE BREAD

makes 2 loaves

2 cups warm milk
2 tablespoons sugar
1 package active dry yeast
¼ cup melted sweet butter
1 tablespoon salt
5 to 6 cups flour
1 large egg white, slightly beaten

In a small bowl combine ½ cup of the warm milk and the sugar. Add the yeast and stir until it is completely dissolved. Set aside and allow it to proof for 3 minutes.

Pour the remaining milk, the melted butter and the salt into a large bowl. Add the flour, 1 cup at a time, stirring with a wooden spoon. After you have added 3 cups, stir in the yeast mixture. Continue to stir in more flour until the dough is firm. This should require 4 to 5 cups of flour.

Turn the dough out on a floured surface and knead, adding more flour as necessary. Continue kneading and adding flour until the dough is no longer sticky, but supple and smooth. This may take as long as 10 minutes.

Generously butter a bowl and place the dough in it. Turn the dough in the bowl so that all sides are coated with the butter. Cover the dough with a clean towel and let rise in a warm draft-free place for 1½ to 2 hours or until doubled in size.

Punch down the dough with your fist. Turn the dough out on a floured surface and knead for 4 to 5 minutes. Divide the dough in half and shape into loaves.

Generously butter two 9 × 5 × 3-inch loaf pans. Place the loaves in the pans. Cover with a clean towel and let rise in a warm draft-free place for 45 minutes or until doubled in size.

Preheat the oven to 400°F.

Using a sharp knife, slash the tops of the loaves and brush with the egg white. Bake for 40 to 45 minutes or until the bread sounds hollow when lightly tapped. For an extra crisp crust carefully remove the bread from the pans and return them to the oven for 3 to 5 minutes. Cool the breads on wire racks. Slice when cool.

ONE-RISE BREAD

makes 2 free-form loaves

2 cups lukewarm water
1 tablespoon sugar
1 package active dry yeast
1¼ tablespoons salt
6 to 7 cups flour (plain flour)
corn meal

Pour the water into a large bowl. Sprinkle in the sugar and yeast. Stir until well blended. Let the mixture stand at room temperature for 10 minutes.

Stir the salt into the mixture. Add the flour, 1 cup at a time, stirring until a stiff dough forms.

Turn the dough out onto a lightly floured surface and knead for 8 to 10 minutes or until smooth and elastic. Add additional flour as needed to prevent the dough from sticking.

Generously butter a large bowl. Transfer the dough to the bowl and turn it several times until well coated. Cover the bowl with plastic wrap and let rise in a warm draft-free spot for 1½ hours or until doubled in size.

Preheat the oven to 400°F. Butter two baking sheets and sprinkle them generously with corn meal.

Punch the dough down and transfer it to a lightly floured surface. Knead until smooth, approximately 5 minutes. Divide the dough into two equal parts and shape each into a round loaf.

Transfer the loaves to the baking sheets. Cover with towels and let stand for 5 minutes. Using a sharp knife, slash the top of each loaf.

Bake for 45 minutes, or until the loaves are golden and sound hollow when the bottom is lightly tapped. Transfer the breads to wire racks. Cool completely before slicing.

Onion Herb Bread

makes 1 loaf

½ cup milk
1½ tablespoons sugar
¾ teaspoon salt
1 tablespoon sweet butter
1 package active dry yeast
½ cup warm water
2¼ cups whole wheat flour
1 medium-sized onion, very finely chopped
1 teaspoon dried rosemary, crushed
1 teaspoon dried sweet basil, crushed
½ teaspoon dried dill

In a small saucepan, scald the milk. Add the sugar, salt and butter to the milk. Stir until butter is melted. Cool mixture to lukewarm.

Combine the yeast and warm water in a large bowl. Let stand for 5 to 10 minutes. Add the cooled milk mixture to the yeast. Mix well. Stir in the flour, the onion and the rosemary, basil and dill. Mix very well until the batter is smooth.

Cover bowl with a towel and let rise in a warm draft-free place for 2 hours or until the dough has tripled in size. Stir the dough down with a large wooden spoon. Beat for 2 minutes.

Butter a 9 × 5 × 3-inch loaf pan.

Shape the dough into a loaf and transfer it to the prepared pan. Cover with a towel and let rise in a warm draft-free place for 50 minutes or until doubled in size.

Preheat the oven to 350°F.

Bake for 45 to 50 minutes or until bread sounds hollow when lightly tapped. Remove from the oven. Cool in pan on wire rack for 5 minutes. Turn bread out onto rack and cool completely.

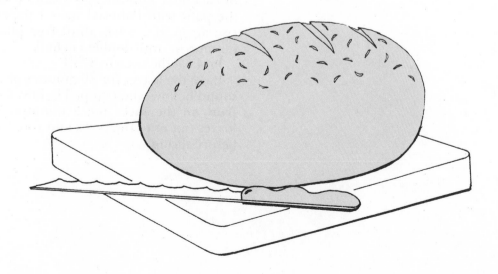

ONION-PARMESAN RYE BREAD

makes 2 loaves

1 teaspoon corn meal
1½ cups warm water
1 tablespoon sugar
2 packages active dry yeast
2 tablespoons sweet butter
1 cup finely chopped onion
2 large eggs
2 tablespoons honey
4 cups flour
1 tablespoon salt
2 cups rye flour
1 cup grated Parmesan cheese
2 tablespoons poppy seeds
1 egg, beaten with 1 tablespoon water and
¼ teaspoon salt

Butter two 9 × 5 × 3-inch loaf pans. Sprinkle each evenly with the corn meal. Set aside.

In a large bowl combine the warm water and sugar. Stir to dissolve the sugar, then sprinkle in the yeast. Stir and let stand for 5 minutes or until foamy.

In a skillet melt the butter over moderate heat. Add the onion and cook, stirring frequently for 5 to 7 minutes or until soft and golden. Remove from the heat.

To the yeast mixture add the 2 eggs and honey. Beat with a whisk to combine. Add 2 cups of the flour along with the salt and the onion. Mix well. Add the rye flour, Parmesan cheese and poppy seeds. Stir with a large wooden spoon until the dough is thick. Slowly work in the remaining flour, adding only enough to make a workable but sticky dough. When the dough forms a ball, knead for 1 minute in the bowl.

Turn the dough out onto a floured surface and knead for 10 minutes; add more flour as necessary.

Oil a large bowl. Place the dough in the bowl and turn until well-coated. Cover the bowl with a clean towel and let rise in a warm draft-free place for 1 hour or until doubled in bulk.

Turn the dough out onto a lightly floured surface and knead gently for 2 minutes. Divide the dough in half and shape into loaves. Put the dough in the pans and brush the top of each loaf with the egg wash. Loosely cover the pans with buttered waxed paper and let rise again in a warm draft-free place for 45 minutes or until doubled in bulk.

Preheat the oven to 375°F.

Bake the loaves for 30 minutes or until they sound hollow when tapped lightly. Cool in the pans on the racks for 5 minutes. Turn the loaves out onto the racks and cool completely before slicing.

ONION AND PARSLEY BREAD

makes 1 round loaf

4 tablespoons sweet butter
1 cup coarsely chopped onion
½ cup very warm water
2 packages active dry yeast
4 tablespoons light brown sugar
1½ cups milk
1 teaspoon salt
1 egg, beaten
5 cups sifted flour
⅓ cup finely chopped parsley
2 tablespoons melted butter

Generously butter an 8-cup soufflé or casserole dish. Set aside.

Melt the butter in a skillet. Add the onion and sauté over moderate heat until lightly browned, about 5 to 8 minutes. Remove from the heat and set aside.

Put the very warm water into a small bowl. Add the yeast and 2 tablespoons of the brown sugar and stir until dissolved. Let stand at room temperature for 10 minutes. The mixture will be bubbly.

Heat the milk in a saucepan over moderate heat until bubbles start to form. Add the salt and the remaining brown sugar to the saucepan. Stir to dissolve. Remove the saucepan from the heat and cool to room temperature. Pour the mixture into a large bowl.

Add the yeast mixture, onions, egg and flour to the milk mixture. Mix with a wooden spoon or electric mixer until very well blended, about 3 to 4 minutes. Add the parsley and stir.

Turn the dough into the prepared dish. Cover the dough with a sheet of buttered waxed paper and then a clean towel. Put the dish in a warm place and let rise until doubled in size, about 45 minutes.

Preheat the oven to 375°F.

Bake the bread until it sounds hollow when tapped, about 35 to 40 minutes. Remove from the oven and carefully turn the bread out onto a wire rack. Brush the top of the loaf with melted butter and serve warm.

ORANGE RYE BREAD

makes 2 small loaves

2 packages active dry yeast
1½ cups warm water
½ cup dark honey
2 tablespoons vegetable oil
2 tablespoons grated orange rind
1 tablespoon salt
1 teaspoon ground cardamom
2½ cups rye flour
2½ cups whole wheat flour
yellow corn meal
softened butter

Place the warm water in a bowl and sprinkle in the yeast. Let stand for 2 minutes and then stir to dissolve.

Pour the yeast mixture into a large bowl and add the honey, oil, orange peel, salt and cardamom. Mix well. Add 1 cup of the rye flour and 1 cup of the whole wheat flour. Stir until smooth, about 2 to 3 minutes. Stir in the remaining flour. Combine thoroughly.

Turn the dough out onto a lightly floured surface. Knead until the dough is smooth and elastic, about 15 to 20 minutes. Form the dough into a ball and place in a lightly buttered bowl. Cover with a clean towel and let rise until doubled in bulk, about 1½ hours.

Punch down the dough. Divide it in half and form the halves into small ovals.

Butter a baking sheet and sprinkle it with corn meal. Place the loaves on the sheet. Make 3 slashes across the top of each loaf with a sharp knife. Cover with a clean towel and let rise again in a warm place until almost doubled in bulk, about 45 minutes.

Preheat the oven to 375°F.

Bake the loaves for 45 minutes or until golden. Remove from oven and brush with softened butter. Cool completely before slicing.

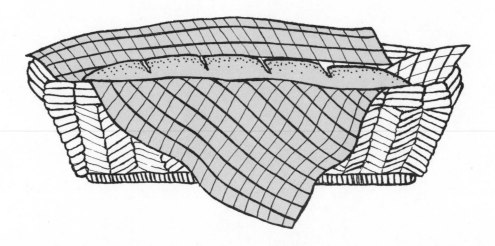

PORTUGUESE SWEET BREAD

makes 3 free-form loaves

2 cups milk
1 package active dry yeast
1½ cups sugar
9 cups or more flour
1 tablespoon salt
4 large eggs
¼ cup sweet butter, melted and cooled

Scald the milk in a saucepan. Remove from the heat and cool to lukewarm.

In a bowl combine ½ cup of the milk, the yeast and 1 tablespoon of the sugar. Stir and let stand for 15 minutes. The mixture will be foamy.

Into a bowl sift 8 cups of the flour with the salt. Set aside.

In a large bowl, beat the eggs until foamy. Add the remaining sugar and beat until mixture is light in color and thick, approximately 5 minutes. Add the yeast mixture and beat until blended. Add the melted butter and stir.

Add the flour alternately with the remaining milk, stirring until a dough forms.

Turn the dough out onto a floured surface and knead, adding more flour to keep it from sticking, for 10 minutes or until elastic and smooth.

Generously butter a large bowl. Transfer the dough to the bowl and turn the dough until well coated. Cover the bowl with plastic wrap and let rise in a warm draft-free area for 1½ hours or until doubled in size.

Punch down the dough. Cover it again and let rise in a warm draft-free area for 1 to 1½ hours or until doubled in size.

Punch the dough down again. Divide the dough into three equal parts and shape each into a round loaf.

Lightly butter 2 to 3 baking sheets. Arrange the loaves on the sheets and cover with towels. Let rise again in a warm draft-free area for 1 hour or until doubled in size.

Preheat the oven to 350°F.

Bake in the oven for 35 to 40 minutes or until golden and hollow-sounding when the bottoms are lightly tapped. Remove from the oven. Transfer to wire racks and cool completely.

POTATO BREAD

makes 1 free-form loaf

3 to 4 medium-sized potatoes
2½ cups warm water
1 package active dry yeast
8 cups flour
1½ tablespoons salt
1½ tablespoons caraway seeds
water

Wash the potatoes. Place them in a saucepan of boiling water, and boil for 30 minutes or until just soft. Drain and when cool enough to handle, peel them. Place the potatoes in a bowl and mash them until they are smooth. Set aside and let cool.

In a large bowl combine ½ cup of the warm water and the yeast. Stir to dissolve the yeast. Add 3 tablespoons of the flour and mix very well. Let the mixture stand at room temperature for 30 minutes.

Add the remaining warm water, the salt and caraway seeds and mix well. Add the flour and 1 cup of the mashed potatoes. Mix very well.

Turn the dough out onto a floured surface and knead for 15 minutes or until the dough is smooth and elastic. Form the dough into a ball.

Generously oil a bowl. Transfer the dough to the bowl and turn several times until well coated. Cover with a towel and place in a warm draft-free place to rise for 1 to 1½ hours or until the dough doubles in size.

Transfer the dough to a board and punch down. Knead for 5 minutes. Shape the dough into a large round loaf.

Generously butter a 12-inch heatproof skillet with well-rounded sides. Transfer the dough to the skillet and cover with a towel. Let rise again in a warm draft-free place for 30 minutes.

Preheat the oven to 400°F.

Brush the top of the loaf with water. Make a deep cross shape in the center of the loaf with a sharp knife.

Bake for 1 to 1¼ hours or until the bread is brown and sounds hollow when lightly tapped. Turn the bread out of the skillet and cool on a wire rack.

PUMPERNICKEL

makes 2 loaves

2 packages active dry yeast
1½ cups very warm water
½ cup dark molasses
2 tablespoons caraway seeds
1 tablespoon salt
2 cups rye flour
4 cups flour
3 tablespoons softened sweet butter

Add the yeast to the warm water in a bowl. Let stand for 2 minutes and then stir to dissolve.

In a large bowl combine the yeast, molasses, caraway seeds and salt. Stir to mix well. Add the rye flour and 2 cups flour. Beat until well mixed. Add the butter and mix well. Stir in the remaining flour. Turn the dough out onto a lightly floured surface and knead until smooth, about 5 to 7 minutes.

Place the dough in an oiled bowl. Cover with a clean towel and let rise in a warm place until doubled in bulk, about 2 hours.

Turn the dough out onto a lightly floured surface. Divide into halves and let rest, covered with a clean towel, for 10 minutes. Shape each half into a loaf.

Butter 2 9 × 5 × 3-inch loaf pans. Place the dough into the pans and cover. Let rise until doubled in bulk, about 50 minutes.

Preheat the oven to 450°F.

Bake the loaves for 10 minutes. Lower the temperature to 350°F and continue baking for 30 minutes.

Remove to cooling racks. Cool in the pan for 10 minutes. Turn out onto racks and cool completely.

SAFFRON BREAD

makes 2 loaves

¼ teaspoon crumbled saffron threads
½ cup boiling water
2 cups milk
½ cup melted sweet butter
1 package active dry yeast
2 tablespoons warm water
1 cup sugar
½ teaspoon salt
½ teaspoon nutmeg
6 to 6½ cups sifted flour
grated rinds of 2 lemons
2 cups currants
1 tablespoon melted sweet butter

Steep the saffron in the boiling water for 1 hour. Strain and reserve the saffron liquid.

In a saucepan, scald the milk and place it in a large mixing bowl. Add the saffron liquid and the melted butter. Stir well. Dissolve the yeast in the warm water. Stir it into the warm milk mixture. Add the sugar, salt and nutmeg. Sift in the flour and mix well. Add the grated lemon rind and the currants. Mix until well blended. The dough should be stiff.

Cover the mixing bowl with a clean towel. Let rise in a warm place until doubled in bulk, about 1½ hours.

Remove the dough from the bowl and punch it down. Knead on a lightly floured surface until smooth, about 2 minutes.

Butter 2 9 × 5 × 3-inch loaf pans.

Divide the dough and shape each half into a loaf. Place in loaf pans. Let the dough rise a second time, about 50 to 60 minutes.

Preheat the oven to 350°F.

Bake the loaves for 1 hour or until they are golden and sound hollow when tapped.

Remove the pans to cooling racks and brush the tops of the loaves with melted butter. Cool in the pans for 10 minutes. Turn loaves out onto racks and continue cooling. Cool completely before slicing.

SEASONED FLAT BREAD

makes 2 loaves

1½ cups warm water
1 package active dry yeast
6 cups flour
1 teaspoon olive oil

SEASONING:
2 teaspoons dried oregano
2 teaspoons dried basil
½ teaspoon dried savory
½ teaspoon dried rosemary
2 teaspoons dried lemon peel

In a large bowl, combine the yeast and the warm water. Let rest for 2 minutes.

Add 5 cups of the flour to the yeast mixture. Stir until well combined. Add the remaining flour, a little at a time, stirring until a dough forms. Do not add all the flour if it is not needed.

Transfer the dough to a floured surface and knead for 10 minutes or until dough is no longer sticky and is smooth. Shape the dough into a ball. Place ½ teaspoon of the olive oil into your hand. Roll the dough around in your hand until it is coated with the oil. Place dough in a large bowl and cover with a towel. Let rise in a warm draft-free place for 35 minutes or until doubled in size.

In a small bowl combine the dried oregano, basil, savory, rosemany and lemon peel.

Punch the dough down and divide it in half. Flatten each half until it resembles a plate-sized round. Brush the tops of the loaves with the remaining oil. Sprinkle the tops of the loaves with the remaining oil. Sprinkle the tops of the loaves with the seasoning mixture.

Place the loaves on baking sheets. Cover loaves with bowls and let rise in a warm draft-free place for 30 minutes or until doubled in size.

Preheat the oven to 400°F. Bake for 30 minutes or until tops are golden brown. Remove from the oven. Cool or serve warm.

Sourdough Rye Bread

makes 2 free-form loaves

2 packages active dry yeast
3¼ cups warm water
6 cups flour
2 cups rye flour
2 teaspoons salt
1 tablespoon caraway seeds
1½ teaspoons poppy seeds
2 tablespoons melted sweet butter
2½ tablespoons sugar
corn meal
1 egg beaten with 1 tablespoon water

Prepare the starter 4 days before you wish to make the bread. In a bowl combine 1 package of the yeast, 2 cups of the warm water and 2 cups of the flour. Mix well and cover tightly. Allow the starter to stand for 2 days at room temperature. Refrigerate the starter for at least 1 day. There will be more starter than this recipe needs. If you wish to keep it, add equal parts of warm water and flour equal to what has been used. Let stand at room temperature as above and then refrigerate.

The day before making the dough, combine 1 cup of the starter, the rye flour and 1 cup of the warm water in a bowl. Cover and let stand at room temperature overnight.

The next day, stir down the mixture. Dissolve the remaining package of yeast in the remaining ¼ cup warm water. Add the yeast mixture, salt, caraway seeds, poppy seeds, butter and sugar to the starter mixture. Stir until well combined.

Stir in up to 4 cups of the remaining flour, adding 1 cup at a time. This will produce a stiff but workable dough. Knead the dough for 10 minutes in the bowl and form a ball.

Generously butter a bowl. Transfer the dough to the bowl and turn until it is well coated. Cover with a clean towel and let rise in a warm draft-free area for 2 hours or until doubled in bulk.

Punch down the dough with your fist and divide it in half. Shape each half into a round loaf.

Generously butter two baking sheets and sprinkle them with corn meal. Place the loaves on the sheets and cover with a clean towel. Let rise again in a warm draft-free place for 1 hour or until doubled in bulk.

Preheat the oven to 375°F. Brush each loaf with the egg wash and bake in the oven for 30 minutes or until golden and hollow-sounding when tapped lightly.

Transfer to wire racks and cool, covered with towels. Covering the breads will prevent the crust from becoming too hard.

SPIRAL BREAD

makes 1 loaf

2 tablespoons softened sweet butter
2 shallots, finely chopped
1 cup finely chopped fresh parsley
1 garlic clove, crushed
2 teaspoons finely chopped fresh thyme or
1 teaspoon crumbled dried thyme
15 finely chopped basil leaves or
1 tablespoon crumbled dried basil
1 egg, beaten
salt to taste
cayenne pepper to taste
black pepper to taste
Tabasco sauce to taste
½ cup very warm water
1 package active dry yeast
½ cup scalded milk
1 tablespoon sugar
1 tablespoon salt
4 tablespoons sweet butter
3 to 4 cups flour
1 egg, beaten

Melt the 2 tablespoons softened butter in a large skillet. Add the shallots, parsley, garlic, thyme and basil. Sauté over medium heat, stirring often, for 10 minutes. Put the mixture into a bowl.

Add the egg, salt, cayenne pepper, black pepper and Tabasco sauce to the bowl. Stir to mix well. Set the filling aside.

Put the warm water into a large bowl and add the yeast. Stir to dissolve. Let the mixture stand at room temperature for 10 minutes.

Add the milk, sugar, salt and 4 tablespoons butter to the yeast. Stir until well blended. Add 3 cups of the flour and mix well. Add more flour as needed to form a solid dough. Let the dough rest in the bowl for 10 minutes.

Turn the dough onto a lightly floured surface and knead for 12 to 15 minutes. Put the kneaded dough into a lightly buttered bowl and turn it to coat with the butter. Cover the bowl with a clean towel and let rise in a warm place until doubled in size, about 1 hour.

Punch the dough down and let it rest in the bowl for 12 to 15 minutes.

Turn the dough out onto a lightly floured surface and roll it out into a rectangle that is ¼-inch thick and 10 inches long. Brush the surface of the dough with half the beaten egg. Spread the filling over the dough, leaving a thin border all around. Carefully roll the dough up and seal the edges.

Put the dough into a well-greased 9 × 5 × 3-inch loaf pan. Brush the top of the loaf with the remaining beaten egg. Let the loaf rise in a warm spot for 1 hour.

Preheat the oven to 375°F.

Bake the bread until the top is golden brown, about 50 to 60 minutes. Remove from the oven and cool for 15 minutes on a wire rack. Carefully remove the loaf from the pan and cool completely on the rack.

SPICE BREAD

makes 2 loaves

¾ cup warm water
⅓ cup sugar
2 packages active dry yeast
1¼ cups milk
1½ tablespoons salt
¼ cup softened sweet butter
1 tablespoon ground cinnamon
2 teaspoons freshly grated nutmeg
5 to 6 cups to flour

In a large bowl combine the warm water, sugar and yeast. Stir and dissolve sugar and yeast and let stand for 5 minutes.

In a small saucepan, heat the milk until it is warm. Stir in the salt and butter. Continue stirring until butter melts. Remove from the heat. Add to the yeast mixture and mix well. Add the cinnamon, nutmeg and 4½ cups of the flour, one cup at a time, mixing well after each addition.

Transfer dough to a lightly floured surface and knead for 10 to 12 minutes, adding as much of the remaining flour as needed to keep the dough from sticking. When dough is smooth and slightly elastic, shape it into a ball.

Generously butter a large bowl. Transfer dough to bowl and turn in bowl until well coated. Cover the bowl with plastic wrap and let rise in a warm draft-free area for 50 to 60 minutes or until doubled in size.

Generously butter two 8 × 4 × 2-inch loaf pans.

Punch dough down in the center. Divide dough in half and shape each half into a loaf. Transfer loaves to prepared pans. Cover pans loosely with a towel and let rise in a warm draft-free spot for 30 to 40 minutes or until doubled in size.

Preheat the oven to 425°F.

Bake breads for 10 minutes. Reduce the temperature to 350°F and continue baking for 25 minutes longer or until breads sound hollow when tapped lightly. Remove from the oven. Cool in pans on wire racks for 5 minutes. Turn loaves out of pans onto racks and cool completely.

SUMMER SQUASH BREAD

makes 1 loaf

½ cup lukewarm water
1 tablespoon active dry yeast
1 teaspoon sugar
1½ cups summer squash or zucchini
1 large egg, slightly beaten
¼ cup corn meal
½ cup chopped fresh basil or
2 tablespoons dried basil
3 tablespoons grated Parmesan cheese
1 tablespoon olive oil
1½ teaspoons salt
3 cups flour
1 egg, beaten lightly with 1 teaspoon water

Combine the water, yeast and sugar in the large bowl of an electric mixer. Let the mixture stand for 10 to 15 minutes or until foamy.

Stir in the squash, egg, corn meal, basil, Parmesan cheese, oil and salt. Mix very well.

Add the flour, 1 cup at a time, beating well after each addition. When all the flour has been added, beat the mixture for 5 minutes. Continue beating and add more flour, very gradually, until the dough begins to pull away from the sides of the bowl.

Cover the bowl with plastic wrap and let rise in a warm draft-free place for 1 hour or until doubled in size.

Generously butter a 9 × 5 × 3-inch loaf pan.

Stir the dough down with a wooden spout and transfer to the prepared pan. Using lightly floured hands, pat the dough evenly into the pan. Cover with a towel and let rise again in a warm draft-free place for 45 minutes or until bread sounds hollow when lightly tapped. Remove bread from the oven. Cool in pan on wire rack for 10 minutes. Turnout onto rack and cool completely.

—QUICK BREADS—

APPLE-NUT BREAD

makes 1 loaf

2 cups flour
¾ cup firmly packed light brown sugar
3 teaspoons baking powder
1 teaspoon cinnamon
1 teaspoon salt
½ teaspoon baking soda
1 cup chopped pecans or walnuts
¾ cup unsweetened applesauce
¼ cup apple cider
2 tablespoons melted sweet butter
1 egg, beaten

Preheat the oven to 350°F. Butter a 9 × 5 × 3-inch loaf pan and set aside.

In a large bowl combine the flour, brown sugar, baking powder, cinnamon, salt, baking soda and nuts. Stir until thoroughly mixed.

In another bowl combine the applesauce, apple cider, melted butter and egg. Stir mixture until well blended.

Stir the dry ingredients into the applesauce mixture, a little at a time. Continue stirring until well blended.

Pour batter into the loaf pan and bake for 1 hour or until a cake tester inserted into the center of the bread comes out clean.

Remove bread to a cooling rack. Cool in the pan for 15 minutes. Turn bread out and cool completely.

APRICOT LOAF

makes 1 loaf

3 cups flour
1 tablespoon plus ½ teaspoon baking powder
1 teaspoon salt
1 tablespoon plus 1 teaspoon grated orange rind
1 cup sugar
2 tablespoons softened sweet butter
1 egg, beaten
¾ cup milk
¾ cup orange juice
1 cup chopped dried apricots
¾ cup chopped walnuts

Preheat the oven to 350°F.

In a mixing bowl combine the flour, baking powder, salt and orange rind. Mix well and set aside.

In a mixing bowl cream together the butter and sugar. Add the egg and mix well.

Combine the milk and orange juice.

Add the flour mixture alternately with the milk mixture to the creamed butter and sugar. Stir in the apricot and walnuts.

Turn the batter into a buttered 9 × 5 × 3-inch loaf pan. Let the bread rest for 20 minutes.

Bake for 60 to 70 minutes or until a cake tester inserted into the center of the bread comes out clean.

Remove from the oven to a cooling rack. Cool in the pan for 10 minutes. Turn bread out onto the rack and cool completely.

APRICOT AND PECAN LOAF
makes 1 loaf

1½ cups sifted flour
2 teaspoons baking powder
½ teaspoon salt
¼ teaspoon baking soda
½ cup sugar
½ cup coarsely chopped dried apricots
½ cup coarsely chopped pecans
1 teaspoon grated orange rind
1 egg, lightly beaten
¾ cup milk
¼ cup vegetable oil

Preheat the oven to 350°F. Generously butter a 9 × 5 × 3-inch loaf pan. Set aside.

Sift the flour together with the baking powder, salt and baking soda. Add the sugar, apricots and pecans and mix well.

Add the orange rind, egg, milk and vegetable oil. Stir until the mixture is well blended. Pour the batter into the prepared pan.

Bake until a cake tester inserted into the center of the bread comes out clean, about 45 to 50 minutes. Remove from the oven and cool in the pan for 10 minutes. Carefully turn the loaf out from the pan and cool thoroughly on a wire rack before slicing.

HUCKLEBERRY BREAD
makes 1 loaf

2 eggs
1 cup sugar
3 tablespoons melted sweet butter
1 cup milk
3 cups flour
1 teaspoon salt
4 teaspoons baking powder
1 cup fresh huckleberries or blackberries, cleaned
½ cup chopped walnuts

Preheat the oven to 350°F.

In a large bowl beat the eggs. Gradually add the sugar and continue beating for 1 minute. Add the butter and milk. Stir until well blended.

In a bowl combine the berries and the chopped nuts.

Combine the flour with salt and baking powder. Add to the berries and nuts and stir gently. Add the mixture to the egg and milk mixture. Stir only until dry ingredients are moistened.

Turn dough into a buttered 5 × 12-inch loaf pan. Bake for 50 to 60 minutes or until a cake tester inserted into the center comes out clean.

Remove to a cooling rack and cool in the pan for 10 minutes. Turn out onto rack and cool completely.

BLUEBERRY-LEMON BREAD

makes 1 loaf

¼ cup softened sweet butter
¾ cup sugar
2 large eggs, beaten
coarsely grated peel of 1 large lemon
2 cups flour
2½ teaspoons baking powder
1 teaspoon salt
¾ cup milk
½ cup fresh blueberries or blackberries,
cleaned
2 tablespoons lemon juice
2 tablespoons sugar

Preheat the oven to 350°F. Butter a 9 × 5-inch loaf pan. Set aside.

In a large bowl cream together the butter and sugar until light and fluffy. Add the eggs, one at a time, beating well after each addition. Add the lemon peel and blend.

Onto a piece of waxed paper sift together all but 2 tablespoons of the flour with the baking powder and salt.

Add flour mixture alternately with the milk to the creamed mixture, beating well after each addition.

Sprinkle the remaining 2 tablespoons of flour over the berries. Toss until well coated.

Gently fold berries into the batter. Turn batter into the prepared pan and bake in the oven for 1 hour or until a cake tester inserted into the center comes out clean.

Transfer pan to wire rack and cool for 10 minutes. Carefully prick the top of the bread with a fork. In a small bowl combine the lemon juice and the sugar. Spoon the mixture over the top of the bread. When bread is completely cool turn out of pan and serve or wrap in aluminum foil and store.

BLACK OLIVE BREAD

makes 1 loaf

1½ cups flour
1½ cups whole wheat flour
1½ teaspoons salt
2 teaspoons baking powder
½ teaspoon baking soda
½ cup light molasses
1¾ cups milk
1 cup pitted and coarsely chopped
black olives

Preheat the oven to 350°F.

In a bowl combine the flour, whole wheat flour, salt and baking powder.

In a large mixing bowl, combine the molasses and baking soda. Add the milk and stir. Gradually add in the dry ingredients. Mix thoroughly. Stir in the olives.

Turn the batter into a buttered 9 × 5 × 3-inch loaf pan. Bake for 1 hour or until a cake tester inserted into the center of the bread comes out clean.

Remove from the oven to a cooling rack. Cool in the pan for 10 minutes, then turn out onto the rack and cool completely.

BLACK WALNUT BREAD

makes 1 loaf

3 cups flour
4½ teaspoons baking powder
½ cup sugar
1 teaspoon salt
1 cup coarsely chopped black walnuts
¼ cup melted sweet butter
2 eggs
1 cup milk

Preheat the oven to 350°F.

In a large mixing bowl combine the flour, baking powder, sugar and salt. Add the chopped nuts and stir.

In a bowl combine the eggs, milk and melted butter. Beat until well blended. Add to the flour mixture. Stir until well blended. Do not try to break up the lumps.

Gently spoon the batter into a buttered 9 × 5 × 3-inch loaf pan. Bake for 1 hour or until a cake tester inserted into the center comes out clean.

Remove from oven to a cooling rack. Cool in pan for 10 minutes. Turn out onto cooling rack and cool completely.

BOSTON BROWN BREAD

makes 3 loaves

1 cup rye flour
1 cup corn meal
1 cup whole wheat flour
¾ teaspoon baking soda
1 teaspoon salt
¾ cup dark molasses
2 cups buttermilk
1 cup dark seedless raisins

Into a large bowl sift the rye flour, corn meal, whole wheat flour, baking soda and salt. Add the molasses, buttermilk and raisins. Stir well.

Divide the batter into 3 equal parts. Place each part into a buttered 1-pound coffee can, filling the can about three-quarters of the way full (large juice cans also work well). Cover the top of each can with buttered waxed paper and then aluminum foil. Puff the foil and allow approximately 1 inch of space so that the bread has room to rise. Tie the foil and waxed paper in place with string.

Place the cans on a rack set in a very large pot. Fill the pot with enough boiling water to reach three-quarters of the way up the cans. Return water to a boil, cover pot, reduce heat, and steam for 2½ hours. Check the pot occasionally and add water if needed to keep the water at the original level.

When the bread is done, carefully remove the cans and cool just enough to remove the bread. Serve the bread hot with butter.

Carrot Coconut Bread

makes 1 loaf

2 cups flour
1¼ cups sugar
2 teaspoons ground cinnamon
2 teaspoons baking soda
½ teaspoon salt
½ cup grated unsweetened coconut
½ cup currants
½ cup coarsely chopped pecans
2 cups coarsely grated carrot
1 cup vegetable oil
2 eggs
2 teaspoons pure vanilla extract

Preheat the oven to 350°F. Generously butter an 8 × 4 × 2½-inch loaf pan.

Combine the flour, sugar, cinnamon, baking soda and salt together in a large mixing bowl. Add the grated coconut, currants, and pecans, Mix until well blended.

Add the grated carrots, oil, eggs and vanilla extract. Mix well, using a wooden spoon, until all the ingredients are thoroughly combined.

Pour the batter into the prepared pan. Bake until the bread shrinks slightly from the sides of the pan and a cake tester inserted into the center of the bread comes out clean, about 30 to 40 minutes.

Remove the pan from the oven and put it on a wire rack. Cool the bread in the pan for 10 minutes. Turn the loaf out onto the rack and cool completely. This loaf slices best if it is aged for a day.

Cheddar Soda Bread

makes 1 round loaf

4 cups flour
1 tablespoon baking powder
1 teaspoon salt
¾ teaspoon baking soda
6 tablespoons softened sweet butter
2 cups coarsely grated Cheddar cheese
2 large eggs
1½ cups buttermilk

Preheat the oven to 350°F. Generously butter a 1½-quart round baking dish that is 3 inches deep. Set aside.

In a large bowl combine the flour, baking powder, salt and baking soda. Add the butter and, with a pastry blender or two knives, cut it in until the mixture looks like a coarse meal.

Add the grated cheese and stir until well blended.

In a bowl beat the eggs together. Remove 1 tablespoon and use later for brushing the bread. Add the buttermilk to the beaten eggs. Mix well.

Add buttermilk mixture to the flour mixture. Stir well. Transfer dough to a lightly floured surface and knead for 3 minutes. Form the dough into a round and fit into the prepared dish. Using a sharp knife, slit the loaf in the center to form a cross. Brush the top of the bread with the reserved egg.

Bake for 1 hour 15 minutes or until a cake tester inserted into the center of the bread comes out clean. Remove from the oven. Cool in pan on wire rack for 15 minutes. Turn out on rack and cool completely.

Chocolate-Pecan Bread

makes 2 loaves

3 cups flour
1 teaspoon baking powder
1 teaspoon salt
½ teaspoon baking soda
3 ounces unsweetened chocolate
½ cup softened sweet butter
1 cup sugar
2 large eggs, lightly beaten
1 cup milk
1½ teaspoons pure vanilla extract
½ cup coarsely chopped pecans

Preheat the oven to 350°F. Butter and lightly flour two 8 × 4-inch loaf pans. Set aside.

Sift together the flour, baking powder, salt and baking soda.

In the top of a double boiler, melt the chocolate together with the butter over hot not boiling water. Stir until mixture is smooth. Remove from the heat and cool.

In a large bowl beat together the sugar, eggs, milk and vanilla extract. Add the flour mixture and stir until well blended. Add the cooled chocolate mixture and stir until the batter is well blended and smooth. Gently fold in the pecans.

Turn the batter into the prepared pans; divide evenly. Bake in the oven for 40 to 45 minutes or until a cake tester inserted into the center of each loaf comes out clean.

Remove from the oven. Cool in the pans on wire racks for 5 minutes. Turn out onto the racks and cool thoroughly.

Coconut Bread

makes 1 loaf

1 cup unsweetened grated coconut
2 cups flour
¾ cup sugar
1 tablespoon baking powder
½ teaspoon salt
1 cup milk
¼ cup vegetable oil
1 large egg
1 teaspoon pure vanilla extract

Preheat the oven to 350°F. Generously butter and lightly flour a 9 × 5 × 3-inch loaf pan. Set aside.

Spread the coconut in a shallow baking dish. Toast in the oven for 4 minutes or until lightly browned. Shake the pan to ensure that coconut toasts evenly. Remove from the oven and cool.

In a large bowl combine the flour, sugar, baking powder, salt and coconut.

In a small bowl combine the milk, oil, egg and vanilla extract. Whisk until well combined. Add to the flour mixture and stir until well blended.

Transfer batter to prepared pan and bake for 1 hour or until bread is golden brown. Remove from the oven.

Cool bread in the pan on wire rack for 5 minutes. Turn out on rack and cool completely.

CORN BREAD

makes 1 bread

2 tablespoons sweet butter
1½ cups corn meal
1½ teaspoons baking powder
3 tablespoons flour
½ teaspoon salt
1½ cups milk
1 egg

Preheat the oven to 450°F.

Melt the butter in a heavy 12-inch iron skillet.

In a mixing bowl combine the corn meal, flour, salt and baking powder. Add the milk and egg. Mix well.

Add the melted butter and stir to blend. Pour the batter into the hot iron skillet.

Place the skillet in the oven and bake 20 to 25 minutes or until golden brown. Serve warm with butter.

Although this bread can be made in a baking dish, for true authenticity it must be made in a cast-iron skillet.

CRANBERRY NUT LOAF

makes 1 loaf

3 cups flour
4 teaspoons baking powder
¼ cup sugar
1 teaspoon salt
½ cup chopped walnuts
1 egg
1 cup milk
2 tablespoons melted sweet butter
1 cup cranberries
¼ cup sugar
1 teaspoon pure almond or vanilla extract

Preheat the oven to 350°F.

In a large bowl, mix the flour with the baking powder, ¼ cup sugar and salt. Add walnuts and mix lightly.

In a small mixing bowl beat the egg, add the milk and butter, and mix well.

Chop the cranberries or currants finely and mix with ¼ cup sugar. Add the cranberries or currants and the almond extract to the egg mixture.

Stir the flour mixture into the egg-cranberry mixture. Mix until well blended. Pour batter into a buttered 9 × 5 × 3-inch loaf pan. Bake for 1 hour or until bread tests done with a cake tester. When done, remove from oven and place pan on cooling rack. Cool in pan for 10 minutes; turn loaf out and continue to cool on rack.

DATE NUT BREAD

makes 2 loaves

2 cups boiling water
1 cup sugar
1 cup pitted and chopped dates
1 teaspoon salt
2 tablespoons sweet butter
2 teaspoons baking soda
1 egg, beaten
2 teaspoons pure vanilla extract
2 teaspoons baking powder
3 cups flour
1 cup coarsely chopped walnuts

Preheat the oven to 350°F.

In a mixing bowl combine the sugar, chopped dates, salt, butter and baking soda. Pour the boiling water over the mixture. Stir well and set aside to cool.

When mixture is cool add the egg, vanilla extract, baking powder, flour and chopped walnuts. Mix well.

Turn the batter into two buttered and floured 8 × 4 × 3-inch loaf pans. Bake for 45 minutes or until a cake tester inserted into the center of the bread comes out clean.

Remove from the oven to cooling racks. Cool in the pan for 10 minutes, then turn out onto the racks and cool completely.

FOUR-GRAIN BREAD

makes 2 loaves

½ cup bran cereal
1 cup buttermilk
½ cup whole wheat flour
½ cup flour
½ cup rye flour
1 teaspoon baking powder
1 teaspoon baking soda
1 teaspoon caraway seeds
¾ teaspoon salt
¼ cup softened sweet butter
3 tablespoons sugar
1 large egg

Preheat the oven to 375°F. Generously butter two 8 × 4 × 3-inch loaf pans. Set aside.

In a small bowl, combine the bran and the buttermilk. Set aside.

In a bowl mix together the whole wheat flour, plain flour, rye flour, baking powder, baking soda, caraway seeds and salt. Set aside.

In a large bowl cream the butter until light and fluffy. Add the sugar and beat until well blended. Add the egg and beat until completely blended.

Add the flour mixture in three parts, alternately with the bran mixture in two parts. Beat well after each addition. Scrape down the sides of the bowl with a rubber spatula when necessary. Be sure to begin and end with the flour.

Transfer batter evenly to the prepared pans. Bake for 20 to 25 minutes or until cake tester inserted into the center of each loaf comes out clean.

Remove from the oven and turn loaves out on wire racks. Cool on racks. Serve warm or cool completely.

HONEY CINNAMON BREAD

makes 1 loaf

2 cups flour
1 teaspoon baking soda
1 teaspoon baking powder
1 teaspoon salt
1 teaspoon ground ginger
½ teaspoon cinnamon
1 cup milk
1 cup honey
1 egg, slightly beaten

Preheat the oven to 375°F.
Into a large bowl sift the flour, baking soda,

baking powder, salt, ginger and cinnamon. Stir in the milk, honey and egg. Place in the bowl of an electric mixer and beat for 20 minutes or until all ingredients are well blended and the batter is smooth.

Pour into a buttered 9 × 5 × 3-inch loaf pan. Bake for 45 minutes or until bread tests done when a cake tester is inserted in the middle.

Remove bread from oven and cool in pan for 10 minutes. Turn out onto a rack and continue cooling. Serve bread sliced thin.

INDIAN BREAD

makes 1 loaf

½ cup flour
1½ cups corn meal
½ teaspoon salt
4 tablespoons sugar
2 large eggs, beaten
1 cup sour cream
1 teaspoon baking soda
1½ cups milk

Preheat the oven to 400°F.

Combine the flour, corn meal, salt and sugar in a large bowl. Add the eggs and sour cream and beat well until smooth.

Dissolve the baking soda in the milk in a small bowl. Add to the flour mixture and mix well.

Pour the mixture into a buttered 12-inch loaf pan. Bake for 25 minutes or until a cake tester comes out clean and the bread is lightly browned.

IRISH SODA BREAD

makes 3 round loaves

2 pounds flour
4 tablespoons baking powder
1 tablespoon salt
2 tablespoons caraway seeds
2 cups milk
¾ cup very soft sweet butter
4 large eggs, lightly beaten
½ to ¾ cup raisins

Preheat the oven to 400°F. Have ready three 8-inch round pans. Do not butter.
In a large bowl combine the flour, baking

powder, salt, caraway seeds, milk, butter, eggs and raisins. Using your hands, mix well for 5 minutes.

Divide the dough evenly among the three pans. Pat gently. Sprinkle the top of each loaf with flour. Using a short knife, carefully slit the top of each loaf, forming a cross.

Bake for 30 minutes or until golden and cake tester inserted into the center of each comes out clean.

Remove from the oven. Cool in pans on wire racks for 5 minutes. Turn out onto racks and cool completely.

LEMON-GLAZED BREAD

makes 1 loaf

2½ cups flour
3 tablespoons baking powder
1 teaspoon salt
⅓ cup softened sweet butter
1¼ cups sugar
2 tablespoons grated lemon peel
2 eggs
1 cup milk
½ cup finely chopped walnuts
⅓ cup lemon juice

Preheat the oven to 325°F.

Sift together the flour, baking powder and salt in a bowl. Set aside.

In a mixing bowl cream the butter with 1 cup sugar and 1 tablespoon lemon peel. Add the eggs, 1 at a time. Beat well after each addition. Add the flour mixture and milk alternately. Stir just until the batter is smooth. Fold in the nuts.

Turn the batter into a buttered 9 × 5 × 3-inch loaf pan. Bake for 60 to 70 minutes or until a cake tester inserted into the center of the bread comes out clean.

When the bread has approximately 5 minutes of baking time left, prepare the glaze. In a saucepan combine the lemon juice, the remaining sugar, and the remaining lemon peel. Heat slowly, stirring constantly, until the sugar dissolves.

Remove the bread from the oven and glaze with the lemon syrup.

Cool in the pan on a cooling rack for 30 minutes. Carefully remove bread from pan and place on rack to cool completely.

NUTTED BANANA BREAD

makes 1 loaf

2½ cups flour
2 teaspoons baking powder
½ teaspoon baking soda
½ teaspoon salt
½ cup softened sweet butter
1 cup sugar
2 eggs
3 very ripe bananas, mashed with
½ teaspoon water
1 teaspoon pure vanilla extract
½ cup coarsely chopped walnuts

Preheat the oven to 375°F. Generously butter a 9 × 5 × 3-inch loaf pan. Set aside.

Sift the flour together with the baking powder, baking soda and salt onto a large sheet of waxed paper. Set aside.

Cream the butter and sugar together in a large mixing bowl. Add the eggs, one at a time, beating well after each addition. Add the mashed bananas and the vanilla extract. Stir until well mixed.

Stir in the sifted flour mixture. Mix until well combined. Add the walnuts and stir.

Turn the batter into the prepared pan and bake until a cake tester inserted into the center of the bread comes out clean, about 35 minutes. Remove from the oven and cool in the pan for 10 minutes. Carefully turn out the loaf from the pan and cool completely on a wire rack.

NUTTED CORN BREAD

makes 1 square bread

¾ cup pecans
3 tablespoons lard or sweet butter
2 cups milk
2 large eggs, slightly beaten
3 cups yellow cornmeal
1 teaspoon cream of tartar
1½ teaspoons salt

Preheat the oven to 400°F.

Place pecans in a shallow pan. Toast in the oven for 5 to 8 minutes or until lightly golden. Remove from the oven. Cool pecans; coarsely chop and set aside.

Place the lard or butter in 9-inch square baking pan. Heat the dish in the oven for 5 minutes.

In a large bowl combine the milk and the eggs; beat well.

Mix together the cornmeal, cream of tartar and salt. Add the corn meal mixture and the pecans to the milk-egg mixture. Stir until just mixed.

Carefully remove the pan from the oven. Turn the batter into the prepared pan and smooth the top with a rubber spatula.

Bake for 25 to 30 minutes or until bread is golden and lightly puffed. Remove from the oven and transfer to a wire rack. Run a knife around the edge of the bread. Turn bread out onto rack and cool for 5 minutes. Cut into squares and serve hot.

OLD-FASHIONED RAISIN BREAD

makes 1 loaf

1 cup dark seedless raisins
1 teaspoon baking soda
1 cup boiling water
1½ cups flour
½ cup sugar
½ teaspoon salt
1 large egg
½ teaspoon pure vanilla extract
1 tablespoon vegetable oil

Preheat oven to 350°F.

Combine the raisins and baking soda in a mixing bowl. Add the water, cover and set aside until cool, about 1 hour.

In a mixing bowl stir together the flour, sugar and salt. Add the raisins with their soaking liquid, the egg, vanilla and oil. Stir until well mixed.

Pour into a greased and floured 9 × 5 × 3-inch loaf pan and bake for 35 to 45 minutes, or until the bread is lightly browned and firm to the touch.

PEACH AND WALNUT BREAD

makes 1 loaf

¼ cup softened sweet butter
½ cup sugar
1 egg
2½ cups flour
3 teaspoons baking powder
1 teaspoon salt
1 cup milk
¾ cup chopped walnuts
1 cup chopped dried peaches

Preheat the oven to 375°F.

Combine the flour with the baking powder and salt in a large bowl.

In a mixing bowl cream together the butter, sugar and egg. Add the flour mixture to the creamed mixture alternately with the milk. Stir in the walnuts and peaches.

Turn the batter into a buttered 9 × 5 × 3-inch loaf pan. Bake for 50 to 55 minutes or until a cake tester inserted in the center of the loaf comes out clean.

Remove from oven to a cooling rack. Cool in the pan for 10 minutes, then turn out onto the rack and cool completely.

PEAR AND NUT BREAD

makes 1 loaf

2 fresh ripe pears
2 eggs, beaten
1 cup whole bran
1½ cup flour
½ cup sugar
1 teaspoon baking powder
½ teaspoon salt
½ teaspoon baking soda
¼ cup softened sweet butter
½ cup coarsely chopped walnuts

Preheat the oven to 350°F.

Core and chop the pears. There should be about 1¼ cups. Place the pears in a bowl and add the eggs and bran. Mix well and set aside.

In a large bowl combine the flour, sugar, baking powder, salt and baking soda. Add the softened butter and the pear mixture. Mix well. Stir in the walnuts and mix well.

Butter an 8 × 4 × 2-inch loaf pan. Turn the batter into the pan and let rest for 20 minutes.

Bake loaf for 1 hour or until a cake tester inserted into the center comes out clean.

Remove to cooling rack. Let cool in pan for 10 minutes. Turn out onto rack and cool completely.

PECAN BREAD

makes 1 loaf

3½ cups flour
1 cup sugar
1 teaspoon salt
3 teaspoons baking powder
1 cup milk
¼ cup melted sweet butter
1 egg
2 cups coarsely chopped pecans

Preheat the oven to 350°F.

In a large bowl combine the flour, sugar, salt and baking powder. Mix well. Add the milk, egg and melted butter. Stir until well blended and smooth. Stir in the pecans.

Butter a 9 × 5 × 3-inch loaf pan. Pour batter into the pan and bake for 1 hour or until cake tester inserted into the middle comes out clean.

Remove from oven. Cool in the pan for 10 minutes. Then turn loaf out onto a rack and cool completely.

PRUNE BREAD

makes 1 loaf

1 cup flour
½ cup whole wheat flour
½ teaspoon baking soda
½ teaspoon baking powder
½ teaspoon salt
½ cup sugar
1 egg, slightly beaten
2 tablespoons melted sweet butter
½ cup milk
½ cup chopped cooked prunes
½ cup prune juice

Preheat the oven to 375°F.

In a bowl combine the flour, whole wheat flour, baking soda, baking powder, salt and sugar.

Using an electric mixer, combine the egg, butter, milk, prunes and prune juice in a large mixing bowl. Mix until well blended. Add the flour mixture and beat at medium speed until well combined.

Turn the batter into a buttered 9 × 5 × 3-inch loaf pan. Bake for 40 to 60 minutes or until a cake tester inserted into the center of the bread comes out clean.

Remove from the oven to a cooling rack. Cool in the pan for 10 minutes. Turn out onto the rack and cool completely.

PUMPKIN BREAD

makes 2 loaves

¼ cup vegetable oil
2 cups sugar
2 eggs
1½ cups flour
½ teaspoon salt
½ teaspoon cinnamon
2 teaspoons baking soda
1¾ cups canned pumpkin
¾ cup coarsely chopped walnuts

Preheat the oven to 350°F.

Cream the oil and sugar together in a large mixing bowl. Add the eggs and beat well.

Combine the flour with the salt, cinnamon and baking soda. Add it alternately with the pumpkin to the creamed mixture. Stir in the nuts.

Pour the batter into two well-greased 9 × 5 × 3-inch loaf pans and bake for 1 hour. When done, remove pans and place on cooling racks. Cool for 15 minutes in the pan; then turn loaves over, remove pans and continue cooling.

RICE BREAD

makes 1 loaf

3 eggs
2¼ cups milk
2 cups white corn meal
1 teaspoon salt
2½ teaspoons baking powder
1 tablespoon melted sweet butter
1 cup cooked cold rice, pushed through a sieve

Preheat the oven to 400°F.

In a bowl beat the eggs lightly. Gradually pour in the milk and mix well.

In another bowl combine the corn meal, salt and baking powder. Add to egg mixture and beat well. Add the melted butter and sieved rice. Beat until the batter is very light.

Butter a shallow 9 × 9-inch baking pan and fill with the batter. Bake for 30 minutes or until golden. Serve hot with butter.

SPICED APPLE BREAD

makes 1 loaf

1 cup flour
1 teaspoon baking soda
1 teaspoon cinnamon
¼ teaspoon salt
¼ teaspoon grated nutmeg
¼ teaspoon ground cardamom
⅓ cup softened sweet butter
1 egg, beaten
¾ cup honey
½ teaspoon pure vanilla extract
2 tart apples, peeled, cored and thinly sliced
¼ cup ground hazelnuts

Preheat the oven to 350°F.

In a bowl combine the flour, baking soda, cinnamon, salt, nutmeg and cardamom. Set aside.

In a large mixing bowl cream the butter. Add the egg, honey and vanilla. Cream until well blended. Add the apples and ground hazelnuts. Stir well until combined. Stir in the flour mixture. Mix well until thoroughly blended.

Pour the batter into a buttered 9 × 5 × 3-inch loaf pan.

Bake for 30 minutes. Reduce the temperature to 325°F and bake 20 minutes longer or until a cake tester inserted into the center comes out clean.

Remove from oven to a cooling rack. Let cool in the pan for 10 minutes. Turn out onto the rack and cool completely.

SPOON BREAD

makes 1 bread

1 tablespoon sweet butter
1½ cups milk
½ cup yellow corn meal
2 eggs
2 teaspoons baking powder
1 teaspoon salt

Preheat the oven to 350°F.

Melt the butter in a 1-quart casserole in the oven.

In a saucepan, scald 1 cup milk. Mix in the corn meal. When mixture thickens, remove from heat and cool slightly.

Beat in ½ cup milk, the eggs, baking powder and salt. Pour the melted butter into the saucepan. Pour the entire mixture back into the casserole and bake for 1 hour or until golden.

SWEET NUT LOAF

makes 1 loaf

2 cups flour
1 teaspoon baking powder
½ teaspoon baking soda
1 teaspoon salt
1 cup firmly packed light brown sugar
2 eggs, beaten
1 cup buttermilk
3 tablespoons melted sweet butter
¾ cup chopped pecans

Preheat the oven to 350°F.

Combine the flour, baking powder, baking soda and salt in a large bowl. Add the brown sugar, breaking up any lumps. Stir mixture well.

In another bowl combine the eggs, buttermilk and melted butter. Stir until well blended. Add to the dry ingredients. Stir well. Add the pecans and continue mixing only until well blended. Do not beat the mixture.

Butter a 9 × 5 × 3-inch loaf pan. Pour batter into the pan and bake for 1 hour or until a cake tester inserted into the center of the bread comes out clean.

Remove the bread to a cooling rack and cool 10 to 15 minutes in the pan. Then turn the loaf out onto a rack and continue cooling.

WHOLE WHEAT NUT BREAD

makes 2 loaves

2 tablespoons sweet butter, melted
½ cup sugar
½ cup molasses
2 cups buttermilk
2 teaspoons baking soda
2 cups whole wheat flour
1⅔ cups flour
1 teaspoon salt
1 teaspoon baking powder
1 cup coarsely chopped walnuts

Preheat the oven to 350°F.

In a large bowl combine the butter, sugar and molasses. Mix well. Dissolve the baking soda in the buttermilk and add to the molasses mixture. Stir until well blended.

Combine the whole wheat flour, white flour, salt and baking powder in a bowl or on a large piece of waxed paper. Add to the molasses-buttermilk mixture. Add the nuts and stir well.

Pour the batter into two 9 × 5 × 3-inch greased loaf pans. Bake for about 50 minutes or until a cake tester comes out clean. Cool before serving.

ROLLS

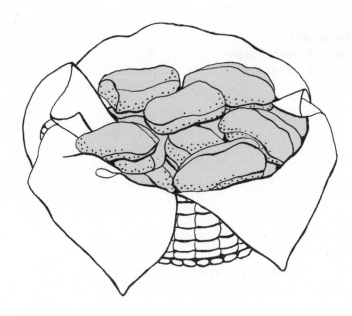

BREAKFAST ROLLS

makes 36 rolls

4 cups sifted flour
¼ cup sugar
1 teaspoon salt
1 teaspoon grated lemon peel
1 cup sweet butter, cut into pieces
1 package active dry yeast
¼ cup very warm water
1 cup lukewarm milk
2 large eggs, well beaten
1 cup sugar
1 tablespoon cinnamon

In a large bowl mix together the flour, sugar, salt and lemon peel. Add the butter and using a pastry blender or two knives, cut it in until the mixture resembles a coarse meal.

Add the yeast to the water and stir to dissolve. Let stand for 3 minutes.

To the flour mixture add the yeast mixture, lukewarm milk and beaten eggs. Mix well but lightly until the mixture is thoroughly combined. Cover the bowl and refrigerate at least 8 hours or overnight.

Remove dough from the refrigerator. Divide in half. Transfer one half to a generously floured surface and roll out to form an 18 × 12-inch rectangle.

Sprinkle the top of the dough evenly with ½ cup of the sugar and 1½ teaspoons of the cinnamon. Starting at the wide side, roll the rectangle up tightly.

Cut the roll into 1-inch slices. Place each slice, cut-side up, on a buttered baking sheet. Flatten the slices with the palm of your hand.

Repeat the above steps with the remaining dough, sugar and cinnamon.

Preheat the oven to 400°F.

Bake for 12 to 15 minutes or until golden. Remove from the oven and serve warm.

CARAWAY ROLLS

makes 24 rolls

2 cups boiling water
½ cup firmly packed dark brown sugar
1½ teaspoons sweet butter
1 cup and 2 tablespoons rye flour
5 cups flour
1 package active dry yeast
1 tablespoon caraway seeds
1 tablespoon salt
1 egg white lightly beaten with 1 tablespoon water for egg wash

In a large bowl, combine the boiling water, brown sugar and butter. Stir mixture until both sugar and butter are completely dissolved. Let stand at room temperature until lukewarm.

Into a large bowl sift together the rye flour and 2½ cups of the flour. Repeat and set aside.

Sprinkle the yeast into the lukewarm butter-sugar mixture; stir to dissolve. Add the caraway seeds and the sifted flour mixture, 1 cup at a time. Stir until well mixed. Cover the bowl and let the mixture rise in a warm, draft-free space for 1 to 1½ hours or until doubled in size.

Sift 2 cups of the remaining flour and the salt over the yeast-flour mixture. Stir down. Slowly stir in the remaining flour or as much as needed to make a stiff dough.

Transfer the dough to a floured surface and knead for 10 minutes or until dough is elastic and smooth. Add flour as needed.

Break the dough into 24 equal pieces. Form each piece into a small round. Place rounds approximately 2 inches apart on lightly buttered baking sheets. Cover sheets and let rise in a warm draft-free place for 1 to 1½ hours or until doubled in size.

Preheat the oven to 425°F.

Brush each round with the egg wash mixture. Bake in the oven for 15 to 20 minutes or until rolls sound hollow when lightly tapped. Remove from sheets to wire racks and cool slightly before serving.

ONION-FILLED ROLLS

makes 24 rolls

½ cup lukewarm water
1 teaspoon sugar
1 package active dry yeast
5 tablespoons softened sweet butter
2 tablespoons sugar
1 teaspoon salt
1 large egg, beaten
4 cups sifted flour

FILLING:
½ cup sweet butter
2 cups finely chopped scallions
¼ teaspoon salt
⅛ teaspoon black pepper

In a small bowl combine the lukewarm water and the 1 teaspoon of sugar. Stir to dissolve. Sprinkle in the yeast and let the mixture stand for 10 minutes. Stir very well.

In a large bowl cream the butter until soft. Add the remaining sugar and salt and beat until light and fluffy. Beat in the egg; continue beating until mixture is smooth. Add the yeast mixture and stir until thoroughly combined.

Add the flour and stir until well mixed. When dough is stiff enough to handle, transfer it to a lightly floured surface and knead for 5 minutes.

Generously butter a large bowl. Transfer dough to bowl, turn until well coated. Cover and let rise in a warm draft-free area for 1½ hours or until doubled in bulk.

While the dough rises prepare the filling. In a saucepan, melt the butter. Add the scallions and sauté over moderate heat until soft, approximately 5 minutes. Do not brown. Remove from the heat and stir in the salt and pepper. Allow the mixture to cool before using.

Punch the dough down. Transfer to a lightly floured surface and knead for 3 minutes. Roll the dough out to ¼-inch thickness. Cut dough into circles using a 3-inch round cookie or biscuit cutter. There will be 24 circles. Place 1 teaspoon of the filling in the center of each circle. Using your fingers, dampen the edge of half of each circle with water. Fold over the other half and press edges together.

Transfer to buttered baking sheets. Cover with a clean towel and let rise in a warm draft-free place for 30 minutes or until doubled in size.

Preheat the oven to 400°F.

Bake for 15 minutes or until lightly browned. Remove from the oven and transfer to wire racks. Cool completely or serve warm.

Parker House Rolls

makes 24 rolls

½ cup scalded milk
½ cup boiling water
1 teaspoon salt
1 tablespoon sweet butter
1 teaspoon sugar
1 package active dry yeast dissolved in
¼ cup lukewarm water
3 cups flour
½ cup sweet butter, melted

Preheat the oven to 400°F.

Place the milk, water, salt, butter and sugar in a mixing bowl and mix well. Add the yeast. Add the flour and mix until the dough is stiff enough to knead. Cover and let the dough rise until it is doubled in bulk, about 20 minutes.

Shape the dough into 24 balls and place them on buttered baking sheets or in buttered muffin tins. Cover with a clean cloth and let rise in a warm place for 15 to 20 minutes or until doubled in bulk.

Flour the handle of a wooden spoon and press it against the dough balls until they are almost cut in half.

Brush one half of each ball with melted butter. Fold over the other half and press the halves together. Let rise once more for 15 to 20 minutes.

Bake for 15 minutes. Brush the tops with butter after baking. Serve warm.

Seeded Sandwich Rolls

makes 12 rolls

1½ cups water
1 package active dry yeast
4 to 5 cups flour
½ teaspoon salt
1 tablespoon sugar
2 tablespoons sweet butter, melted and cooled
1 egg yolk beaten with 1 tablespoon water
for egg wash
sesame seeds or poppy seeds

In a small bowl combine the water and the yeast. Let stand for 3 to 5 minutes.

In a large bowl combine 4 cups of the flour, salt and sugar. Add the melted butter and then the yeast mixture. Stir well. Add as much of the remaining flour as is needed to make a dough. When dough is stiff transfer it to a lightly floured surface.

Knead dough for 5 to 8 minutes or until smooth and elastic.

Butter a large bowl. Transfer dough to bowl and let rise in a warm draft-free place for 1 hour or until doubled in bulk.

Punch dough down in the center; divide into 4 equal pieces. On a lightly floured surface, roll each piece into a rectangle measuring 12 inches wide. Cut the rectangle into 3 equal pieces. Form each 4-inch piece into a miniature bread loaf. Seal the edges by pressing gently.

Transfer the rolls to buttered baking sheets and cover with a clean towel. Let rise in a warm draft-free place for 1 hour or until doubled in bulk.

Preheat the oven to 375°F.

Brush each roll with the egg wash and sprinkle with sesame seeds or poppy seeds. Bake for 15 to 20 minutes or until tops are brown.

Remove from the oven. Transfer rolls to wire racks. Cool completely or serve warm.

SWEET POTATO ROLLS

makes 20 rolls

1 large sweet potato
1 package active dry yeast
¾ teaspoon salt
3 tablespoons sugar
1 tablespoon sweet butter, softened
1 cup milk
3½ to 4½ cups flour

Peel the sweet potato and cut it into thirds. Place the pieces into a saucepan and add enough water to cover. Cook until tender, about 15 to 20 minutes. Drain and reserve ¼ cup of the cooking water.

When the cooking water has cooled to lukewarm, add the yeast to it and stir to dissolve.

Place the sweet potato pieces into a large mixing bowl. Mash the pieces with a fork and then add the salt, sugar and butter. Beat well.

Place the milk in a saucepan and heat until a skin begins to form on top. Skim the milk and stir it into the sweet potato mixture. Allow the mixture to cool to lukewarm. When cooled, stir in the yeast and water mixture.

Add to the sweet potato mixture as much flour as necessary, 1 cup at a time, to make a dough dense enough to knead. Turn the dough out onto a floured surface and knead until smooth and elastic. Place the dough in a large, oiled bowl and cover with a clean towel. Let dough rise in a warm place until it is doubled in bulk, about 1½ hours.

Remove the dough from the bowl and punch it down.

Grease the cups of two 10-cup muffin tins. Pinch off 20 small pieces of dough and place one in each cup. Set the tins aside and let the dough rise again until almost doubled or until the cups are almost filled, about 45 to 50 minutes.

Preheat the oven to 425°F.

Bake the muffins for 13 to 15 minutes or until golden. Cool slightly before serving.

ZUCCHINI ROLLS

makes 12 to 16 rolls

⅔ cup coarsely grated zucchini
3½ cups flour
½ teaspoon salt
2 tablespoons vegetable oil
½ cup warm water
1 teaspoon flour
2 teaspoons honey
1 package active dry yeast
1 cup warm milk

Drain the grated zucchini in a colander for 30 minutes.

In a large bowl combine the flour, salt, grated zucchini and vegetable coil.

In a small bowl combine the warm water, 1 teaspoon flour, honey and yeast. Stir until the ingredients are dissolved. Add the warm milk and stir again. Quickly pour the mixture into the zucchini mixture in the large bowl. Stir until well blended.

Turn the dough out onto a lightly floured surface and knead until the dough is soft and firm, about 10 minutes. Add more flour as needed.

Put the kneaded dough into a generously buttered bowl. Turn the dough to coat it with the butter. Cover with a clean towel and let the dough rise in a warm place until it is doubled in size, about 50 to 60 minutes.

Turn the dough out onto a lightly floured surface and knead for 5 minutes. Shape the dough into 12 to 16 small rolls. Put the rolls into well-greased muffin tins. Cover with a clean towel and let rise in a warm place for 30 minutes.

Preheat the oven to 400°F.

Put the rolls into the oven and reduce the heat to 375°F. Bake until the rolls are golden brown, about 15 to 20 minutes.

Remove the rolls from the oven, turn them out of the muffin tins and serve warm.

MUFFINS

APPLE MUFFINS

makes approximately 16 muffins

2 cups flour
4 teaspoons baking powder
¼ teaspoon baking soda
½ teaspoon grated nutmeg
½ teaspoon salt
4 tablespoons softened sweet butter
¼ cup sugar
2 eggs
1 cup sour cream
2 to 3 tart apples, peeled, cored and chopped

Preheat the oven to 425°F.

Grease the muffin tins and set them aside.

In a large bowl combine the flour, baking powder, baking soda, nutmeg and salt.

In another large mixing bowl, cream the butter and sugar until the mixture is light and fluffy. Beat in the eggs, 1 at a time. Add the flour mixture, 1 cup at a time, beating it in alternately with the sour cream. End with the sour cream.

Stir the chopped apples into the mixture. Spoon the batter into the muffin pans, filling each cup about halfway. Bake for 15 to 20 minutes or until a cake tester comes out clean. Turn the muffins out while hot and serve.

BASIC MUFFINS

makes 12 muffins

2 cups flour
1 tablespoon baking powder
1 tablespoon sugar
½ teaspoon salt
1 egg, lightly beaten
1 cup milk
¼ cup melted sweet butter

Preheat the oven to 425°F.

In a large bowl combine the flour, baking powder, sugar and salt.

In a small bowl combine the egg, milk and butter. Stir gently.

Make a well in the middle of the flour mixture and pour the egg and milk mixture into it all at once. Stir gently but quickly with a fork. The batter should be lumpy.

Lightly butter the bottoms of 12 muffin cups. Spoon the batter into each cup until two-thirds full.

Bake for 20 minutes or until golden brown. Serve hot.

BLUEBERRY MUFFINS

makes 20 muffins

1½ cups fresh blueberries or blackberries, cleaned
2 cups flour
2 teaspoons baking powder
½ teaspoon salt
½ cup softened sweet butter
1 cup sugar
2 eggs
½ cup milk

Preheat the oven to 375°F.

Rinse the berries and remove any stems and blemished berries. Dry the berries completely on paper towels.

Mash ½ cup of the berries in small bowl with 2 tablespoons of the flour. Toss to coat the berries and set aside.

Combine the remaining flour with the baking powder and salt in a bowl or on a large piece of waxed paper.

In a mixing bowl cream the butter and sugar together until light and fluffy. Add the eggs, 1 at a time. Beat well after each addition.

Add 1 cup of the flour mixture to the creamed mixture. Mix well. Beat in half the milk. Beat in the remaining flour and the rest of the milk. Continue to beat until the batter is smooth. Add the mashed berries and beat again. Fold the whole berries into the batter. Mix gently.

Spoon the batter into 20 well-buttered muffin cups, filling each about three-quarters full.

Bake for 20 to 25 minutes or until a cake tester inserted into the center of a muffin comes out clean.

Remove from the oven. Turn the muffins out of the tins and serve warm.

BRAN AND BANANA MUFFINS

makes 12 muffins

¾ cup flour
¼ cup sugar
3 tablespoons baking powder
½ cup whole wheat flour
1½ cups natural bran cereal
¾ cup milk
1 cup mashed ripe bananas
1 large egg
¼ cup vegetable oil
½ cup coarsely chopped pecans.

Preheat the oven to 400°F. Butter 12 muffin cups.

Into a large bowl sift together the flour, sugar and baking powder. Add the whole wheat flour and stir until evenly mixed.

In a separate bowl, combine the bran, milk and mashed banana. Allow the mixture to stand for 5 minutes, or until the bran has softened. Add the egg and the vegetable oil to the bran mixture. Beat well.

Add the flour mixture to the bran-egg mixture and stir just until combined. Add the nuts and stir. Fill the prepared cups approximately three-quarters full.

Bake for 20 to 25 minutes or until golden. Remove from the oven. Turn muffins out onto wire racks. Cool completely or serve warm.

CHOPPED CHERRY MUFFINS

makes 12 muffins

2 cups flour
3 teaspoons baking powder
½ teaspoon salt
3 tablespoons sugar
1 egg, well beaten
1 cup milk
3 tablespoons melted sweet butter
¾ cup fresh cherries, pitted and chopped

Preheat the oven to 425°F.

In a large bowl combine the flour, baking powder, salt and sugar.

In a small bowl combine the egg, milk and melted butter. Mix well and add to the flour mixture. Stir quickly and only until the dry ingredients are just moistened. Gently fold in the chopped cherries.

Spoon the batter into 12 buttered muffin cups until each cup is two-thirds full. Bake for 20 to 30 minutes or until golden. Serve hot or cold.

FRESH CORN MUFFINS

makes 12 muffins

1 cup fresh corn (about 2 to 3 ears)
1 cup flour
½ cup yellow corn meal
½ cup sugar
1 tablespoon baking powder
½ teaspoon salt
2 eggs, beaten
½ cup milk
½ cup butter, melted

Preheat the oven to 400°F.

Using a small sharp knife, cut the corn kernels from the cobs. Scrape the cobs with the side of a spoon to remove all the kernel. Set the kernels aside.

Combine the flour, corn meal, sugar, baking powder and salt together in a large bowl. Mix well. Add the corn kernels and stir until they are well coated.

Add the milk and melted butter to the beaten eggs in a bowl. Mix until well blended. Pour into the flour mixture and stir only until the mixtures are just combined; muffin batter should be lumpy.

Divide the batter among 12 buttered muffin tins. Bake the muffins until a cake tester inserted into the center of a muffin comes out clean, about 15 to 20 minutes.

Remove the muffins from the oven and cool in the tin on a wire rack for 5 minutes. Turn the muffins out of the tin onto a wire rack and cool slightly before serving.

HONEY WHOLE WHEAT MUFFINS

makes 12 muffins

¾ cup whole wheat flour
¾ cup flour
2 teaspoons baking powder
½ teaspoon salt
1 large egg
½ cup milk
½ cup honey
¼ cup melted sweet butter

Preheat the oven to 400°F. Butter 12 muffin cups.

In a large bowl combine the whole wheat flour, flour, baking powder and salt.

In another bowl beat the egg. Add the milk, honey and butter and beat until well mixed. Add to the flour mixture and stir just until mixed.

Turn batter into prepared cups, filling them about two-thirds full. Bake in the oven for 25 to 30 minutes or until a cake tester inserted in the center of a muffin comes out clean.

Remove from the oven. Turn muffins out onto wire racks. Cool completely or serve warm.

MACADAMIA NUT AND CHOCOLATE MUFFINS

makes 12 muffins

2 cups sifted flour
⅓ cup sugar
1 tablespoon baking powder
1 teaspoon salt
½ cup cold shortening, cut into small pieces
½ cup semisweet chocolate bits
¾ cup coarsely chopped macadamia nuts
1 large egg, lightly beaten
1 cup milk
1 teaspoon dark rum

Preheat the oven to 400°F.

Sift the flour together with the sugar, baking powder and salt into a large bowl. Add the shortening pieces, cutting them in with a pastry blender or two knives until the mixture resembles a coarse meal. Add the chocolate pieces and stir. Add ½ cup of the macadamia nuts and stir again.

Combine the egg, milk and rum together in a bowl. Beat lightly until blended. Add to the flour mixture and stir only until the mixtures are just combined; muffin batter should be lumpy.

Divide the batter among 12 buttered muffin tins. Sprinkle the tops of the muffins with the remaining macadamia nuts.

Bake the muffins until a cake tester inserted into the center of a muffin comes out clean, about 25 minutes.

Remove the muffins from the oven and cool in the tin on a wire rack for 5 minutes. Turn the muffins out of the tin onto a wire rack and cool completely before serving.

MOLASSES MUFFINS

makes 12 muffins

2 cups flour
½ teaspoon baking soda
1 teaspoon baking powder
½ tablespoon ground ginger
½ teaspoon cinnamon
½ teaspoon salt
½ teaspoon black pepper
¼ teaspoon ground cloves
2 tablespoons softened sweet butter
¾ cup sugar
2 eggs, well beaten
⅓ cup molasses
¼ cup buttermilk

Preheat the oven to 350°F.

In a bowl combine the flour, baking soda, baking powder, ginger, cinnamon, salt, pepper and ground cloves.

Cream the butter and sugar together in a mixing bowl until light and fluffy. Beat in the eggs. Add the molasses and stir until blended. Add the flour mixture and the buttermilk alternately. Stir well after each addition.

Spoon the batter into 12 buttered muffin cups. Bake for 25 to 30 minutes or until a cake tester inserted into the center of a muffin comes out clean. Serve warm.

OATMEAL MUFFINS

makes 12 muffins

1 cup quick-cooking oats
1 cup buttermilk
1 cup flour
1 teaspoon baking powder
½ teaspoon salt
½ teaspoon baking soda
1 egg, slightly beaten
⅓ cup light brown sugar, firmly packed
⅓ cup vegetable oil

Preheat the oven to 400°F.

Place the oats in a mixing bowl and pour the buttermilk over them. Let soak for 15 minutes.

In a bowl combine the flour with baking powder, salt and baking soda. Stir into the oats and buttermilk mixture. Stir in the egg, brown sugar and vegetable oil. Mix until just blended.

Spoon the batter into 12 buttered muffin cups. Bake for 20 to 25 minutes or until golden. Serve hot or cold.

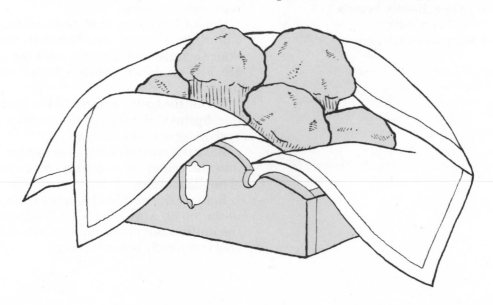

PECAN GINGER MUFFINS

makes 12 muffins

1 cup pecans
1 cup flour
1 teaspoon salt
1 teaspoon baking powder
½ teaspoon baking soda
¾ teaspoon ground cinnamon
¾ teaspoon ground ginger
½ teaspoon nutmeg
¾ cup whole wheat flour
½ cup packed light brown sugar
1 egg, lightly beaten
1 cup buttermilk
⅓ cup butter melted

Preheat the oven to 400°F.
Put the pecans in a shallow dish or on a baking sheet. Toast them in the oven until golden, about 5 minutes. Let the nuts cool, then chop them coarsely and set aside.

Combine the flour, salt, baking powder, baking soda, cinnamon, ginger and nutmeg in a large bowl. Mix well. Add the whole wheat flour, sugar and chopped pecans. Mix well.

Add the buttermilk and melted butter to the beaten egg in a bowl. Beat until well combined. Pour into the flour mixture and stir only until the mixtures are just combined; muffin batter should be lumpy.

Divide the batter among 12 buttered muffin tins. Bake the muffins until a cake tester inserted into the center of a muffin comes out clean, about 25 minutes.

Remove the muffins from the oven and cool in the tin on a wire rack for 5 minutes. Turn the muffins out of the tin onto a wire rack and cool slightly before serving.

PUMPKIN-RAISIN-PECAN MUFFINS

makes 24 muffins

2 cups sifted flour
1 teaspoon baking soda
½ teaspoon baking powder
½ teaspoon ground cinnamon
½ teaspoon grated nutmeg
¼ teaspoon ground ginger
2 large eggs, lightly beaten
⅓ cup buttermilk
⅓ cup melted sweet butter
1 tablespoon molasses
½ teaspoon pure vanilla extract
1 cup sugar
1 cup canned pumpkin
½ cup raisins
½ cup coarsely chopped pecans

Preheat the oven to 350°F. Butter 24 muffin cups. Set aside.

Into a large bowl sift together the flour, baking soda, baking powder, cinnamon, nutmeg and ginger.

In another large bowl combine the eggs, buttermilk, butter, molasses, vanilla, sugar and pumpkin. Beat until well blended. Add the flour mixture and stir just until mixed. Add the raisins and pecans and fold in gently.

Turn batter into prepared cups, filling them about three-quarters full. Bake in the oven for 20 minutes or until a cake tester inserted into the center of a muffin comes out clean.

Remove from the oven. Turn muffins out onto wire racks and cool completely or serve warm.

ACORN SQUASH MUFFINS

makes approximately 18 muffins

2 cups flour
2 teaspoons baking powder
½ teaspoon salt
½ cup sugar
¼ teaspoon cinnamon
¼ teaspoon grated nutmeg
1 egg, beaten
1 cup mashed, cooked acorn squash
1 cup milk

Preheat the oven to 400°F.

In a large mixing bowl combine the flour, baking powder, salt, sugar, cinnamon and nutmeg.

In another bowl beat the egg; add the squash and milk and blend well.

Add the squash mixture to the dry ingredients and stir just until the mixtures are combined. Muffin batter should be lumpy.

Fill the cups of greased muffin pans three-quarters full. Bake for 20 to 25 minutes. Serve hot or cold.

WALNUT CORN MUFFINS

makes 18 muffins

3½ cups whole wheat flour
1 cup yellow corn meal
1 package active dry yeast
1 teaspoon baking powder
1 teaspoon salt
1 cup milk
½ cup sweet butter
½ cup water
⅓ cup honey
2 eggs
1 cup coarsely chopped walnuts

Grease 18 muffin-tin cups. Sprinkle each cup with a little bit of corn meal. Set aside.

In a large bowl, combine 1 cup whole wheat flour, the corn meal, yeast, baking powder and salt.

Place the milk, butter, water and honey in a saucepan. Heat the mixture until the butter melts. Set aside and cool until lukewarm.

When mixture has cooled, pour it into the flour mixture. With an electric mixer, beat the batter at medium speed for 2 minutes. Beat in the eggs. Stir in the remaining flour. Add the walnuts and stir.

Fill each muffin cup three-quarters full with the dough. Smooth the tops. Cover the muffin tins with clean towels and let the dough rise in a warm place for 40 to 50 minutes or until the dough almost fills the tins.

Preheat the oven to 350°F.

Bake the muffins for 20 minutes or until golden brown. Serve warm.

ZUCCHINI MUFFINS

makes 12 muffins

2 cups flour
½ cup sugar
1 tablespoon baking powder
1 teaspoon salt
1 teaspoon grated lemon rind
½ teaspoon grated nutmeg
½ cup coarsely chopped walnuts
¼ cup dark raisins
¼ cup golden raisins
2 eggs, beaten
½ cup milk
⅓ cup vegetable oil
1 cup coarsely grated zucchini

Preheat the oven to 400°F.

Combine the flour, sugar, baking powder, salt, lemon rind and nutmeg in a large bowl. Add the raisins and walnuts and stir well.

Add the milk and oil to the beaten eggs in a bowl. Beat until well blended. Pour the mixture into the bowl with the flour mixture; do not stir. Add the grated zucchini. Stir only until the ingredients are just combined; muffin batter should be lumpy.

Divide the batter among 12 buttered muffin tins. Bake the muffins until a cake tester inserted into the center of a muffin comes out clean, about 15 to 20 minutes.

Remove the muffins from the oven and cool in the tin on a wire rack for 5 minutes. Turn the muffins out of the tin onto a wire rack and cool completely before serving.

BISCUITS

BUTTERMILK BISCUITS

makes 12 to 14 biscuits

2 cups flour
1 teaspoon baking powder
½ teaspoon baking soda
1 teaspoon salt
4 tablespoons softened sweet butter
1 cup thick buttermilk

Sift the flour, baking powder, baking soda and salt into a mixing bowl. Cut in the butter with a pastry blender or two knives until the mixture resembles a coarse meal. Add enough of the buttermilk to make a soft dough. Mix lightly.

Turn the dough out onto a lightly floured surface. Knead for 5 minutes.

Preheat the oven to 450°F.

Roll out the dough on a floured surface to ½-inch thickness. Cut biscuits from the dough with a 2-inch floured biscuit cutter.

Place the biscuits on lightly greased baking sheets. Bake for 10 to 12 minutes. Serve hot.

CHEDDAR CHEESE BISCUITS

makes approximately 24 biscuits

1 cup flour
¼ teaspoon salt
⅓ cup sweet butter
1 cup finely grated Cheddar cheese

Preheat the oven to 350°F.

Combine the flour and salt in a large bowl. Cut in the butter with a pastry blender or two knives. Add the cheese and mix lightly with your hands until the dough holds together.

Roll the dough out about ½-inch thick on a lightly floured surface. Cut out biscuits with a small, greased biscuit cutter. Prick the tops with a fork.

Place the biscuits on an ungreased baking sheet and bake for 12 to 15 minutes or until the biscuits are a rich Cheddar color, but not brown. Allow the biscuits to cool before serving.

DROP BISCUITS

makes 12 biscuits

2 cups flour
2 teaspoons baking powder
1 teaspoon salt
4 tablespoons sweet butter
1 cup milk

Preheat the oven to 450°F.

Combine the flour with the baking powder and salt in a large bowl. Cut in the butter with a pastry blender or two knives until the mixture resembles a coarse meal. Add the milk and stir to form a soft dough.

Drop the dough by well-rounded tablespoons onto a lightly buttered cookie sheet. There should be 12 biscuits.

Bake for 12 to 15 minutes or until golden. Serve hot.

OLD FASHIONED SOUR CREAM BISCUITS

makes 12 biscuits

2 cups flour
2 teaspoons baking powder
½ teaspoon baking soda
1 teaspoon salt
1 tablespoon sweet butter
1 cup and 2 tablespoons sour cream

Preheat the oven to 450°F.

Combine the flour with the baking powder, baking soda and salt in a large bowl. Cut in the butter with a pastry blender or two knives until the mixture resembles a coarse meal. Stir in the sour cream and mix well to form a soft dough.

Roll the dough out on a lightly floured surface to form a 6 × 8-inch rectangle that is ¾-inch thick. Cut approximately 12 rounds from the dough with a lightly floured 2-inch biscuit cutter.

Place the rounds on a greased baking sheet and bake for 12 to 15 minutes or until golden. Serve hot.

ORANGE SUGAR BISCUITS

makes 16 biscuits

2 cups flour
5 teaspoons baking powder
1 teaspoon salt
2 tablespoons softened sweet butter
½ cup milk
juice of 1 large orange
grated rind of 1 orange
16 small sugar cubes

Preheat the oven to 375°F.

In a large bowl combine the flour, baking powder and salt. Cut in the butter with a pastry blender or two knives until the mixture resembles a coarse meal. Add enough milk to make a soft dough. Mix well.

Turn the dough out onto a lightly floured surface. Roll the dough out ¾-inch thick and cut out 16 rounds with a lightly floured biscuit cutter.

Place the biscuits into 16 buttered muffin cups. Sprinkle the grated orange rind over the biscuits.

Place the orange juice in a bowl. Dip the sugar cubes into the juice and quickly press 1 cube into the center of each biscuit.

Bake for 20 minutes or until golden. Turn out of the tins and serve at once.

SPICY CHEESE BISCUITS

makes 10 to 12 biscuits

½ cup sweet butter
¾ cup grated Swiss cheese
½ tablespoon Dijon-style mustard
2 egg yolks, beaten
⅛ teaspoon cayenne pepper
1 cup flour

Preheat the oven to 300°F.

In a bowl beat the butter until very creamy. Add the egg yolks and mix well. Add the cheese, mustard and cayenne. Gradually stir in the flour. Mix thoroughly to make a stiff dough.

Roll out the dough on a lightly floured surface. Cut biscuits out with a floured 1-inch biscuit cutter.

Place the biscuits on a greased baking sheet and bake for 20 minutes or until golden. Serve hot.

SWEET POTATO BISCUITS

makes 10 to 12 biscuits

1 small sweet potato
2 tablespoons sweet butter
1 cup flour
1 teaspoon baking powder
½ teaspoon salt
1 to 3 tablespoons milk

Preheat the oven to 425°F.

Wrap the sweet potato in aluminum foil and bake for 40 to 45 minutes or until soft. Turn the oven down to 400°F.

When the potato has cooled, peel and dice it.

Sift the flour, baking powder and salt together in a large bowl. Cut the sweet potato pieces and butter into the mixture, using a pastry blender or two knives. Add the milk and stir until well blended.

Turn the dough out onto a lightly floured surface and knead for 2 minutes. Roll out to ½-inch thickness. Cut biscuits from the dough with a floured 2-inch biscuit cutter.

Place the biscuits onto a greased baking sheet and bake for 12 minutes or until golden. Serve hot.

—UNUSUAL BREADS—

BUCKWHEAT PANCAKES

makes 12 to 16 cakes

¾ cup buckwheat flour
¾ cup flour
½ teaspoon salt
3½ teaspoons baking powder
2 tablespoons sugar
1 egg beaten
3 tablespoons sweet butter, melted
1¼ cups milk
1 tablespoon molasses

In a large bowl combine the buckwheat with the flour, baking powder, salt and sugar.

In a mixing bowl combine the egg, butter, milk and molasses. Beat until well blended. Add the flour mixture to the egg mixture and stir gently until well mixed.

Heat an ungreased griddle over medium heat. Drop the batter by teaspoons onto the griddle. Cook the pancakes about 1 minute on each side. Turn when the pancakes are bubbly on top and dry around the edges.

Serve hot with butter and honey.

CORNSTICKS

makes 12 cornsticks

1½ cups corn meal
½ cup flour
1 teaspoon baking soda
½ teaspoon salt
1 teaspoon baking powder
2 teaspoons sugar
2 eggs, beaten
2 cups buttermilk
3 tablespoons melted sweet butter

Preheat the oven to 425°F.

In a large bowl combine the flour, baking soda, salt, baking powder and sugar. Stir in the corn meal.

In another bowl combine the eggs, buttermilk and melted butter. Add to the flour mixture and beat well.

Butter the molds of a 12-stick cast-iron cornstick pan. Spoon the batter into the molds, filling them two-thirds full.

Bake for 20 to 25 minutes or until golden brown. Serve at once.

GRIDDLE CAKES

makes approximately 18 cakes

2 cups flour
4 teaspoons baking powder
½ teaspoon salt
2 tablespoons sugar
2 large eggs
1¾ cups milk
2 tablespoons sweet butter

In a large mixing bowl combine flour, baking powder, salt and sugar.

Beat the eggs in another large bowl and add the milk. Melt the butter in a saucepan and add it to the egg-milk mixture. Blend in the dry ingredients. Stir gently only until the ingredients are well mixed. Do not overbeat.

Heat an ungreased griddle over medium-high heat. Drop the batter from a large spoon onto the griddle. Cook about 1 minute on each side. The cakes will bubble on top and be dry around the edges; they are ready to be turned at this point.

Remove the cakes from the griddle when done. Serve hot with butter and pure maple syrup.

LEFSE (SWEDISH POTATO BREADS)

makes approximately 30 lefse

6 medium-sized potatoes, peeled and halved
¼ cup softened sweet butter
¼ cup milk
1½ teaspoons salt
1 teaspoon sugar
⅛ teaspoon black pepper
2½ to 3 cups flour
softened butter

Place the potatoes in a skillet with enough water to cover. Cook, covered, for 20 minutes or until the potatoes are tender. Drain well. Return the potatoes to skillet and dry them over low heat, shaking the skillet back and forth.

Mash the potatoes thoroughly. Add the ¼ cup butter, milk, salt, sugar and pepper. Whip the mixture until it is light and fluffy.

Chill the mixture for 4 hours.

Heat a large griddle over very low heat until it is very hot.

Remove the potato mixture from the refrigerator. Add about half the flour and beat until smooth. Beat in enough of the remaining flour to form a soft dough. Form the dough into a ball and turn it out onto a lightly floured surface. Roll the dough out into a round sheet about ⅛-inch thick. Cut 24 to 30 6-inch rounds out of the dough.

Place a round on the very hot griddle. Cook until it is lightly browned. This will take only a moment or two. Turn the round over and brown the other side. Brown the rest of the rounds.

Transfer the rounds to a clean towel as they are cooked. Cool completely. Serve spread with softened butter and loosely rolled.

Old Fashioned Johnny Cakes

makes 12 to 16 cakes

1 teaspoon salt
1 tablespoon sweet butter
1 cup yellow corn meal
1 cup boiling water
¼ cup milk
2 tablespoons bacon drippings or butter

Preheat the oven to 475°F.

Place the corn meal in a mixing bowl. Add the salt and butter.

Pour the *boiling* water over the corn meal. Stir immediately. It is crucial that the water be boiling when it is poured. Add milk and stir until well mixed.

Melt the bacon drippings in a 8- or 9-inch round cake pan. Grease the sides of the pan and pour in the batter. Place the pan over the heat until the batter begins to bubble around the edges.

Place the pan in the oven. Bake for about 30 minutes. After the first 10 minutes, dot the top with butter if desired.

Popovers

makes 12 popovers

1½ cups flour
¼ teaspoon salt
2 eggs, lightly beaten
1½ cups milk
2 tablespoons sweet butter, melted

Preheat the oven to 425°F.

In a large bowl sift together the flour and salt. Add the eggs, milk and butter. Blend well to make a smooth batter.

Beat the batter with an electric mixer for 3 minutes.

Lightly butter a 12-cup muffin tin that has been warmed in the oven for 5 minutes. Fill the cups two-thirds full with the batter.

Bake for 30 minutes. Do not open the oven while the popovers bake. They will brown and pop when done. Serve hot.

SCONES

makes 12 scones

1½ cups flour
1½ tablespoons sugar
¾ teaspoon baking powder
¼ teaspoon baking soda
⅛ teaspoon salt
4 tablespoons very cold sweet butter
7 to 8 tablespoons milk

Preheat the oven to 400°F. Generously butter one large or two small baking sheets.

Into a large bowl sift together the flour, sugar, baking powder, baking soda and salt.

Add the butter to the flour mixture. Using a pastry blender or two knives, cut the butter in until the mixture resembles a fine meal. Sprinkle in 7 tablespoons of the milk. Toss gently with a fork until all ingredients are well moistened. Add more milk if necessary. Continue to toss until the dough forms a ball.

Transfer the dough to a floured board. Knead two to three times. Roll the dough out on the floured board to a ½-inch thickness. Using a 2-inch round cookie or biscuit cutter, cut out 12 scones. Reroll scraps as necessary.

Transfer scones to the prepared sheet and bake for 12 to 15 minutes or until the bottoms are lightly browned. Remove from the oven and serve warm.

CURRANT SCONES

makes 12 scones

2 cups flour
2 teaspoons baking powder
1 teaspoon baking soda
½ teaspoon salt
¼ cup sweet butter, very cold and cut into small pieces
½ cup dried currants
1 large egg
⅔ to 1 cup heavy cream
heavy cream for brushing

Preheat the oven to 400°F. Generously butter two baking sheets. Set aside.

Into a large bowl sift together the flour, baking powder, baking soda and salt.

Add the butter pieces and using a pastry blender or two knives, cut in until the mixture resembles a coarse meal. Stir in the currants.

In a separate bowl combine the egg and ⅔ cup of the cream. Beat until well combined. Add this to the flour mixture, tossing with a fork until a manageable dough forms. Add the remaining cream only if needed.

Turn the dough out onto a floured board and knead for 30 seconds. Shape the dough into a ¾-inch thick rectangle.

Using floured 2 to 2½ inch round biscuit or cookie cutter, cut out 12 rounds. Reroll scraps and cut scones in the same manner as above.

Arrange the scones 1 inch apart on the baking sheet. Brush the top of each scone with cream. Bake for 12 to 14 minutes or until golden. Serve warm.

LEMON GINGER SCONES

makes 12 scones

2 cups flour
4 tablespoons sugar
2½ teaspoons baking powder
2 teaspoons ground ginger
½ teaspoon baking soda
½ teaspoon salt
½ cup sweet butter, very cold and cut into pieces
¾ cup sour cream
1 large egg
2 teaspoons grated lemon peel

Preheat the oven to 425°F.

In a large bowl combine the flour, 2 tablespoons of the sugar, the baking powder, ginger, baking soda and salt.

Add the butter to the flour mixture and using a pastry blender or two knives, cut in until the mixture resembles a fine meal.

Add the sour cream, egg and lemon peel. Using a fork, toss the mixture until moist and well blended. Toss until the dough forms a ball.

Divide the dough into two equal parts. Working on a generously floured surface, put each piece into a 7-inch circle. Using a floured knife, cut each circle into 6 wedges.

Arrange the wedges 1 inch apart on an unbuttered baking sheet. Sprinkle the tops of each wedge with the remaining 2 tablespoons sugar.

Bake for 12 to 14 minutes or until lightly golden. Remove from the oven and serve hot.

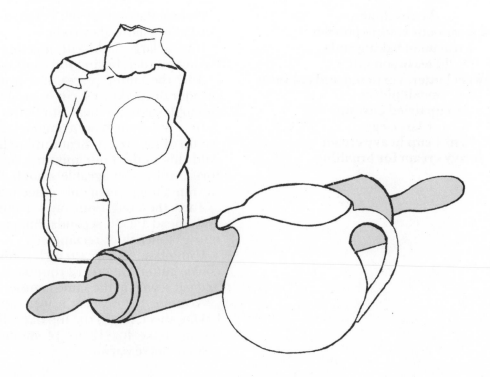

LEMON-SCENTED SCONES

makes 16 to 20 scones

**4 cups flour
2 tablespoons baking powder
¼ cup sugar
¼ teaspoon salt
3 tablespoons grated lemon rind
½ cup sweet butter, very cold and cut into
small pieces
2 large eggs, well beaten
⅔ cup buttermilk
heavy cream for brushing**

Preheat the oven to 450°F. Generously butter and lightly flour two baking sheets. Set aside.

Into a bowl sift the flour 3 times with the baking powder.

Into a large bowl sift together the flour, sugar and salt. Add the lemon rind and stir.

Add the butter pieces and using a pastry blender or two knives cut the butter in until the mixture resembles a coarse meal. Add the eggs and enough of the buttermilk to form a soft dough; toss with a fork until the dough forms a ball.

Transfer the dough to a floured board. Carefully roll out to ½-inch thickness. Add flour as necessary to prevent dough from sticking.

With a 2-inch round biscuit cutter, cut circles out of the dough. Place rounds ½-inch apart on the prepared sheets. Brush the tops of each round with the heavy cream.

Bake for 12 to 14 minutes or until golden. Remove from the oven and serve hot or lukewarm.

CAKES

——PLAIN CAKES——

ALMOND LEMON CAKE

makes 1 9-inch cake

½ cup chopped almonds
1⅔ cups sifted, finely ground almonds
1⅔ cups sifted confectioners' sugar
1 egg white
3 very large eggs
2 teaspoons orange-flavored liqueur
2 teaspoons finely grated lemon rind
6 tablespoons cornstarch, sifted together
with ½ teaspoon baking powder
6½ tablespoons sweet butter, melted and
cooled
confectioners' sugar

Preheat the oven to 350°F. Generously butter a 9-inch round layer-cake pan. Line the bottom of the pan with a piece of waxed paper cut to size. Butter the top of the paper and sprinkle it with flour. Rotate the pan to distribute the flour evenly over the sides. Shake out any excess flour. Press the chopped almonds around the sides of the pan; remove any pieces that fall to the bottom. Set the pan aside.

In the container of a food processor or blender combine the almond meal and sugar.

Process until a very fine powder is formed. With the motor running, add the egg white and process until a smooth paste is formed. The paste should feel sticky to the touch.

Put the almond mixture into the large bowl of an electric mixer. Add the eggs, one at a time, beating well after each addition. Continue to beat until the mixture is very light and smooth, about 10 minutes.

Add the orange-flavored liqueur and the lemon rind. Beat for 1 minute longer.

Sift the cornstarch mixture over the bowl and gently fold it into the mixture with a rubber spatula. Shake the batter off the spatula often to avoid lumps. Gently fold in the melted butter.

Turn the batter into the prepared pan. Bake for 40 to 45 minutes, or until a cake tester inserted into the center of the cake comes out clean.

Remove the cake from the oven and cool completely in the pan on a wire rack. Cover the top of the pan with a serving plate. Carefully invert the pan and unmold the cake. Dust the top of the cake with confectioners' sugar and serve.

ALMOND-TOPPED GLAZED ORANGE CAKE

makes 1 9-inch cake

1¾ cups sifted flour
2 teaspoons baking powder
½ cup plus 6 tablespoons sweet butter, softened
1 cup sugar
4 large eggs
1 teaspoon pure vanilla extract
1 teaspoon grated orange rind
⅛ teaspoon salt
¾ cup orange juice
¼ cup orange-flavored liqueur
⅔ cup toasted sliced almonds
¼ cup sweet orange marmalade

Preheat the oven to 375°F. Generously butter and flour a 9-inch springform pan.

In a small bowl combine the flour and baking powder. Set aside.

In a large bowl cream the butter until light in color and fluffy, approximately 3 minutes. Beat in the sugar, a little at a time, until well blended. Add the eggs, one at a time, beating well after each addition. Scrape sides of bowl with a rubber spatula as necessary. Add the vanilla extract, orange rind and salt. Beat just to blend.

Add the flour mixture to the butter-egg mixture. Fold in until well blended. Turn batter into the prepared pan and bake for 30 to 40 minutes or until a cake tester inserted into the center of the cake comes out clean.

Remove from the oven. Cool in pan on wire rack for 10 minutes. Turn out onto rack and cool slightly.

In a glass combine the orange juice and orange liqueur. Transfer the cake to a serving platter and with a fork pierce the top in several places. Spoon the liquid over the cake. Allow cake to stand until all the liquid is absorbed.

In a small saucepan over a low heat, warm the marmalade until it melts. Brush the marmalade over the entire cake. Sprinkle the top and sides with the toasted almonds. Serve at room temperature.

APPLE PECAN CAKE

makes 1 12-inch cake

¼ cup flour
1 teaspoon baking powder
¼ teaspoon salt
3 eggs
1½ cups sugar
1 teaspoon pure vanilla extract
1 cup apples, peeled, cored and finely chopped
1 cup finely chopped pecans
1 cup heavy cream
2 tablespoons chopped pecans

Preheat the oven to 400°F. Generously butter a 12 × 8 × 2-inch baking pan. Set aside.

Sift together the flour, baking powder and salt. Set aside.

Beat the eggs briefly. Then add the sugar and vanilla and beat until mixture is thick, about 4 to 5 minutes.

Beat in the flour mixture until well blended. Add the chopped apples and 1 cup chopped pecans. Mix gently but thoroughly into the batter with a rubber spatula.

Turn batter into the pan and bake for 30 to 35 minutes or until a cake tester inserted into the center comes out clean.

Remove from oven and cool slightly.

Beat the cream in a chilled mixing bowl until stiff. Transfer to a serving bowl and sprinkle with 2 tablespoons chopped pecans. Serve cake directly from the pan while still warm. Serve whipped cream on the side.

BLACKBERRY CAKE

makes 1 sheet cake

1½ cups sugar
½ cup softened sweet butter
2 eggs
1 cup fresh blackberries
2 cups flour
½ teaspoon baking powder
1 teaspoon grated nutmeg
½ teaspoon cinnamon
⅔ cup buttermilk
1 teaspoon baking soda

Preheat the oven to 350°F. Butter and flour a 13 × 9 × 2-inch baking pan. Set aside.

In a mixing bowl combine the sugar, butter, eggs and blackberries. Beat mixture with an electric mixer at medium-high for 2 minutes.

In a separate bowl combine the flour, baking powder, nutmeg and cinnamon.

Combine the buttermilk and baking soda. Add alternately with the flour mixture to the berries. Beat for 2 minutes.

Pour batter into the pan and bake for 25 to 30 minutes or until a cake tester inserted into the center of the cake comes out clean.

Remove and let cool. Serve from baking pan.

BLACK WALNUT–CITRUS BUTTER CAKE

makes 1 10-inch cake

2 cups sifted flour
1¼ cups sifted cake flour
1½ teaspoons baking soda
1 teaspoon baking powder
¾ teaspoon salt
1 cup softened sweet butter
2 cups sugar
4 extra-large eggs, separated
1½ teaspoons grated lemon rind
1½ teaspoons grated orange rind
1 teaspoon pure vanilla extract
1 cup buttermilk
1 cup coarsely chopped black walnuts
confectioners' sugar

Preheat the oven to 325°F. Generously butter and flour a 10-inch tube pan.

Into a large bowl sift together the flour, cake flour, baking soda, baking powder and salt. Set aside.

In the large bowl of an electric mixer, beat the butter at a high speed until light and fluffy. Add the sugar in three parts, beating well after each addition.

Add the egg yolks, one at a time, beating well after each addition. Scrape down sides of the bowl with a rubber spatula. Beat mixture at high speed for 4 minutes. Add the lemon rind, orange rind and vanilla extract. Beat to blend.

With mixer on low speed, add the flour mixture in 3 parts, alternately with the buttermilk. Begin and end with the flour. Add the black walnuts and stir.

In a small bowl beat the egg whites until firm but not stiff. Stir about 4 tablespoons of the egg whites into the batter. Fold in the remaining egg whites. Mix gently.

Turn batter into prepared pan. Bake for 1 hour 15 minutes or until a cake tester inserted into the center of the cake comes out clean.

Remove from the oven. Cool in pan on wire rack for 15 minutes. Turn cake out onto rack and cool completely. Dust top of the cake with confectioners' sugar before serving.

BLACK WALNUT AND DATE CAKE

makes 1 9 × 13-inch cake

2 cups very coarsely chopped black walnuts
2 cups coarsely chopped dates
1 cup flour
2 teaspoons baking powder
4 large eggs, lightly beaten
1 cup sugar
1 teaspoon pure vanilla extract

Preheat the oven to 325°F. Generously butter a 9 × 13-inch baking pan. Set aside.

In a large bowl combine the black walnuts and dates. Set aside.

In a bowl combine the flour and baking powder. Mix well. Set aside.

In a large bowl beat together the eggs, sugar and vanilla extract until very well blended; approximately 2 minutes. Add the flour mixture and beat until mixed. Stir in the black walnut and date mixture. Mix until evenly distributed.

Transfer batter to the prepared pan and bake for 1 hour or until a cake tester inserted into the center of the cake comes out clean.

Remove from the oven. Cool in pan on wire rack. Cut into pieces and serve from the pan.

BLUEBERRY BUTTER CAKE

makes 1 8-inch cake

1 cup softened sweet butter
2½ cups flour
1¼ cups sugar
4 eggs
2½ teaspoons baking powder
¼ teaspoon salt
1½ teaspoons pure vanilla extract
1½ cups fresh blueberries
1 cup chilled heavy cream

Preheat the oven to 375°F.

Using an electric mixer, cream the butter and sugar together in a large mixing bowl until light and fluffy. Beat in the eggs, one at a time.

In a bowl combine 2¼ cups flour with the baking powder and salt. Beat the flour mixture into the creamed mixture, a little at a time. Beat in the vanilla extract.

Place the blueberries in a small bowl and toss with the remaining ¼ cup flour. Coat berries evenly. Gently fold the berries into the batter.

Turn the batter into a generously buttered and floured 8-inch springform cake pan. Bake for 1 hour or until a cake tester inserted into the center comes out clean.

Remove from oven. Remove the sides of the pan. Cool cake for 15 minutes.

Beat the chilled cream in a chilled mixing bowl. Sweeten with a little confectioners' sugar if desired. Beat the cream until it is thick enough to form peaks. Serve the cream with the warm cake.

BRAZIL NUT ORANGE CAKE

makes 1 9-inch cake

2 cups and 2 tablespoons Brazil nuts
¾ cup and 2 tablespoons sugar
¼ cup flour
5 eggs, separated
1 tablespoon orange juice
1 teaspoon grated orange rind
¼ teaspoon cream of tartar
confectioners' sugar for dusting

Preheat the oven to 350°F. Place the nuts in a baking pan and toast in the oven for 10 minutes. Remove ⅓ cup of the nuts to a large strainer. Turn off the oven, leaving the remaining nuts inside. Using a terry cloth towel, rub the nuts against the strainer to remove most of their skins. Repeat the process with the remaining nuts, working in batches. Allow nuts to cool completely.

Preheat the oven to 325°F. Butter a 9-inch springform pan. Line the bottom with foil. Butter the foil and flour the entire pan. Set aside.

In a blender or food processor, grind half the nuts with 3 tablespoons of the sugar until fine. Transfer nut mixture to a bowl. Repeat the process with the remaining nuts and an additional 3 tablespoons sugar. Sift the flour over the nut mixture and stir until well blended.

In a large bowl beat the egg yolks with ¼ cup of sugar for 5 minutes or until very light in color. Add the orange juice and orange rind. Beat to blend.

In a separate bowl beat the egg whites with the cream of tartar until soft peaks form. Gradually add the remaining ¼ cup sugar, beating until egg whites are stiff but not dry.

Add the nut mixture to the egg yolk mixture alternately with the egg whites, folding it in 3 batches. Fold until just blended.

Gently transfer batter to the prepared pan and bake for 45 minutes or until a cake tester inserted into the center comes out clean. Remove from the oven. Cool in pan on wire rack for 10 minutes. Run a knife around the side of the cake and remove sides. Invert again so cake is right-side up. Cool thoroughly. Dust cake with confectioners' sugar before serving.

BUTTERMILK RAISIN CAKE

makes 1 9-inch cake

½ cup softened sweet butter
1 cup sugar
3 eggs, separated
½ cup buttermilk
2 tablespoons prune juice
2 cups flour
½ teaspoon baking soda
1 cup chopped raisins

Preheat the oven to 350°F.
In a mixing bowl cream the butter and sugar together until light and fluffy.

In a separate bowl beat the egg yolks. Stir into the butter and sugar mixture. Add the buttermilk and prune juice. Stir until well mixed. Add the flour and baking soda.

In a small bowl beat the egg whites until stiff but not dry. Fold gently into the batter. Stir in raisins.

Turn the batter into a buttered 9-inch square baking pan. Bake for 35 to 40 minutes or until a cake tester inserted into the center comes out clean.

Remove from oven and cool.

Parker House Rolls

Sand Cookies

Toll House Cookies

Pound Cake

Black Bread

Apple Crumb Cake

Holiday Fruitcake

Corn Bread

BUTTER CAKE WITH HAZELNUT
CHOCOLATE SWIRL

makes 1 9-inch cake

2½ cups sifted flour
2 teaspoons baking powder
1½ cups finely ground hazelnuts
¼ cup Dutch-process unsweetened cocoa
¼ cup milk
1 tablespoon rum
1 cup sweet butter, softened
1⅓ cups sugar
4 eggs
1½ teaspoons pure vanilla extract
confectioners' sugar for dusting cake

Preheat the oven to 375°F. Butter and lightly flour a 9-inch ring mold pan. Set aside.

In a small bowl combine the flour and baking powder. Set aside.

In another small bowl combine the ground hazelnuts and cocoa. Add the milk and rum and stir to moisten. Set aside.

In a large bowl cream the butter until light in color and fluffy, approximately 3 minutes. Beat in the sugar, a little at a time, until well blended. Add the eggs, one at a time, beating well after each addition. Scrape down the sides of the bowl as needed. Add the vanilla extract and beat until well blended.

Add the flour mixture to the batter and gently fold in until well mixed.

Measure out 1½ cups of the batter and mix it with the hazelnut-cocoa mixture.

Place half the remaining plain batter into the prepared pan. Smooth the top with a rubber spatula. Then add the hazelnut batter on top and smooth. Carefully place a fork down into the pan and with a swirling motion lift it up. This should partially mix both batters. Repeat this process about six times around the pan. Top with the remaining plain batter and smooth the top.

Bake for 50 minutes or until a cake tester inserted into the center of the cake comes out clean. Remove from the oven. Let cake cool in the pan on a wire rack for 10 minutes. Invert cake out onto wire rack and cool completely. Dust with confectioners' sugar before serving.

BUTTERY COCOA CAKE

makes 1 10-inch cake

3¼ cups sifted flour
1 cup Dutch-process unsweetened cocoa
3⅛ teaspoons baking powder
¾ teaspoon salt
¾ cup heavy cream
2½ teaspoons pure vanilla extract
1 cup softened sweet butter
2¾ cups sugar
3 extra-large eggs
1 cup milk
confectioners' sugar for dusting

Preheat the oven to 325°F. Generously butter and flour a 10-inch tube pan.

Into a large bowl sift together the flour, cocoa, baking powder and salt. Set aside.

In a small bowl combine the cream and vanilla.

In a large bowl cream the butter until light and fluffy, approximately 3 minutes. Add the sugar in 3 parts, beating for 2 minutes after each addition. Add the eggs, one at a time, beating well after each addition. Scrape down sides of the bowl with a rubber spatula and beat mixture for 3 minutes. Scrape down sides of bowl often.

Add the flour mixture in three parts, alternately with the milk and then the cream mixture. Begin and end with the flour mixture. Beat until blended.

Pour batter into prepared pan and bake for 1 hour 20 minutes or until a cake tester inserted into the center of the cake comes out clean.

Remove from the oven and turn cake out of pan onto wire rack to cool completely. Dust top of cake with confectioners' sugar before serving.

CHOCOLATE BUNDT CAKE

makes 1 bundt cake

3 cups sifted cake flour
1 cup Dutch-process unsweetened cocoa
1 tablespoon baking powder
1 teaspoon salt
2¾ cups sugar
1 cup softened sweet butter
1½ cups milk
1 tablespoon pure vanilla extract
3 large eggs
¼ cup light cream
1 cup coarsely chopped walnuts
1¼ cups semisweet chocolate pieces
½ cup dark raisins
½ cup golden raisins

Preheat the oven to 325°F. Generously butter and flour a 12-cup bundt pan. Set aside.

Into a large bowl sift together the flour, cocoa, baking powder and salt. Add the sugar and stir to combine. Make a well in the center of the dry ingredients and add the butter. Stir to mix.

Using an electric mixer, gradually beat in the milk and the vanilla extract. Beat for 7 minutes. Scrape down sides with a rubber spatula when necessary.

Add the eggs, one at a time, beating well after each addition. Add the cream and beat to blend.

Add the walnuts, chocolate pieces, raisins and golden raisins. Stir until thoroughly incorporated into the batter.

Turn the batter into the prepared pan and bake in the oven for 1 hour 40 minutes or until a cake tester inserted into the center of the cake comes out clean.

Remove cake from the oven and cool in pan on wire rack for 10 minutes. Turn cake out onto rack and cool completely.

COCONUT CHOCOLATE RING

makes 1 9-inch cake

2 cups sifted flour
2 teaspoons baking powder
1 cup softened sweet butter
1¼ cups sugar
4 large eggs
1½ teaspoons pure vanilla extract
1 cup shredded unsweetened coconut
4 ounces semisweet chocolate, finely grated
4 ounces semisweet chocolate pieces
3 tablespoons softened sweet butter
¼ cup shredded unsweetened coconut
(optional)

Preheat the oven to 375°F. Generously butter and lightly flour a 9-inch springform pan with a tube bottom.

In a bowl combine the flour and the baking powder. Set aside.

In a large bowl cream the 1 cup butter until light in color and fluffy, approximately 3 minutes. Add the sugar, a little at a time, and beat until well blended. Add the eggs, one at a time, beating well after each addition. Scrape down the sides of the bowl with a rubber spatula when necessary. Add the vanilla and beat until blended.

Fold the flour mixture into the batter, mixing only until blended. Add the 1 cup coconut and grated chocolate. Gently fold into the batter. Turn cake into prepared pan.

Bake for 45 to 50 minutes or until a cake tester inserted in the center of the cake comes out clean. Remove from the oven. Cool in pan on wire rack for 10 minutes. Remove sides of pan and invert onto wire rack. Remove bottom and cool completely.

When the cake is cool make the frosting. In the top part of a double boiler combine the chocolate pieces and the 3 tablespoons butter. Melt over hot not boiling water, stirring constantly until smooth and shiny. Remove from the heat and let cool to spreading consistency, about 30 minutes.

Spread the frosting over the top and sides of the cake. Sprinkle the ¼ cup shredded coconut over the top if desired.

FLOURLESS POPPY SEED CAKE

makes 1 8-inch cake

½ cup softened sweet butter
¾ cup sugar
6 large eggs, separated
1 tablespoon grated orange peel
¼ teaspoon ground cinnamon
½ teaspoon pure vanilla extract
1 cup ground poppy seeds
1 cup ground walnuts
¼ cup fine unflavored breadcrumbs
2 tablespoons rum
salt
cream of tartar
⅓ cup apricot jam
confectioners' sugar for dusting

Preheat the oven to 350°F. Generously butter an 8-inch springform pan. Line the bottom of the pan with waxed paper and butter again. Set aside.

In a large bowl cream the butter with an electric mixer. Gradually add the sugar; beat until light and fluffy. Add the egg yolks, one at a time, beating well after each addition. Add the orange peel, cinnamon and vanilla extract. Continue beating until the mixture is thick and light in color.

Add the poppy seeds, walnuts, breadcrumbs and rum. Stir until well blended.

In a small bowl beat the egg whites with a pinch of salt until foamy. Add a pinch (about ⅛ teaspoon) of cream of tartar and beat until whites are stiff but not dry. Stir one-third of the egg whites into the first mixture. Fold the remaining egg whites in gently.

Turn batter into prepared pan and bake for 45 to 50 minutes or until a cake tester inserted into the center comes out clean.

Remove from the oven. Cool in pan on wire rack for 15 minutes. Remove sides of pan and invert the cake onto the rack. Remove the bottom of the pan and the waxed paper and cool completely.

Carefully cut the cake in half to form two layers. Heat the apricot jam and spread it evenly on the bottom layer. Replace the top layer and dust the cake with confectioners' sugar.

FUDGE NUT CAKE

makes 1 9-inch cake

¾ cup sweet butter, softened
2 teaspoons pure vanilla extract
1½ cups sugar
3 large eggs, separated
3 ounces unsweetened chocolate, melted
3 tablespoons hot water
½ cups sifted flour
¾ cup coarsely chopped walnuts
⅛ teaspoon salt
⅛ teaspoon cream of tartar
confectioners' sugar for dusting

Preheat the oven to 350°F. Line the bottom of a 9-inch round cake pan with foil cut to size. Butter the foil and set aside.

In a large bowl cream the butter until light and fluffy. Add the vanilla extract and mix well. Add the sugar, a little at a time, and beat well. Add egg yolks, one at a time, beating well after each addition. Scrape down the sides of the bowl with a rubber spatula.

Add melted chocolate and water. Stir to blend. Add flour and stir until batter is smooth. Add walnuts and stir.

In a bowl beat the egg whites with the salt and cream of tartar until stiff but not dry.

Fold half of the egg whites into the chocolate mixture. Add remaining whites and fold in gently.

Turn batter into prepared pan and smooth the top. Bake for 45 minutes or until cake is firm and top is cracked. Remove from the oven. Cool in pan on wire rack for 1 hour.

Turn out onto another rack. Remove foil. Invert onto a serving plate. Dust top with sugar and serve.

HICKORY NUT CAKE

makes 1 9-inch cake

3½ cups flour
2 teaspoons baking powder
½ teaspoon salt
2 cups sugar
1 cup sweet butter, softened
1 cup milk
4 cups chopped hickory nuts
4 egg whites, slightly beaten
2 teaspoons pure vanilla extract

Preheat the oven to 325°F. Generously butter a deep 9-inch round baking pan. Line the bottom with waxed paper and butter the paper. Flour pan and set aside.

Into a bowl sift together the flour, baking powder and salt.

In a large mixing bowl cream together the butter and sugar until light and fluffy.

Add the flour mixture to the butter mixture alternately with the milk. Mix until well blended. Stir in the nuts and the vanilla extract.

In a separate bowl beat the egg white until stiff but not dry. Gently fold whites into batter.

Turn cake batter into prepared pan and bake for 1 hour or until cake tester inserted into the center of the cake comes out clean. Be careful not to cook the cake too long. Cake should not be dry.

Remove from the oven. Cool cake in pan or wire rack for 10 minutes. Carefully invert cake onto another wire rack and remove the paper. Invert to right-side up and cool completely.

MOLASSES CAKE

makes 1 bundt cake

2½ cups flour
1 cup sugar
4 teaspoons baking soda
½ teaspoon ground ginger
½ teaspoon grated nutmeg
½ teaspoon ground cinnamon
½ teaspoon salt
1 cup boiling water
½ cup sweet butter, melted and cooled
½ cup molasses
2 large eggs, lightly beaten

Preheat the oven to 350°F. Generously butter and flour a 2-quart bundt pan.

Into a large bowl sift together the flour, sugar, baking soda, ginger, nutmeg, cinnamon and salt. Mix well. Make a well in the center of the mixture and add the boiling water, butter and molasses. Mix until well blended. Add the eggs and stir.

Turn the batter into the prepared pan and bake for 45 to 50 minutes or until a cake tester inserted into the center of the cake comes out clean.

Remove from the oven. Let cake cool in pan on wire rack for 15 minutes. Turn cake out onto rack and cool completely.

MOCHA SPICE CAKE

makes 1 9-inch square

2 cups flour
½ teaspoon salt
½ teaspoon baking soda
1 teaspoon ground cinnamon
1 teaspoon grated nutmeg
2 cups strong coffee
2 cups sugar
2 tablespoons Dutch-process unsweetened cocoa
1 cup golden raisins
½ cup softened sweet butter
½ teaspoon pure vanilla extract
2 large eggs
confectioners' sugar for dusting

Preheat the oven to 350°F. Butter a 9 × 9 × 2-inch square pan. Set aside.

Into a bowl sift together the flour, salt, baking soda, cinnamon and nutmeg. Set aside.

In a saucepan combine the coffee, 1 cup sugar, cocoa and raisins. Heat to the boiling point; reduce heat and simmer for 15 minutes over a low heat. Remove from the heat and cool.

In a large bowl cream the butter. Gradually add the remaining 1 cup sugar, beating until mixture is light and fluffy. Add the vanilla extract and mix well.

Add the eggs, one at a time, beating well after each addition. Scrape down sides of the bowl with a rubber spatula when necessary. Add the flour mixture and stir well until well blended. Add the cooled cocoa mixture and stir well. Turn batter into the prepared pan and bake for 1 hour or until cake tester inserted into the center of the cake comes out clean.

Remove from the oven. Cool completely in pan or wire rack. When cool turn cake out of pan and invert onto plate. Dust with confectioners' sugar before serving.

OLD-FASHIONED SOUR CREAM CAKE

makes 1 9-inch cake

**2½ cups flour
2½ teaspoons baking powder
½ teaspoon baking soda
½ teaspoon salt
1 cup sour cream
1½ teaspoons pure vanilla extract
1 cup sweet butter, softened
1¾ cups sugar
3 large eggs
½ cup finely chopped walnuts
1½ teaspoons ground cinnamon
confectioners' sugar (optional)**

Preheat the oven to 325°F. Butter and lightly flour a 9-inch tube pan. Set aside.

Into a large bowl sift together the flour, baking powder, baking soda and salt. Set aside.

In a small bowl mix together the sour cream and vanilla extract. Set aside.

In a large bowl beat the butter at a high speed until light in color and fluffy, approximately 2 to 3 minutes. Add 1½ cups of the sugar, in two parts, beating very well after each addition. Add the eggs, one at a time, beating well after each addition. Scrape down the sides of the bowl with a rubber spatula and beat mixture for 3 minutes.

Add the flour mixture in two parts alternately with the sour cream mixture. Begin and end with the flour. Beat only until blended.

Place the chopped walnuts and cinnamon in a small bowl. Add the remaining ¼ cup sugar and mix well.

Turn half the batter into the prepared pan. Sprinkle with half of the sugar-nut mixture. Pour in remaining batter and sprinkle with remaining sugar-nut mixture. Bake for 55 minutes or until a cake tester inserted into the center of the cake comes out clean.

Remove from the oven and cool in the pan on a wire rack. Turn out onto wire rack and cool completely. If desired dust with confectioners' sugar before serving.

ONE-LAYER APPLE-RAISIN CAKE

makes 1 8-inch cake

1¾ cups flour
⅓ cup sugar
1 teaspoon baking powder
½ teaspoon salt
½ cup boiling water
¼ cup golden raisins
½ cup cold sweet butter
1 large tart apple
1 large egg
3 tablespoons milk
1 tablespoon sugar
⅛ teaspoon ground cinnamon
whipped cream (optional)

Preheat the oven to 375°F. Butter and lightly flour an 8-inch round pan.

Into a large bowl sift together the flour, sugar, baking powder and salt. Set aside.

Place raisins in a small bowl and pour the boiling water over them. Plump for 10 minutes, drain and gently pat dry. Set aside.

Cut the butter into the flour mixture with a pastry blender or two knives until the mixture resembles a coarse meal.

Peel, core and quarter the apple. Using a grater, coarsely shred the apple into the flour mixture. Add the raisins and mix until well blended.

In a small bowl beat the egg and milk together. Gently pour over the flour mixture and toss with a fork just until the dry ingredients are moistened. Mixture will be sticky.

Using a rubber spatula, scrape the batter into the prepared pan. Spread evenly and smooth the top.

In a small bowl combine the sugar and cinnamon. Sprinkle mixture evenly over the top of the cake. Bake for 30 minutes or until top is lightly golden and cake begins to pull away from the sides.

Remove from the oven. Cool in pan on wire rack for 10 minutes. Turn cake out onto wire rack and invert into a plate. Serve warm with whipped cream.

PEAR CAKE

makes 1 10-inch cake

1½ tablespoons sweet butter, softened
⅔ cup sugar
3 tablespoons lemon juice
3 tablespoons dark rum
4 to 5 semiripe pears
8½ tablespoons sweet butter, softened
½ cup sugar
1 teaspoon grated lemon rind
⅓ teaspoon salt
2 large eggs
1 cup plus 2 tablespoons flour
1 teaspoon baking powder

Preheat the oven to 375°F. Butter a 10-inch deep glass pie plate with the 1½ tablespoons butter. Sprinkle the ⅔ cup sugar, lemon juice and 2 tablespoons of the rum on the bottom of the dish.

Peel the pears. Cut them in half and core.

Cut halves crossways into 1¼ inch slices. Arrange the slices, round-side down, in concentric circles in the pie dish. Bake for 1 hour or until pears are slightly carmelized and tender. Remove from the oven and cool. Reduce oven temperature to 350°F.

In a medium-sized bowl cream the 8½ tablespoons butter. Add the ½ cup sugar, the remaining rum, the lemon rind and salt. Beat until well blended. Add the eggs, one at a time, beating well after each addition.

Sift the flour with the baking powder over the butter mixture; gently fold in. Spoon flour mixture over the slightly cooled pears.

Bake for 25 to 30 minutes or until a cake tester inserted into the center comes out clean. Remove from the oven and immediately turn out onto a plate. If any caramel is left in the dish spread it over the pears. Serve at room temperature.

PEAR-ALMOND CAKE

makes 1 9-inch cake

2 pounds ripe pears
juice of 1 lemon
1 cup flour
½ teaspoon baking powder
½ teaspoon salt
⅔ cup sweet butter, softened
1 cup sugar
2 large eggs
½ teaspoon almond extract
½ cup sliced almonds

Preheat the oven to 350°F. Generously butter and flour a 9-inch springform pan.

Peel, core and slice the pears. Toss the pears with half the lemon juice and set aside.

Into a large bowl sift together the flour, baking powder and salt.

In a bowl cream ½ cup of the butter with ¾ cup of the sugar. Add the eggs, one at a time, beating well after each addition.

Add the flour mixture, remaining lemon juice and almond extract. Stir until all ingredients are well blended.

Turn the batter into the prepared pan and cover the top with the pears. Dot with 1 tablespoon of the remaining butter and sprinkle with 2 tablespoons of the remaining sugar. Scatter the sliced almonds on top. Top almonds with the remaining butter and sugar.

Bake for 50 minutes or until top is lightly golden. Remove cake from the oven and cool for 15 minutes on wire rack. Remove sides of pan and serve warm or at room temperature.

PLUM AND NECTARINE CAKE

makes 1 9-inch cake

1 cup flour
1 teaspoon baking powder
¼ teaspoon salt
½ cup sweet butter, softened
¾ cup sugar
1 large egg, lightly beaten
⅓ cup milk
2 tablespoons brandy
1 teaspoon pure vanilla extract
2 plums, pitted and thinly sliced
1 nectarine, pitted and thinly sliced

Preheat the oven to 350°F.

Into a bowl sift together the flour, baking powder and salt. Set aside.

In a large bowl cream 6 tablespoons of the butter. Add ½ cup of the sugar and beat until light and fluffy. Add the egg and beat well.

Add the flour mixture alternately with the milk to the butter mixture. Beat until smooth. Add the brandy and the vanilla extract. Beat well.

Place the remaining butter in a nonstick 9-inch round pan. Place the pan over low heat and melt the butter. Add the remaining sugar and cook, stirring constantly, for 2 minutes. Remove from the heat. Arrange the plum and nectarine slices in an overlapping pattern in the bottom of the pan. Return to the heat and cook for 2 minutes. Remove the pan from the heat.

Spoon the batter into the pan evenly over the fruit. Bake for 30 to 40 minutes or until a cake tester inserted into the center comes out clean.

Remove from the oven. Cool cake in pan on wire rack for 10 minutes. Turn cake out onto dish and serve warm or at room temperature.

RAISIN-PECAN TUBE CAKE

makes 1 10-inch cake

3¾ cups flour
1 teaspoon baking powder
4 teaspoons grated nutmeg
4 cups chopped pecans
5 cups golden raisins
1 cup dark raisins
1 cup softened sweet butter
2 cups sugar
6 eggs
½ cup brandy

Preheat the oven to 275°F. Butter a 10-inch tube pan and set aside.

In a large bowl stir together the flour, baking powder and nutmeg.

Remove ½ cup of the flour mixture and add it to the pecans and raisins in a separate bowl. Mix and set aside.

Cream the butter and sugar until light and fluffy. Add the eggs, two at a time. Beat thoroughly after each addition.

Add the flour mixture to the creamed butter alternately with the brandy. Mix after each addition until well blended. Add the pecan-raisin mixture and mix thoroughly.

Turn the batter into the tube pan. Bake in the center of the oven for 2 hours.

Remove to a cooling rack. Cool in the pan for 15 minutes. Turn cake out and cool completely on rack.

PLUM CARAMEL CAKE

makes 1 13-inch cake

¾ pound Italian plums
¼ cup water
¼ cup sugar
2 cups sifted flour
1 teaspoon baking powder
1 teaspoon freshly grated nutmeg
1 teaspoon ground cinnamon
¼ teaspoon salt
1¼ cups sugar
1 cup oil
3 large eggs
1 teaspoon pure vanilla extract
1 cup buttermilk
1 cup coarsely chopped pecans
Caramel Topping (see page 169)

Pit the plums and then chop them into small pieces. In a small saucepan combine the plums, water and sugar. Cook over high heat to the boiling point. Reduce the heat to medium and continue to boil until mixture becomes syrupy and the plums are soft, about 10 minutes. Stir with a spoon and mash. Remove from the heat and set aside.

Preheat the oven to 315°F. Generously butter and flour a 13 × 9-inch pan.

Into a bowl sift together the flour, baking powder, nutmeg, cinnamon and salt. Set aside.

In a large bowl beat together the sugar and oil until well blended. Add the eggs, one at a time, beating well after each addition. Add the vanilla extract and beat until blended. Add the flour mixture in two parts, alternately with the buttermilk. Mix until ingredients are moistened. Do not overmix. Add the chopped pecans and the plums. Fold in gently but thoroughly.

Turn batter into the prepared pan. Bake for 45 to 50 minutes or until a cake tester inserted into the center comes out clean. When cake has approximately 10 minutes left, make the caramel topping.

Remove cake from the oven and place pan on a wire rack. Prick cake all over with a fork. Pour hot caramel topping over the cake. Let cool to room temperature before cutting.

RUM NUT CAKE

makes 1 10-inch cake

3½ cups cake flour
4 teaspoons baking powder
2 teaspoons grated nutmeg
1 teaspoon salt
4 cups coarsely chopped walnuts
1½ cups dark raisins
1½ cups golden raisins
½ cup flour
1 cup sweet butter, softened
2 cups sugar
6 large eggs
1 cup dark rum

Preheat the oven to 315°F. Generously butter and lightly flour a 10-inch tube pan. Set aside.

In a large bowl combine the cake flour, baking powder, nutmeg and salt. Set aside.

In another bowl combine the walnuts, raisins and golden raisins. Toss the ½ cup flour over them and mix to coat evenly. Set aside.

In a large bowl beat together the butter and sugar until light and smooth. Add the eggs, one at a time, beating well after each addition. Scrape down the sides of the bowl with a rubber spatula. Beat until fluffy.

Add the flour mixture alternately with the rum to the butter-egg batter. Do this in 3 additions. Add the nut-raisin mixture and stir until thoroughly incorporated.

Transfer batter to the prepared pan. Smooth the top. Bake for 1 hour 10 minutes or until a cake tester inserted into the center comes out clean.

Remove from the oven. Cool in the pan on a wire rack for 10 minutes. Turn cake out onto rack and cool completely. Wrap in aluminum foil or plastic wrap and store at least one day before slicing.

TART APPLE SHEET CAKE

makes 1 sheet cake

2½ cups sifted flour
2 teaspoons baking powder
1½ pounds tart baking apples
2 tablespoons lemon juice
1 cup sweet butter, softened
1 cup sugar
4 large eggs
1 teaspoon pure vanilla extract
1 teaspoon grated lemon rind
1½ cups apple jelly
1½ tablespoons sugar
1 tablespoon dark rum

Preheat the oven to 375°F. Generously butter and flour a 16 × 11 × 1-inch jelly roll pan. Set aside.

In a small bowl, combine the flour and the baking powder. Set aside.

Peel the apples and slice them lengthwise into eight wedges. Core the wedges and make three long, shallow cuts lengthwise on the outside of each wedge. Brush wedge with lemon juice and set aside.

In a large bowl cream the butter until light and fluffy. Add the 1 cup sugar, a little at a time, beating until well blended. Add the eggs, one at a time, beating well after each addition. Scrape down the sides of the bowl with a rubber spatula when necessary. Add the vanilla extract and the lemon rind and beat until blended.

Add the flour mixture to the batter and fold in gently. Turn batter into prepared pan and smooth top with rubber spatula.

Place the apples, cut side up, in four rows about ¾ inch apart. Press apples lightly into the batter.

Bake for 30 to 35 minutes or until top of cake is golden and a cake tester inserted into the center of the cake comes out clean. Remove from the oven. Cool cake in pan on wire rack.

While cake cools prepare the glaze. Combine the apple jelly, sugar and rum in a saucepan, boil and cook, stirring constantly, over medium heat until the glaze is thick enough to coat the back of a spoon. If you do not use the glaze right away, warm briefly to spreading consistency before using.

Place 1 tablespoon of the hot glaze onto each piece of apple. Serve cake warm or at room temperature.

WHISKEY TUBE CAKE

makes 1 10-inch cake

1½ cups softened sweet butter
2 cups sugar
2¼ cups firmly packed light brown sugar
6 eggs
5½ cups flour
¼ teaspoon salt
1 teaspoon grated nutmeg
2 cups whiskey
3½ cups coarsely chopped pecans

Preheat the oven to 300°F. Heavily grease a 10-inch tube pan. Flour lightly and shake out excess. Set aside.

In a very large mixing bowl cream the butter until soft.

In a medium bowl combine the sugar and brown sugar. Mix well. Add half the sugar mixture to the butter and cream until smooth.

In another bowl beat the eggs until light and fluffy. Slowly beat in the remaining sugar mixture. Continue beating until mixture is smooth and creamy. Add to the butter mixture and stir until thoroughly combined.

Sift the flour, salt and nutmeg together. Add the flour and whiskey alternately to the batter, beginning and ending with the flour. Mix thoroughly. Stir in the pecan pieces.

Turn batter into the tube pan and bake for 1½ to 1¾ hours or until the cake begins to shrink from the pan.

Remove from oven and cool in pan for 15 minutes. Turn out onto rack and cool completely. This cake improves with age. Wrap tightly in aluminum foil and store.

——FROSTED CAKES——

ALMOND CHOCOLATE CAKE WITH ORANGE-SCENTED CREAM

makes 1 9-inch cake

4 ounces semisweet chocolate, cut into pieces
¼ cup sweet butter
½ cup blanched almonds
⅔ cup sugar
3 tablespoons cornstarch
3 large eggs, separated
2 tablespoons orange liqueur
¼ teaspoon cream of tartar

TOPPING:
¾ cup very cold heavy cream
1½ teaspoons sugar
1½ teaspoons orange liqueur
½ ounce semisweet chocolate, finely grated

Preheat the oven to 350°F. Generously butter a 9-inch round cake pan. Line the bottom of the pan with foil cut to size. Lightly butter the foil. Set aside.

In the top part of a double boiler melt the chocolate together with the butter over hot but not boiling water. Stir until smooth. Remove from the heat and cool for 10 minutes.

In a food processor or blender grind the almonds with 3 tablespoons of the sugar. Turn into a bowl. Add 4 tablespoons of the sugar and the cornstarch. Mix thoroughly. Add the nut–sugar mixture to the melted chocolate and stir well. Add the egg yolks, one at a time, using a wooden spoon; beat until smooth. Blend in the orange liqueur.

In a bowl beat the egg whites with cream of tartar until soft peaks begin to form. Beat in the remaining sugar, a little at a time, and continue beating until whites are stiff but not dry.

Stir 3 tablespoons of the egg whites into the chocolate mixture. Fold chocolate mixture back into egg whites. Mix until just blended.

Turn batter into prepared pan and bake for 20 to 25 minutes or until a cake tester inserted into the center of the cake comes out clean.

Remove from the oven. Run a knife around the sides of the cake to separate the edges from the pan. Turn out onto a wire rack and remove pan and foil. Turn right-side up onto a rack and cool completely. Chill for at least 1 hour before frosting.

To make the topping in a well-chilled bowl beat the cream together with the sugar and liqueur until firm peaks form. Turn the cake onto a serving plate. Spread the cream on the top and sides of cake. Sprinkle grated chocolate over the top. Keep refrigerated. Serve at room temperature. The cake will keep for approximately 8 hours once it has been frosted. If you wish to keep cake the longer, do not frost it; serve the cream on the side.

BLACK WALNUT APPLESAUCE CHOCOLATE CAKE

makes 1 9-inch cake

½ cup sweet butter, softened
1 cup sugar
1 large egg
1⅔ cups sifted cake flour
1 cup chopped black walnuts
½ teaspoon salt
1 teaspoon pure vanilla extract
1 teaspoon baking soda
1 teaspoon ground cinnamon
½ teaspoon allspice
2 tablespoons Dutch-process cocoa
2 cups applesauce, heated

Preheat the oven to 350°F. Butter and flour a 9-inch tube pan. Set aside.

In a large bowl cream the butter until light and fluffy. Gradually add the sugar and beat well. Add the egg and beat until well blended.

Add 2 tablespoons of the flour to the chopped nuts. Mix.

Onto a piece of waxed paper sift together the remaining flour, salt, baking soda, cinnamon, allspice and cocoa. Mix to blend.

Add the flour mixture alternately with the applesauce to the creamed mixture. Mix well. Add the vanilla extract and walnuts. Mix until nuts are evenly distributed.

Turn batter into the prepared pan and bake for 40 minutes or until a cake tester inserted near the center comes out clean.

Remove from the oven. Cool in pan on wire rack for 10 minutes. Invert cake and turn out onto rack to cool completely.

CHOCOLATE-GLAZED RUM CAKE

makes 1 10-inch cake

¾ cup and 2 tablespoons flour
½ teaspoon baking powder
½ teaspoon salt
¼ teaspoon baking soda
2 ounces unsweetened chocolate, melted
¾ cup sweet butter, softened
1¼ cups sugar
2 large eggs
1 tablespoon cocoa
½ cup sour cream
⅓ cup boiling water
1 tablespoon dark rum
Chocolate Glaze (see page 170)

Preheat the oven to 325°F. Butter a 10-inch springform pan. Line the bottom with a piece of waxed paper cut to size. Butter the paper. Set aside.

Onto a piece of waxed paper sift together the flour, baking powder, salt and baking soda. Resift and set aside.

In a large bowl cream together the butter and sugar until light. Add the eggs, one at a time, beating well after each addition, until fluffy.

Add the cocoa and sour cream. Beat until smooth. Add the melted chocolate and mix well.

Add the flour mixture alternately with the boiling water and rum. Mix well after each addition.

Turn batter into prepared pan and bake for 45 to 50 minutes or until cake begins to pull away from the sides of the pan. Remove from the oven. Cool in pan on wire rack.

While cake cools, prepare the Chocolate Glaze.

Remove bottom of pan and waxed paper. Pour the glaze over the cake and spread evenly over top and sides. Allow glaze to set before slicing.

CHOCOLATE AND MARMALADE CAKE

makes 1 8-inch cake

1½ cups flour
1 teaspoon baking powder
⅛ teaspoon salt
3 ounces semisweet chocolate
3 ounces unsweetened chocolate
¾ cup sweet butter, softened
⅔ cup sugar
5 large eggs, separated
¾ cup bitter orange marmalade
¼ cup ground blanched almonds

Preheat the oven to 350°F. Butter an 8-inch springform pan. Line the bottom of the pan with a piece of waxed paper cut to size. Butter the paper and flour the pan.

Into a bowl sift together the flour, baking powder and salt. Set aside.

In the top part of a double boiler melt both chocolates together over hot but not boiling water. Stir until melted and smooth. Remove from the heat and cool to room temperature.

In a large bowl, cream the butter until light. Add the sugar, a little at a time, and beat until mixture is light and fluffy. Add egg yolks, one at a time, beating well after each addition. Scrape down sides of bowl with a rubber spatula as needed. Add chocolate and ¼ cup of the marmalade. Beat until well blended.

Stir in the flour mixture, a little at a time, until well mixed. Add the ground almonds and stir.

In a bowl beat the egg whites until stiff but not dry. Add 3 tablespoons of the whites to the chocolate mixture. Fold in. Gently fold in the remaining whites.

Transfer the batter to the prepared pan and bake for 40 to 45 minutes or until a cake tester inserted into the center of the cake comes out clean. Remove from the oven. Cool in pan on wire rack for 5 minutes. Remove sides of pan and turn cake out onto a wire rack. Remove bottom and waxed paper. Invert onto another rack and cool completely.

In a small saucepan heat the remaining marmalade over a low heat. Stir constantly until melted. Brush marmalade over the cooled cake in several thin layers. Allow marmalade to set for 30 minutes at room temperature before serving.

CHOCOLATE MOUSSE CAKE

makes 1 8-inch cake

4 ounces semisweet chocolate, coarsely chopped
1 cup sweet butter, cut into pieces
4 large egg yolks
½ cup sugar
3 egg whites

ICING:
4 ounces unsweetened chocolate, coarsely chopped
1 cup sweet butter, cut into pieces
4 large egg yolks
½ cup sugar
3 egg whites
1 tablespoon Dutch-process unsweetened cocoa
1 teaspoon confectioners' sugar

Preheat the oven to 325°F. Generously butter an 8-inch springform pan. Set aside.

In the top of a double boiler combine the chocolate and the butter. Heat over hot but not boiling water, stirring constantly, until chocolate is melted and mixture is smooth. Remove from the water.

In a large bowl beat together the egg yolks and sugar until light and lemon-yellow in color; approximately 3 to 5 minutes. Add the melted chocolate mixture to the yolks and stir until well blended.

In a separate bowl, beat the egg whites until stiff but not dry. Add half the egg whites to the chocolate mixture and beat. Gently fold in the remaining whites.

Pour batter into prepared pan and bake for 1 hour or until the cake pulls away from the sides of the pan.

Remove from the oven. Cool in pan on wire rack for 20 minutes. Turn cake out onto a serving plate and cool completely.

For the icing, in the top of a double boiler combine the unsweetened chocolate and butter. Heat over hot not boiling water, stirring constantly, until chocolate is melted and mixture is smooth. Remove from the water.

In a large bowl beat together the egg yolks and sugar until light and lemon-yellow in color; approximately 3 to 5 minutes. Add the melted chocolate mixture to the yolks and stir until well blended.

In a separate bowl, beat the egg whites until stiff but not dry. Add half the egg whites to the chocolate mixture and beat. Gently fold in the remaining whites.

Reserve the icing until cake is completely cool.

Ice the sides and top of the cake with the icing. Dust the cocoa and confectioners' sugar over the top, if desired.

Apple Muffins

Currant Scones

Buttermilk Biscuits

Boston Brown Bread

108

Angel Cake

Chopped Cherry Muffins

Old-Fashioned White Bread

Cake Brownies (above)

Crunchy Cracked Wheat Bread (left)

Hazelnut Sheet Cake with Chocolate Frosting

makes 1 sheet cake

2 cups sifted cake flour
2 teaspoons baking powder
½ cup sweet butter, softened
8 ounces cream cheese, softened
1 cup sugar
4 large eggs
1 tablespoon pure vanilla extract
1 cup finely chopped hazelnuts

FROSTING:
½ cup sweet butter
1 pound confectioners' sugar
3 tablespoons Dutch-process unsweetened cocoa
¼ cup milk
½ cup coarsely chopped hazelnuts

Preheat the oven to 350°F. Heavily butter a 15 × 10 × 1-inch jellyroll pan. Set aside.

Into a bowl sift together the flour and baking powder.

In a large bowl beat together the butter, cream cheese, sugar, eggs and vanilla. Beat for 3 minutes or until very light and fluffy.

Add the flour mixture and the hazelnuts to the butter mixture. Fold in until well blended.

Turn batter into the prepared pan and bake for 18 to 20 minutes or until cake springs back when touched lightly. Remove from the oven and cool completely in pan on wire rack.

In the medium-sized bowl of an electric mixer, beat the butter until light. Add the sugar and cocoa alternately with the milk. Beat until smooth and a spreadable consistency. Add more milk if necessary.

Spread icing evenly over the top of the cake. Sprinkle evenly with chopped hazelnuts. Cut cake into pieces and serve from pan.

Jam Cake

makes 2 9-inch square cakes

¾ cup sweet butter, softened
1 cup sugar
3 eggs
3 cups flour
2 teaspoons baking powder
1 teaspoon baking soda
¼ teaspoon salt
1 teaspoon ground cinnamon
½ cup buttermilk
1 cup thick blackberry jam
Fruit Frosting (see page 171)

Preheat the oven to 350°F. Grease two 9-inch round cake pans. Set aside.

In a large mixing bowl cream the butter and sugar until light and fluffy. Add the eggs and beat well.

In a bowl sift together the flour, baking powder, baking soda, salt and cinnamon three times.

Add the flour mixture to the creamed mixture alternately with the buttermilk. End with the flour. Fold in the jam.

Turn the batter into the prepared cake pans. Distribute evenly. Bake for 35 to 45 minutes or until golden brown.

Remove to cooling racks and cool in the pans for 10 minutes. Turn out onto racks and continue cooling. Frost with fruit frosting.

MAPLE NUT CAKE

makes 2 9-inch square cakes

2¼ cups flour
3 teaspoons baking powder
⅓ cup softened sweet butter
½ cup sugar
¾ cup pure maple syrup
¼ teaspoon salt
½ cup milk
3 egg whites
¾ cup chopped walnuts
Maple Icing (see page 171)

Preheat the oven to 350°F.

Combine the flour with the baking powder and salt in a bowl. Set aside.

In a mixing bowl cream the butter until soft. Gradually add the sugar and beat until light and fluffy. Stir in the syrup. Add the flour mixture alternately with the milk. Stir until well combined.

In a separate bowl beat the egg whites until stiff but not dry. Fold into the batter. Stir in the walnuts.

Butter a 9-inch square baking pan. Line it with waxed paper and butter again. Pour in the batter.

Bake for 35 minutes. Remove to a cooling rack. Cool cake in pan for 5 minutes. Turn out onto a rack and remove wax paper. Turn cake right-side up and cool completely. When cool frost with maple icing.

WELLESLEY FUDGE CAKE

makes 1 9-inch square cake

4 ounces unsweetened chocolate
½ cup hot water
½ cup sugar
2 cups flour
1 teaspoon baking soda
1 teaspoon salt
½ cup sweet butter
1¼ cups sugar
3 eggs
1 teaspoon pure vanilla extract
⅔ cup milk
Fudge Frosting (see page 171)

Preheat the oven to 350°F.

Combine the chocolate and water in the top of a double boiler. Cook over hot, not boiling, water until chocolate is melted. Add ½ cup sugar and cook for 2 minutes longer. Set aside.

Onto a large piece of waxed paper sift the flour, baking soda and salt. Sift together twice more and set aside.

Cream the butter in a mixing bowl. Add 1¼ cups sugar. Cream together until light and fluffy. Add the eggs, 1 at a time, beating well after each addition. Add the vanilla. Add the flour alternately with the milk, beating well after each addition. Begin and end with the flour. Add the chocolate mixture and blend well.

Pour the batter into two greased and floured 9-inch square pans. Bake for 25 to 30 minutes or until cake tester inserted into the center comes out clean. Cool pans on rack for 10 minutes. Turn out and continue to cool. Frost when cool with fudge frosting.

ONE-LAYER CHOCOLATE RAISIN CAKE

makes 1 9-inch cake

2 tablespoons dark raisins
2 tablespoons golden raisins
¼ cup apple brandy
7 ounces bittersweet chocolate
3 tablespoons water
½ cup sweet butter cut into pieces, softened
3 eggs, separated
⅔ cup sugar
⅔ cup finely chopped pecans
4½ tablespoons cake flour
⅛ teaspoon salt
⅛ teaspoon cream of tartar

GLAZE:
3 ounces bittersweet chocolate
3 tablespoons confectioners' sugar
3 tablespoons sweet butter, softened

In a small bowl combine the dark raisins, golden raisins and apple brandy. Let raisins plump for 1 hour.

Preheat the oven to 375°F. Butter a 9-inch round cake pan. Line the bottom of the pan with waxed paper cut to size. Butter the paper.

In the top of a double boiler, melt the chocolate with the water over simmering water. Stir constantly until smooth.

Remove the top of the double boiler. Add the butter, piece by piece, stirring well after each addition.

In a large bowl beat the egg yolks together with the sugar until very pale in color, approximately 3 minutes. Add the chocolate mixture and fold until blended.

Combine the ground pecans and cake flour. Add mixture to the batter and stir well. Add the raisins with the brandy and blend.

In a bowl beat the egg whites with the salt and cream of tartar until stiff but not dry.

Fold 3 tablespoons of the egg whites into the chocolate mixture. Stir to lighten. Gently fold the chocolate mixture back into the egg whites.

Turn batter into prepared pan. Bake for 25 minutes or until cake is firm to the touch. Remove from the oven. Cool in pan on wire rack for 10 minutes. Turn out onto wire rack. Cool completely and then remove waxed paper. To prepare the glaze, in the top of a double boiler melt the chocolate over hot but not boiling water. Remove from the water. Add the confectioners' sugar and stir until smooth. Add the butter in 3 pieces, stirring well after each addition. Blend until glaze is smooth. Let cool.

Place the cake on a serving plate. Spread the glaze on the top and sides of cake. Let glaze set for 30 minutes. Refrigerate until cake is firm. Wrap cake in foil and refrigerate overnight. Remove from the refrigerator 15 minutes before serving.

RAISIN CAKE WITH LEMON CREAM FROSTING

makes 1 8-inch cake

1 cup sifted flour
1½ teaspoons baking powder
⅛ teaspoon salt
5 tablespoons plus 1 teaspoon sweet butter, softened
½ cup sugar
2 large eggs
2 tablespoons lemon juice
1 teaspoon grated lemon rind
½ cup raisins tossed with 1 tablespoon flour

FROSTING:
2 tablespoons plus 2 teaspoons sweet butter
1¾ cups sifted confectioners' sugar
2 tablespoons lemon juice
1 teaspoon grated lemon rind

Preheat the oven to 250°F. Butter an 8-inch round cake pan. Line the bottom of the pan with waxed paper cut to size. Butter the paper and flour the pan.

Into a bowl sift the flour, baking powder and salt.

In a large bowl cream the butter. Add the sugar and beat until the mixture is light and fluffy. Add the eggs, one at a time, beating well after each addition. Scrape down the side of the bowl with a rubber spatula.

Add the flour mixture in four additions to the butter mixture. Mix until well blended. Add the lemon juice and lemon rind; mix until blended. Add the raisins; stir until thoroughly incorporated.

Turn batter into the prepared pan. Bake for 25 minutes or until top is lightly golden and cake pulls away from the side.

Remove from the oven and cool in the pan on a wire rack for 10 minutes. Turn cake out onto the rack and remove paper from the bottom. Turn cake right-side up and cool completely.

To make the frosting, in a small bowl cream the butter until light and fluffy. Add the sugar, a little at a time, and beat until smooth. Add lemon juice and lemon rind. Beat to blend.

Spread the frosting on the sides and top of the cooled cake.

—LAYER CAKES—

BASIC YELLOW CAKE WITH SOFT CHOCOLATE FILLING

makes 1 9-inch cake

1¾ cups sifted cake flour
½ teaspoon salt
2 teaspoons baking powder
½ cup sweet butter, softened
1 cup sugar
2 eggs, lightly beaten
½ cup milk
½ teaspoon pure vanilla extract

CHOCOLATE FILLING:
2 ounces unsweetened chocolate
1 cup milk
6 tablespoons sugar
2 tablespoons flour
¼ teaspoon salt
1 teaspoon butter
½ teaspoon pure vanilla extract
Creamy Chocolate Frosting (see page 170)

Preheat the oven to 375°F. Generously butter and flour two 9-inch round cake pans.

Into a bowl sift together the cake flour, salt and baking powder. Set aside.

In a large bowl cream the butter until soft and light. Add the sugar, a little at a time, and mix until very fluffy. Add the eggs and mix until well blended.

Add the flour alternately with the milk to the butter mixture. Beat well but only until just mixed. Add the vanilla and mix to blend.

Transfer the batter to the prepared pans; divide evenly. Bake for 25 to 30 minutes or until a cake tester inserted into the center comes out clean. Remove from the oven and turn out onto a wire rack. Invert so that layers are right-side up and cool completely. Make the filling and frosting while the layers cool.

In the top part of a double boiler combine the chocolate and milk. Heat over hot but not boiling water until chocolate is melted and mixture is smooth. Remove from the heat and beat very well.

Combine the sugar, flour and salt. Add to the chocolate milk mixture. Return to the heat and cook, stirring constantly, until thick; approximately 3 minutes. Add the butter and vanilla extract and mix well. Cool before using.

Place 1 layer, top-side down, on a serving plate. Spread with the soft chocolate filling. Place the other layer on top, right-side up. Frost the sides and top with the chocolate frosting. Serve cake at room temperature.

Chocolate Cake with White Chocolate Mousse

makes 1 9-inch cake

14 ounces semisweet chocolate
1¾ cups sugar
6 tablespoons and 1 teaspoon sweet butter
3 tablespoons water
1 tablespoon almond extract
10 large eggs, separated

WHITE CHOCOLATE MOUSSE:
5 large egg yolks
½ cup dry white wine
5 tablespoons sugar
14 ounces white chocolate, melted
1½ teaspoons pure vanilla extract
4 cups heavy cream

Preheat the oven to 375°F. Generously butter and flour two 9-inch round pans.

In a large bowl combine the semisweet chocolate, sugar, butter, water and almond extract. Set it over a large saucepan of gently simmering water. Stir constantly until well blended and smooth. Remove from the water. Add the egg yolks, one at a time, stirring well after each addition.

In another large bowl beat the egg whites until stiff but not dry. Add ¼ of the egg whites to the chocolate mixture. Gently stir. Add remaining egg whites and fold gently.

Gently turn the batter into the prepared pans. Bake for 45 to 50 minutes or until cake begins to pull away from the sides of the pan. Remove from the oven. Turn out onto wire racks and cool. When cakes have reached room temperature, refrigerate for 1 hour.

To prepare the mousse, in a large bowl that has been set over a saucepan of simmering water, whisk together the egg yolks, white wine and sugar until very pale in color. Remove from the water.

Add the melted white chocolate to the yolk mixture and stir. Add the vanilla extract and stir until very smooth.

Cool the mixture. In a very cold bowl beat the cream until stiff peaks form. Fold cream into cooled white chocolate mixture. Refrigerate 3 to 5 hours before using.

Transfer 1 cake layer to a serving plate. Spread the top with a generous amount of mousse. Place second layer on top. Spread top and sides with the mousse.

Serve cake with any remaining mousse on the side.

CHOCOLATE GENOISE WITH COFFEE BUTTERCREAM

makes 1 9-inch cake

CAKE:
½ cup sweet butter
2 ounces semisweet chocolate
6 large eggs, slightly beaten
1 cup sugar
1 teaspoon pure vanilla extract
1 cup flour

BUTTERCREAM:
4 large egg yolks
1 cup sweet butter, softened
⅔ cup sugar
¼ cup water
1 tablespoon instant espresso coffee powder

Preheat the oven to 350°F. Butter and lightly flour two 9 × 1½-inch round cake pans.

In a small saucepan melt together the butter and chocolate. Stir until smooth. Remove from the heat and set aside.

In a large bowl stir together the whole eggs, sugar and vanilla extract. Place bowl on top of a large saucepan containing 2 inches of hot but not boiling water. Cook over low heat, stirring frequently, until the mixture is lukewarm. Remove from the heat.

With an electric mixer at a high speed, beat the mixture until it has nearly tripled in volume; approximately 15 minutes. Add the flour and fold in until it is well blended. Add the chocolate mixture, a little at a time, and fold until well blended.

Pour batter into prepared pans and bake for 25 minutes or until a cake tester inserted into the center of the cake comes out clean. Remove from the oven. Cool in pans on wire racks for 10 minutes. Turn cakes out onto racks and cool completely.

When the layers are almost cool, make the buttercream. In a large bowl beat the egg yolks until they are thick and lemon-yellow in color. Set aside.

In a bowl cream the butter until light and fluffy. Set aside.

In a medium-sized saucepan combine the sugar, water and instant espresso. Stir to combine and bring the mixture to a boil. Cook over moderate heat, stirring constantly, until the mixture reaches the softball stage or 236°F on a candy thermometer. Immediately pour the hot mixture, in a slow steady stream, over the egg yolks, beating constantly at high speed. Beat for 15 minutes or until the mixture is thick and smooth. Remove from the heat and cool for 15 minutes.

Add the butter, a little at a time, beating until smooth and well blended. Cover the bowl and refrigerate for 30 minutes or until the butter cream is spreadable.

Place one layer on a serving plate, top-side down. Spread ⅓ of the frosting on top. Place the other layer on top and frost the sides and top of the cake.

CHOCOLATE TRIPLE LAYER CAKE

makes 1 8-inch cake

¾ cup Dutch cocoa
1¾ cups sugar
3 eggs, separated
½ cup milk
1 whole egg
½ cup butter
2 cups flour
1 teaspoon baking soda
1 teaspoon baking powder
½ teaspoon salt
1 cup sour cream
1 teaspoon pure vanilla extract
Chocolate Frosting (see page 169)

Preheat the oven to 350°F.

Combine the cocoa, ¾ cup sugar, 1 egg yolk and milk in a saucepan. Cook over low heat, stirring constantly, until thick. Remove from heat and cool.

In a bowl or on a sheet of waxed paper combine the flour, baking soda, baking powder and salt.

In a large mixing bowl cream the butter until soft. Slowly beat in the remaining sugar. Continue beating until well blended. Add the remaining 2 egg yolks and the whole egg. Mix thoroughly. Add the flour mixture alternately with the sour cream, mixing well after each addition. Stir in the vanilla and the cooled cocoa mixture.

In a small bowl beat the egg whites until stiff but not dry. Gently fold the egg whites into the batter.

Butter three 8-inch layer-cake pans. Line the pans with waxed paper and butter again. Turn the batter into the 3 pans, distributing evenly.

Bake for 30 to 35 minutes or until cake springs back when touched lightly.

Remove from oven and cool 2 minutes in the pans, then turn layers out onto cooling racks. Peel off the waxed paper and cool completely. Frost with Chocolate Frosting.

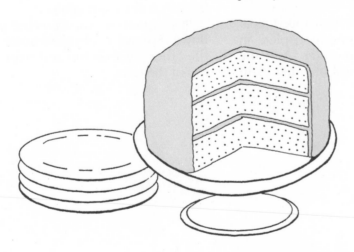

COCONUT LAYER CAKE

makes 1 9-inch cake

2 cups sifted cake flour
2 teaspoons baking powder
½ teaspoon salt
½ cup sweet butter, softened
1 cup sugar
3 large eggs, separated
½ cup milk
1 teaspoon pure vanilla extract

COCONUT FROSTING:
2 large egg whites
1½ cups sugar
5 tablespoons water
1 teaspoon pure vanilla extract
6 ounces shredded coconut

Preheat the oven to 375°F. Butter and flour two 9-inch pans.

Into a bowl sift together the flour, baking powder and salt. Set aside.

In a large bowl cream the butter and sugar together until light and fluffy.

Add the egg yolks, one at a time, beating well after each addition.

Add the flour alternately with the milk, stirring well after each addition with a wooden spoon. Add the vanilla extract and blend.

In a separate bowl beat the egg whites until stiff but not dry. Gently place the egg whites on top of the batter. Carefully fold in until just blended.

Evenly distribute batter between the prepared pans. Bake for 25 minutes or until lightly brown and the layers begin to pull away from the sides of the pan.

Remove from the oven. Turn layers out onto wire racks and immediately turn right-side up. Cool completely.

Prepare the frosting when the layers are cool. In the top part of a double boiler combine the egg whites, sugar and water. Mix well.

Cook over boiling water and beat for exactly 7 minutes. The frosting should be thick and shiny. Remove from the heat. Add the vanilla extract and beat until blended.

Place one cake layer, right-side down, on a serving plate. Spread the layer with some of the frosting and sprinkle with some of the coconut.

Cover with the second layer, right-side up, and frost the sides and the top. Swirl with a knife and sprinkle all over with the remaining coconut.

FOUR-LAYER BUTTER CAKE

makes 1 9-inch cake

2½ cups sifted cake flour
3 teaspoons baking powder
½ teaspoon salt
¾ cup sweet butter, softened
1¼ cups sugar
5 large egg yolks
2 teaspoons pure vanilla extract
1¼ cups milk
¼ cup finely chopped walnuts

FROSTING:
3 ounces semisweet chocolate
½ cup sweet butter
2 teaspoons instant espresso coffee powder
⅓ cup water
1 pound confectioners' sugar

GLAZE:
2 ounces semisweet chocolate
2 tablespoons sweet butter, softened
1 teaspoon pure vanilla extract
1 tablespoon confectioners' sugar
12 walnut halves

Preheat the oven to 350°F. Butter and lightly flour two 9-inch round cake pans. Set aside.

Onto a piece of waxed paper sift together the cake flour, baking powder and salt. Set aside.

In a large bowl beat together the butter, sugar, egg yolks and vanilla with an electric mixer at a high speed until very light and fluffy, approximately 3 minutes. Scrape down the sides of the bowl with a rubber spatula when necessary.

Add the flour mixture alternately with the milk, stirring well after each addition until the batter is smooth. Add chopped nuts and stir.

Transfer batter to prepared pans and bake for 30 minutes or until cake springs back when touched lightly.

Remove from the oven. Cool in pan on wire racks for 10 minutes. Run a knife around the edges of the pan to loosen. Turn layers out onto wire racks and cool completely.

While the layers cool, make the frosting and glaze. In a small saucepan melt the chocolate and butter together over a low heat. Stir until smooth. Remove from the heat.

In a large bowl dissolve the instant espresso in the water. Add the sugar and stir until smooth. Add chocolate mixture and stir vigorously until frosting is thick and spreadable. If frosting doesn't thicken, place bowl in a larger bowl filled with ice and water while stirring. Set frosting aside.

In the top part of a double boiler combine the chocolate, butter and vanilla extract. Melt over hot but not boiling water. Remove from the heat and stir in the sugar.

Carefully split each cake layer in half horizontally. Place the bottom layer, cut-side up, on a serving plate. Spread ⅓ cup of the frosting on top and top with the next layer, cut-side up. Continue making the layers, placing about ⅓ cup of frosting between each layer. Do not spread frosting on top of cake. Spread the glaze evenly on the top of the cake and frost the sides of the cake with the remaining frosting. Place walnut halves on top. Let glaze set before serving.

FOUR-LAYER RASPBERRY CREAM CAKE

makes 1 8-inch cake

⅓ cup sweet butter, softened
1¾ cups flour
1¼ cups sugar
⅔ cup milk
1 large egg
2½ teaspoons baking powder
1 teaspoon pure vanilla extract
¼ teaspoon salt

CREAM FILLING:
⅓ cup sugar
4 teaspoons cornstarch
⅛ teaspoon salt
1 cup milk
2 egg yolks, beaten
1 tablespoon sweet butter, softened
1 teaspoon pure vanilla extract
¼ cup raspberry preserves

ICING:
2 tablespoons sweet butter, softened
½ cup sifted confectioners' sugar
1 tablespoon milk
½ teaspoon pure vanilla extract
½ to ⅓ cup sifted confectioners' sugar

Preheat the oven to 375°F. Butter and flour two 8 × 8 × 2-inch pans.

In a large bowl beat the butter with an electric mixer for 30 seconds at medium speed. Add the flour, sugar, milk, egg, baking powder, vanilla and salt. Beat until blended. Scrape down the sides of the bowl with a rubber spatula. Beat for 2 minutes at a medium speed.

Pour batter evenly into prepared pans. Bake for 20 minutes or until a cake tester inserted into the center comes out clean.

Remove from the oven. Cool in the pans on wire racks for 10 minutes. Turn out into racks and cool completely. While the layers cool make filling and icing.

To make the filling, in a saucepan combine the sugar, cornstarch and salt. Add the milk and stir. Cook, stirring constantly, over moderate heat until thick and bubbly. Cook and stir for 2 minutes longer.

Slowly stir in approximately half of the cooked sugar mixture to the beaten egg yolks. Pour back into the rest of the sugar mixture in the saucepan. Cook, stirring constantly, until thick and bubbly. Cook, stirring constantly, for 2 minutes longer. Remove from the heat. Add the butter and vanilla extract and stir until well blended. Cover the surface with waxed paper and chill.

To make the icing, in a small bowl beat the butter until light and fluffy. Slowly add the confectioners' sugar, beating until smooth. Add the milk and vanilla extract and beat well. Slowly beat in enough of the remaining confectioners' sugar until the icing is spreadable.

To assemble the cake, split each layer in half horizontally. Place one layer on a plate; spread with half the cream filling. Top with a second layer and spread with the raspberry preserves. Top with the third layer and spread with the remaining cream filling. Top with last layer and spread the icing on top. Garnish top of cake with fresh raspberries, if desired.

HAZELNUT CAKE WITH COFFEE BUTTERCREAM

makes 1 9-inch cake

2 cups hazelnuts
¾ cup and 3 tablespoons sugar
3 tablespoons and 2 teaspoons flour
5 large eggs, separated
¼ teaspoon cream of tartar
3 tablespoons sweet butter, melted and
slightly cooled

BUTTERCREAM:
2 teaspoons instant coffee powder
2 tablespoons boiling water
3 large eggs
¾ cup sugar
1 cup and 2 tablespoons sweet butter, softened

Preheat the oven to 350°F.

Place the hazelnuts in a shallow pan and toast in the oven for 8 to 10 minutes or until the skins begin to split. Remove from the oven and transfer to a strainer. Rub nuts with a clean towel against the strainer to remove as much skin as possible. Cool thoroughly.

Generously butter two 9-inch round cake pans. Line the bottoms with foil cut to size. Butter the foil and dust the pans with flour. Set aside.

Measure out 1½ cups of the hazelnuts. Reserve the remaining ½ cup for garnishing the cake. In a blender or food processor, grind the nuts with ¼ cup of the sugar. Remove and transfer mixture to a bowl. Add the flour and mix well.

In a large bowl beat the egg yolks with ½ cup of the sugar until very pale in color; approximately 5 minutes.

In a separate bowl, beat the egg whites with the cream of tartar until soft peaks begin to form. Add the remaining sugar, a little at a time, and continue beating until egg whites are stiff but not dry.

Add ⅓ of the nut mixture to the egg yolks and fold gently. Then add ⅓ of the egg whites and fold. Repeat the process in two more batches, folding in gently and only until just blended. Before adding the last addition of the egg whites, add the melted butter in a slow steady stream and blend.

Evenly distribute the batter between the prepared pans. Bake in the oven for 15 to 17 minutes, or until a cake tester inserted into the center of the cake comes out clean.

Remove from the oven. Run a knife around each cake to separate it from the pan. Turn layers out onto plates and remove pan and foil. Invert quickly onto wire racks and cool completely. When the layers are cool make the buttercream. In a small bowl, dissolve the coffee in the boiling water. Cool.

In a large bowl beat the eggs. Add the sugar and the cooled coffee and beat to blend. Place the bowl in a pan of hot water over very low heat. Beat mixture with an electric mixer for 5 minutes at a medium speed, then at a high speed for 3 minutes. The mixture will be thin. Remove bowl from the water and continue beating.

In a large bowl cream the butter until smooth. Add ½ cup of the cooked mixture and beat. Gradually beat in the remaining mixture. Scrape down sides of bowl with a rubber spatula when necessary. Use at once.

Place 1 cake layer, smooth-side up, on a serving plate. Spread evenly with ⅓ of the frosting. Place second layer, smooth-side up, on top. Spread sides and top of cake with remaining frosting. Using a flat knife, swirl frosting on top. Chop the remaining hazelnuts and sprinkle on top of the cake. Refrigerate for at least 2 hours before serving. Serve at room temperature.

LEMON-FILLED TRIPLE LAYER CAKE

makes 1 8-inch cake

1½ cups cake flour
2 teaspoons baking powder
3 large eggs
1½ cups sugar
1½ cups heavy cream
2 teaspoons pure vanilla extract
¼ teaspoon salt
1 cup finely ground walnuts

FILLING:
½ cup sweet butter, softened
2 cups confectioners' sugar
1 tablespoon lemon juice
½ teaspoon pure vanilla extract
2 large egg yolks
8 walnut halves
1 tablespoon confectioners' sugar

Preheat the oven to 350°F. Generously butter three 8-inch round cake pans. Line the bottom of each pan with waxed paper cut to size. Butter the paper and set aside.

In a bowl combine the cake flour and the baking powder. Set aside.

In a small bowl beat the eggs until lemon yellow in color. Add the sugar, a little at a time, and beat until light and fluffy.

In a large bowl beat together the cream, vanilla extract and salt until just stiff. Gradually fold the egg and sugar mixture into the cream. Fold in the flour, a little at a time. Fold in the ground walnuts.

Transfer batter to the prepared pans and distribute evenly. Bake for 25 minutes or until cake springs back when touched lightly.

Remove from the oven. Cool in pans on wire racks for 5 minutes. Turn out onto racks and remove pans and paper. Cool completely.

Prepare the filling while cake cools. In a bowl combine the butter, sugar, lemon juice and vanilla extract. Cream together until well blended. Add the egg yolks, one at a time, beating well after each addition. Beat until light and fluffy.

Place one layer, top-side down, on a plate and spread with most of the remaining filling. Top with the second layer and spread with most of the remaining filling. Top with remaining layer. Spoon 8 dollops of the remaining lemon filling on top of the cake to form a border. Press a walnut half on top of each dollop. Sprinkle top of cake with the confectioners' sugar. Refrigerate until ready to serve.

MACADAMIA NUT CAKE

makes 1 9-inch cake

2⅓ cups unsalted macadamia nuts
¾ cup plus 2 tablespoons sugar
¼ cup flour
5 large eggs, separated
¾ teaspoon pure vanilla extract
¼ teaspoon cream of tartar

FILLING:
6 tablespoons sweet butter, softened
5 tablespoons sifted confectioners' sugar
1 egg yolk
1 tablespoon nut-flavored or almond liqueur
½ cup unsalted macadamia nuts

TOPPING:
1 cup very cold heavy cream
1 tablespoon sugar
2 teaspoons pure vanilla extract
chopped, toasted, unsalted macadamia nuts

Preheat the oven to 325°F. Butter a 9-inch springform pan. Line the bottom of the pan with foil. Butter the foil and flour the entire pan. Set aside.

To make the cake, in a blender or food processor grind half of the macadamia nuts with 3 tablespoons of the sugar. Process until very fine. Empty nut mixture into a bowl and process the remaining nuts with 3 tablespoons sugar. Process until very fine and add to other nut mixture. Sift the flour over the nut mixture. Stir until blended.

In a medium-sized bowl beat the egg yolks with ¼ cup sugar for 5 minutes or until very light in color. Add the vanilla and beat to blend.

In a small bowl beat the egg whites with the cream of tartar until they form soft peaks.

Add the remaining ¼ cup sugar, a little at a time, beating until the whites are stiff but not dry.

Alternately fold the nut mixture and the egg whites into the egg yolks.

Gently turn batter into the prepared pan. Bake for 50 minutes or until a cake tester inserted into the center of the cake comes out clean.

Remove from the oven. Cool in pan on wire rack for 10 minutes. Carefully run a knife around the cake and remove the sides. Invert cake onto another wire rack. Remove the bottom of the pan and the foil. Invert again so that cake is right-side up. Cool completely.

To make the filling, in a small bowl beat together the butter and ¼ cup of the confectioners' sugar until smooth. Add the egg yolk and beat. Blend in the liqueur.

In a blender or food processor grind the nuts with the remaining 1 tablespoon confectioners' sugar. Process until fine. Add to the butter mixture and stir.

Carefully cut the cooled cake in half, forming two layers. Place the filling on top of the bottom layer and spread evenly. Top with the second layer. Refrigerate for 1 to 1½ hours.

To make the topping, in a well-chilled mixing bowl beat the cream with the sugar until soft peaks begin to form. Add the vanilla extract and continue beating until firm peaks form.

Remove the cake from the refrigerator. Spread topping on sides and top of cake. Sprinkle the chopped macadamia nuts in the center of the cake.

Refrigerate. Remove from refrigerator before serving. Serve at room temperature.

ORANGE-CUSTARD FILLED GENOISE

makes 1 9-inch cake

4 large eggs
½ cup sugar
½ cup sifted flour
½ cup sweet butter, melted

CUSTARD:
2 medium-sized oranges
3 large egg yolks
½ cup and 1 tablespoon sugar
3 tablespoons cornstarch
2 tablespoons flour
2 cups milk
¼ cup and 1 tablespoon orange-flavored liqueur
2 cups whipped cream

Preheat the oven to 375°F. Butter and flour a 9-inch square cake pan. Set aside.

In a large, heat-proof bowl beat together the eggs and sugar until well blended. Place the bowl over very low heat, and using a wire whisk, whisk the mixture 25 times. Remove from the heat and beat at a high speed until cool and more than tripled in volume; approximately 10 to 15 minutes.

Add the flour to the egg mixture and fold in gently. Add melted butter and mix only until combined. Transfer mixture to the prepared pan.

Bake for 20 to 25 minutes or until cake springs back when touched lightly. Remove from the oven. Invert cake onto a wire rack; immediately invert right-side up on another wire rack. Cool completely.

To prepare the custard, grate the rind from the oranges; reserve the oranges.

In a bowl combine the egg yolks, sugar, cornstarch and flour. Beat together until very smooth and lemon-yellow in color; approximately 3 to 5 minutes.

In a large saucepan heat the milk over very low heat. Very slowly add the egg yolk mixture to the milk. Stir constantly until mixture is thick and smooth; about 10 minutes. Add the orange rind and mix well. Remove from the heat and cool.

Carefully cut the cake into three square layers. Brush each layer evenly with some of the orange liqueur. Place one layer, cut-side up, on a serving plate and spread with half the custard. Top with a second layer, cut-side up, and spread with the remaining custard. Place the remaining layer on top, cut-side down. Frost the sides and the top of the cake with the whipped cream. Cut the reserved oranges into very thin slices. Arrange the slices on top of the cake. Refrigerate until ready to use.

SPICED PECAN CAKE

makes 1 9-inch cake

3½ cups pecans
1½ cups sugar
3 tablespoons flour
2 tablespoons Dutch-process unsweetened
cocoa
1 teaspoon cinnamon
1 teaspoon baking powder
¼ teaspoon grated nutmeg
6 large eggs, separated
¼ teaspoon cream of tartar

CREAM FROSTING:
1¼ cups cold heavy cream
2 tablespoons and 1 teaspoon sugar
1 teaspoon Dutch-process unsweetened
cocoa, sifted
½ teaspoon cinnamon
10 pecan halves

Preheat the oven to 350°F. Butter two 9-inch round cake pans. Line bottoms with foil cut to size. Butter the foil and flour the pans.

In a blender or food processor grind half of the nuts with ¼ cup of the sugar. Process until very fine. Transfer to a bowl. Repeat the process with the remaining nuts and ¼ cup of the sugar. Add to the first mixture in the bowl.

Sift the flour, cocoa, cinnamon, baking powder and nutmeg together over the nut mixture. Mix until well blended.

In a large bowl beat the egg yolks with ½ cup of the sugar until very pale in color, approximately 5 minutes.

In another bowl beat the egg whites with the cream of tartar until soft peaks form. Add the remaining sugar, a little at a time, and beat until stiff but not dry.

Fold ⅓ of the nut–flour mixture into the egg yolks. Fold in ⅓ of the egg whites. Repeat the process in two batches, folding until just blended.

Gently turn batter into prepared pans. Bake for 30 minutes or until a cake tester inserted into the center comes out clean. Remove from the oven and cool on wire racks in pans for 10 minutes. Run a knife around the edges to separate cake. Turn layers out onto plates; remove pans and foil. Invert onto wire racks and cool completely.

To make the frosting, in a very cold mixing bowl beat the cream together with the sugar until firm peaks begin to form. Add the cocoa and cinnamon. Beat until blended.

Place one cake layer, top-side down, on a serving plate. Spread with ⅓ of the frosting. Top with second layer, top-side up. Spread the frosting on the sides and top of the cake. Place the pecans around the edge of the cake. Refrigerate until ready to use. Serve cake at room temperature.

—ROLLED CAKES—

ALMOND RASPBERRY CREAM ROLL

makes 1 cake roll

1¼ cups blanched, slivered almonds
¾ cup cake flour
1 teaspoon baking powder
¼ teaspoon salt
3 large eggs
1 cup sugar
⅓ cup water
1½ teaspoons pure vanilla extract
1 teaspoon pure almond extract
confectioners' sugar for dusting
2 cups heavy cream
⅔ cup confectioners' sugar
3 tablespoons almond-flavored liqueur
⅔ cup seedless raspberry jam

Preheat the oven to 375°F. Butter a 15½ × 10½ × 1-inch jelly roll pan. Line the bottom of the pan with foil and butter generously. Set aside.

Toast the almonds in a shallow pan in the oven for 10 minutes or until lightly golden. Remove from the oven and cool.

In a bowl combine the flour, baking powder and salt. Set aside.

In a large bowl beat the egg until very foamy, approximately 3 to 5 minutes. Gradually beat in the sugar.

Add the water, ½ teaspoon of the vanilla extract and the almond extract. Beat to blend. Gradually beat in the flour, combining until smooth.

Turn batter into the prepared pan and bake for 12 to 15 minutes or until a cake tester inserted into the center of the cake comes out clean.

Remove from the oven. Turn cake out onto a towel that has been heavily dusted with confectioners' sugar. Remove the pan and the foil. Carefully roll up the cake and towel together from the narrow end. Cool completely on a wire rack.

In a bowl beat together the cream, confectioners' sugar, remaining vanilla extract and almond liqueur until stiff.

Chop 1 cup of the almonds. Combine almonds with half the cream mixture. Refrigerate remaining half until needed.

Carefully unroll the cooled cake and spread evenly with the raspberry jam, leaving 1 inch along the sides. Spread the whipped cream–almond mixture over the jam. Be sure to leave the same border.

Carefully reroll the cake. Transfer to a plate, seam-side down. Frost cake with remaining whipped cream and decorate with remaining toasted almonds. Serve or refrigerate.

CRANBERRY-APPLE WALNUT ROLL

makes 1 cake roll

FILLING:
2 large cooking apples
1 cup whole cranberries
¼ cup sugar
¼ cup water
2 tablespoons apple brandy
1 teaspoon lemon juice
½ teaspoon ground cinnamon
¼ teaspoon grated nutmeg

CAKE:
⅔ cup sifted flour
1 teaspoon baking powder
¼ teaspoon salt
3 eggs
¾ cup sugar
⅓ cup water
1 teaspoon pure vanilla extract
⅓ cup finely ground walnuts
confectioners' sugar for dusting

TOPPING:
1 cup heavy cream
1 teaspoon pure vanilla extract
½ teaspoon grated nutmeg

Preheat the oven to 375°F. Butter a 15 × 10 × 1-inch jelly-roll pan. Line the bottom with waxed paper cut to size. Butter paper. Set aside.

Peel and core the apples. Cut them into ¼-inch slices. In a saucepan, combine the apples, cranberries, sugar, water, brandy, lemon juice, cinnamon and nutmeg. Cook, stirring constantly, over moderate heat until mixture thickens; approximately 6 to 7 minutes. Remove from the heat and cool.

To make the cake, sift together the flour, baking powder and salt into a bowl. Set aside.

In a large bowl beat the egg for 3 minutes. Add the sugar, a little at a time, beating until thick and light in color; approximately 5 minutes. Add the water and vanilla extract. Stir to blend.

Add the flour mixture and the ground walnuts. Fold in gently. Turn batter into prepared pan and smooth. Bake for 10 to 12 minutes or until the cake springs back when touched lightly.

Remove from the oven. Using a small knife, loosen the cake around the edges. Turn cake out onto a clean towel that has been heavily dusted with sugar. Remove the pan. Carefully remove the wax paper. Starting with the short end, roll the cake up together with the towel. Cool on wire rack for 30 minutes.

Carefully unroll the cooled cake. Spread the apple filling evenly over it, leaving 2 inches along the edges. Reroll cake, using a towel for help, if necessary. Transfer cake to a plate, seam-side down.

In a small bowl beat the cream, vanilla extract and nutmeg together until stiff. Spoon dollops of the cream along the top of the roll. Serve cake accompanied by remaining cream.

LEMON ROLL

makes 1 cake roll

FILLING:
⅔ cup sugar
½ cup sweet butter
⅓ cup lemon juice
2 large eggs
2 egg yolks
⅛ teaspoon salt

CAKE:
¾ cup sugar
3 large eggs
3 eggs, separated
1 teaspoon pure vanilla extract
⅛ teaspoon cream of tartar
2 tablespoons sugar
⅔ cup sifted cake flour

SYRUP:
⅓ cup sugar
6 tablespoons water
1 tablespoon lemon juice
½ cup confectioners' sugar

First prepare the filling. In the top part of a double boiler combine the sugar, butter, lemon juice, eggs, egg yolks and salt. Cook the mixture over boiling water for 10 minutes or until it is thick enough to coat the back of a spoon. Do not allow the mixture to boil. Remove from the heat. Transfer to a container and cool. Refrigerate until ready for use.

To prepare the cake, preheat the oven to 450°F. Generously butter and flour an 11 × 17-inch jelly-roll pan. Line the bottom of the pan with waxed paper cut to size. Butter and flour the paper. Set aside.

In a large bowl whisk together the sugar, whole eggs and egg yolks. Continue to beat until sugar is dissolved and well blended. Add vanilla and blend.

In a bowl beat the egg whites with the cream of tartar until stiff but not dry. Add the sugar and continue beating until egg whites are glossy.

Gently fold the flour into the egg yolk mixture. Add the egg whites and fold until blended. Gently turn mixture into prepared pan and smooth. Bake for 7 to 10 minutes, or until the cake springs back when touched lightly.

Remove from the oven. Loosen cake around the edges with a knife. Cool in pan for 5 minutes. Turn out onto a large wire rack and cool completely.

To make the syrup, combine the sugar and water in a saucepan and cook over a low heat until the sugar dissolves. Stir occasionally. Raise the heat and bring the mixture to the boil. Remove from the heat and cool. Add the lemon juice and mix well.

To assemble the cake, remove the paper from the cake. Brush the cake with some of the syrup, but do not soak it through. Spread the filling evenly over the top.

Carefully roll the cake up lengthwise, seam-side down, making sure it is tight. Wrap the cake in plastic wrap and refrigerate 6 hours. Dust with confectioners' sugar before serving.

TORTES

CHESTNUT CHOCOLATE TORTE

makes 1 9-inch torte

15 ounces unsweetened chestnut purée
(available in specialty food stores)
½ cup brandy
⅓ cup heavy cream
¾ cup sugar
6 tablespoons sweet butter, softened
16 ounces semisweet chocolate, broken
into pieces
5 large eggs
2 egg yolks
2 tablespoons cornstarch

FROSTING:
4 ounces semisweet chocolate, cut up
2 tablespoons sweet butter
1 tablespoon strong coffee
1 tablespoon brandy

Do not preheat the oven. Generously butter and flour a 9-inch round cake pan.

In a large bowl combine the chestnut purée, brandy and cream. Whisk together only until smooth. Do not overbeat. Add sugar and butter and whisk until blended.

In the top of a double boiler, over hot but not boiling water, melt the chocolate. Stir until smooth.

Add chocolate to the chestnut–cream mixture. Stir well. Add the whole eggs and egg yolks, one at a time, beating well after each addition. Scrape down the sides of the bowl with a rubber spatula. Sift the cornstarch over the mixture. Fold it in gently.

Turn batter into the prepared pan. Place in the oven and heat oven to 300°F. Bake for 50 to 60 minutes or until a cake tester inserted into the center comes out not quite clean.

Remove from the oven. Cool in pan or wire rack for 15 minutes. Turn out onto plate and remove pan. Cool. Cover with plastic wrap and let stand overnight.

To prepare the frosting, in the top of a double boiler, over hot but not boiling water, melt the chocolate and butter together. Stir until smooth. Add the coffee and brandy. Stir. Remove from the heat and cool to room temperature.

Unwrap the cake. Spread the sides and top of the cake evenly with the frosting. Serve.

CHOCOLATE-FILLED HAZELNUT
CHOCOLATE TORTE

makes 1 9-inch torte

2 cups hazelnuts
12 large egg yolks
1 cup sugar
4 ounces semisweet chocolate, melted
½ cup unflavored breadcrumbs
8 large egg whites
½ teaspoon salt
2 teaspoons pure vanilla extract

FILLING:

2 cups very cold heavy cream
2 teaspoons pure vanilla extract
¼ cup confectioners' sugar
¼ cup Dutch-process unsweetened cocoa

Preheat the oven to 325°F. Butter two 9-inch round cake pans. Line the bottoms with waxed paper cut to size. Butter paper and flour entire pan. Set aside.

Place hazelnuts in a shallow pan and toast in the oven for 15 minutes or until lightly browned. Remove from the oven and transfer nuts to a clean towel. Cool for 1 minute. Rub in towel until most of the skins come off. Cool. Chop the nuts very finely in a blender or food processor, but do not form a paste.

In a large bowl beat the egg yolks until thick, about 1 minute. Add ¾ cup of the sugar, a little at a time, beating 1 minute longer. Add the melted chocolate, ground nuts and bread-crumbs. Stir until well mixed.

In a large bowl beat the egg whites until frothy. Add the salt, vanilla extract and remaining sugar. Beat until stiff but not dry.

Stir 2 tablespoons of the egg whites into the chocolate–nut mixture. Fold the mixture into the remaining egg whites. Blend gently but thoroughly.

Turn the batter into the prepared pans. Divide evenly. Bake for 20 to 25 minutes or until a cake tester inserted into the center comes out clean.

Remove from the oven. Cool in pans on wire racks for 10 minutes. Run a knife around the edges of the cake. Turn out onto racks, peel off paper and turn right-side up. Cool completely.

In a large bowl combine the heavy cream and vanilla extract. Sift the confectioners' sugar and cocoa over the cream mixture. Beat together until spreading consistency.

Place one layer top-side down on serving plate. Spread ⅓ of the filling evenly on top of the layer. Top with second layer, right-side up. Frost sides and top with remaining filling. Sprinkle cake with chocolate curls or grated chocolate if desired.

CHOCOLATE-NUT RUM TORTE

makes 1 10-inch cake

1¼ cups walnuts
6 tablespoons Dutch-process unsweetened
cocoa
¾ cup sweet butter, softened
1¼ cups sugar
4 large eggs

CREAM FILLING:
1 cup heavy cream
2 egg yolks
¼ cup sugar
1 tablespoon flour
4 ounces semisweet chocolate, cut into pieces
2 tablespoons dark rum
½ cup cold sweet butter, cut into pieces

GLAZE:
2 cups sifted confectioners' sugar
⅔ cup Dutch-process unsweetened cocoa
3 tablespoons hot water
2 tablespoons dark rum
10 to 12 walnut halves for garnish

Preheat the oven to 350°F. Butter a 10 × 15-inch jelly roll pan. Dust with dry unflavored breadcrumbs and set aside.

Toast the walnuts in a shallow pan in the oven for 10 minutes or until lightly golden. Remove from the oven and cool. Grind the cooled nuts in a blender or food processor.

In a large bowl combine the ground nuts and the cocoa.

In another large bowl cream together the butter and sugar until light in color. Add the eggs, one at a time, beating well after each addition. Add nut mixture and fold until well blended.

Turn batter into the prepared pan and bake for 30 minutes or until firm to the touch. Remove from the oven. Cool in pan on wire rack.

To make cream filling, in a saucepan combine the cream, egg yolks, sugar and flour. Over moderate heat bring the mixture to a boil. Stir constantly. Cook for 4 to 5 minutes or until mixture is very thick. Remove from the heat. Add chocolate and stir until chocolate is completely melted. Cool thoroughly. Add the rum and beat. Add the pieces of cold butter and continue beating until fluffy. Refrigerate until filling is of spreading consistency, about 30 minutes.

With the cake still in pan, cut crosswise into 3 equal layers. Place 1 layer , right-side down, on a serving plate. Place half the filling on top and spread evenly. Place second layer on top, right-side down; spread with remaining cream. Top with last layer, right-side up. Refrigerate for 2 hours.

In a small bowl combine the confectioners' sugar, cocoa, water and rum. Stir until very smooth.

Remove cake from refrigerator. Spread the glaze over the top of the cake, allowing some to run down the sides. Place walnut halves on top of cake. Refrigerate for 1 hour or until glaze is firm. Serve at room temperature.

MOCHA-FILLED MERINGUE TORTE

makes 1 9-inch torte

MERINGUE:
4 large egg whites
½ teaspoon cream of tartar
1¼ cups sugar

MOCHA FILLING:
½ cup milk
½ cup heavy cream
½ cup very strong coffee
3 large egg yolks
1½ tablespoons cornstarch
1 cup sweet butter, softened
1 cup sifted confectioners' sugar
1 teaspoon pure vanilla extract
1 cup heavy cream
⅓ cup slivered almonds

Preheat the oven to 250°F. Draw a 9-inch circle on each of two large sheets of parchment paper, waxed paper or foil and cut out. Arrange circles on baking sheets.

In a large bowl beat the egg whites and cream of tartar together until soft peaks begin to form. Gradually add the sugar, beating until egg whites are stiff and glossy. Evenly divide the meringue among the prepared circles. Smooth out tops. Bake for 2½ hours or until meringues are totally dry. When done, turn off the oven and leave meringues in oven for 5 minutes. Remove from the oven and prepare filling.

In a saucepan combine the milk, heavy cream, coffee, egg yolks and cornstarch. Place over moderate heat and beat for 5 minutes or until smooth. Remove from the heat and cool.

In a large bowl cream together the butter and sugar until light and fluffy. Add vanilla extract and blend. Add the mocha mixture, a little at a time, and beat until smooth.

In an oven set at 400°F toast the almonds in a shallow pan for 7 to 10 minutes. Remove from the oven and cool.

Remove one meringue layer from the baking sheet. Be sure to remove the paper or foil. Place it on a serving plate. Spread the layer evenly with 1 cup of the mocha filling. Place the second meringue layer on gently. Top with the remaining filling and smooth. Sprinkle with toasted almonds and refrigerate for 2 to 3 hours. Remove from refrigerator 45 minutes before serving.

PECAN TORTE

makes 1 8-inch torte

2 tablespoons flour
2 teaspoons baking powder
¼ teaspoon salt
3 cups finely chopped pecans
6 eggs, separated
1½ cups sugar
2 cups heavy cream
¼ cup confectioners' sugar
1 teaspoon pure vanilla extract

Preheat the oven to 350°F. Grease two 8-inch round cake pans. Cut waxed paper circles to fit the bottoms and place in pans. Grease again and lightly flour. Set aside.

In a large bowl mix together the flour, baking powder, salt and chopped pecans. Stir until the mixture resembles a fine meal.

In a separate bowl beat the egg yolks with the sugar. Continue beating until thick and lemon-colored, about 3 to 5 minutes.

In a separate bowl beat the egg whites until they are stiff but not dry. Fold into the chopped nut mixture. Then fold egg white and chopped nut mixture into the egg yolk mixture.

Pour the batter evenly into the pans and bake for 20 to 25 minutes. Remove from oven to cooling racks and cool for 5 minutes in pans. Carefully turn cakes out onto cooling racks. Quickly turn right-side up. Cool completely.

When ready to serve, beat the cream with the confectioners' sugar and vanilla. Continue beating until mixture is of spreading consistency.

Turn one of the cakes upside down. Spread with half the mixture. Top with second layer and spread with remaining mixture. Serve immediately.

POUND CAKES

BASIL POUND CAKE

makes 1 loaf cake

2 cups flour
1 tablespoon chopped fresh basil or
1 teaspoon dried basil
1 cup softened sweet butter
1¼ cups sugar
4 large eggs

Preheat the oven to 325°F. Butter and flour a 9 × 5 × 3-inch loaf pan. Set aside.

Combine flour and basil together in a bowl. Stir to mix.

In a bowl cream the butter. Gradually add the sugar, beating constantly until light and fluffy, approximately 7 to 8 minutes.

Add the eggs, one at a time, beating for 2 minutes after each addition. Scrape the side of the bowl with a rubber spatula when necessary. Gradually add the flour mixture to the butter-egg mixture and beat on a low speed until just mixed. Do not overbeat.

Transfer batter to prepared pan. Bake in the oven for 1¼ hours or until the cake springs back when lightly touched. Do not test with cake tester.

Remove from the oven and cool cake in pan on wire rack for 10 minutes. Turn cake out onto rack and cool completely.

COCONUT POUND CAKE

makes 1 10-inch cake

1½ cups softened sweet butter
2½ cups sugar
5 eggs, at room temperature
3 cups flour
1 teaspoon baking powder
1 teaspoon almond extract
1 teaspoon pure vanilla extract
1 cup light cream
1 cup grated coconut

Butter and lightly flour a 10-inch tube pan. Set aside.

In a large bowl cream the butter and sugar together for 15 minutes. Add eggs, one at a time, beating after each addition just enough to blend.

In a bowl or on a sheet or waxed paper, sift together the flour and baking powder.

Add the flour to the creamed mixture alternately with the cream. Continue mixing until well blended. Add the almond and vanilla extracts. Stir well. Fold in the coconut and combine well. Pour into pan.

Place pan in cold oven and set temperature to 300°F. Bake 1¾ hours or until a cake tester inserted into the center of the cake comes out clean.

Remove to cooling rack. Cool in pan for 10 minutes. Turn out onto rack and continue cooling.

GINGERY POUND CAKE

makes 2 loaf cakes

3 cups flour divided into 2½ cups and ½ cup
1 tablespoon baking powder
¾ cup light cream
2 teaspoons pure vanilla extract
2¼ cups sugar
1½ cups softened sweet butter
6 large eggs
1 cup diced crystalized ginger

Preheat the oven to 350°F. Butter two 9 × 5½-inch loaf pans. Line the bottoms with waxed paper; butter the paper. Lightly flour pans and set aside.

Into a bowl sift 2½ cups of the flour with the baking powder. Set aside.

In a small bowl combine the cream and the vanilla extract. Set aside.

In the large bowl of an electric mixer, beat the sugar and butter together until light in color and fluffy. Reduce the speed to medium and add the eggs, one at a time. Scrape down sides of bowl with a rubber spatula when necessary.

With mixer on low, add the flour mixture alternately with the cream, being sure to end with the flour. Increase speed and beat until smooth.

Combine the remaining ½ cup flour with the ginger. Toss until the ginger is coated. Gently fold into the batter.

Pour the batter into the prepared pans, dividing it evenly. Smooth tops with rubber spatula. Bake for 1 hour or until a cake tester inserted into the center comes out clean.

Remove from the oven and transfer pans to wire racks. Cool cake in pans for 30 minutes. Turn cakes out of pans onto wire racks and cool completely. Wrap cake in plastic wrap or aluminum foil and let stand overnight before serving.

ORANGE POUND CAKE

makes 4 small loaf cakes

1 cup flour
½ teaspoon baking powder
½ teaspoon baking soda
½ cup softened sweet butter
½ cup sugar
2 large eggs, separated
½ cup sour cream
1 tablespoon grated orange rind
½ teaspoon orange-flavored orange liqueur
⅛ teaspoon cream of tartar

Preheat the oven to 350°F. Generously butter four 4½ × 2½ × 1½-inch loaf pans. Set aside.

Into a bowl sift together the flour, baking powder and baking soda. Set aside.

In a large bowl cream the butter. Add the sugar, a little at a time, and beat until light and fluffy. Add the egg yolks, one at a time, beating well after each addition.

Stir in the sour cream, orange rind and orange liqueur. Mix well until well blended. Add the flour mixture to the butter-egg mixture and stir until well mixed.

In a small bowl, beat the egg whites with the cream of tartar until they are stiff but not dry.

Stir one-fourth of the egg whites into the batter. Fold the remaining egg whites into the batter. Gently spoon the batter into the prepared pans and bake for 25 to 30 minutes or until a cake tester inserted into the center of the cake comes out clean.

Remove from the oven and transfer to wire racks. Cool in pans for 5 minutes. Turn cakes out onto wire racks and cool completely. Wrap in aluminum foil or plastic wrap when cool.

LEMON-FILLED COCONUT POUND CAKE

makes 1 10-inch tube cake

3 cups flour
¼ teaspoon salt
¼ teaspoon baking soda
1½ cups softened sweet butter
3 cups sugar
6 large eggs
1 cup sour cream
½ cup flaked coconut
2 teaspoons pure vanilla extract

FILLING:
6 large lemons
2 cups sugar
¾ cup sweet butter, cut into pieces
6 large eggs, lightly beaten

Preheat the oven to 300°F. Generously butter and flour a 10-inch tube pan with a removable bottom. Set aside.

Into a bowl sift together the flour, salt and baking soda.

In a large bowl cream the butter. Gradually add the sugar, beating until light and fluffy. Scrape sides of the bowl with a rubber spatula when necessary. Beat in the eggs, one at a time, beating well after each addition.

Add the flour mixture alternately with the sour cream to the butter mixture. Mix well. Add the coconut and vanilla extract; stir to blend.

Turn batter into prepared pan. Bake in the oven for 1½ hours or until a cake tester inserted near the center of the cake comes out clean. Remove from the oven. Cool cake in pan on wire rack for 30 minutes. Turn cake out onto rack and cool completely.

Prepare the filling while the cake cools. Remove the peel from the lemons and chop it very fine. Squeeze the lemons and measure out 1 cup of lemon juice.

In the top of a double boiler combine the lemon peel, juice, sugar and butter. Heat over hot but not boiling water until the sugar dissolves and the butter melts. Stir constantly. Add the beaten eggs through a strainer. Cook, stirring constantly, for 20 minutes or until very thick. Do not boil. Transfer the custard to a bowl and cover with plastic wrap touching the surface to prevent skin from forming. Refrigerate 6 to 8 hours before using.

Cut the cooled cake in half making two layers. Fill the cake with 1¼ cups of the lemon filling. Spread ¼ cup of the filling on the top of the cake. Serve remaining filling with cake or store tightly covered in refrigerator for up to three weeks. Store cake, covered, at room temperature.

POUND CAKE

makes 2 loaf cakes

1 pound softened sweet butter
1 pound sugar
10 eggs, separated
4 cups flour
½ teaspoon salt
1 teaspoon baking powder
1 teaspoon pure vanilla extract
2 tablespoons grated lemon rind

Butter two 12-inch loaf pans and dust them lightly with flour. Set aside.

In a large bowl cream the butter. Gradually add the sugar and continue creaming until the mixture is light and fluffy.

In a separate bowl beat the egg yolks. Add the yolks to the butter mixture, beating constantly.

In a bowl or on a large sheet of wax paper, sift together the flour, salt, and baking powder 4 times.

Gradually add the flour to the butter mixture. Mix thoroughly. Add the vanilla and lemon rind. Mix thoroughly.

Preheat the oven to 300°F.

In a small bowl beat the egg whites until they are stiff but not dry. Fold into the batter.

Pour half the mixture into each of the loaf pans. Bake for 1 to 1¼ hours or until a cake tester inserted into the middle of the loaf comes out clean.

Remove to cooling racks. Cool 10 minutes in the pan. Then turn out onto racks and cool completely.

A traditional pound cake such as this one calls for one pound each of the major ingredients. Ten eggs weigh about 1 pound.

PUMPKIN-APRICOT POUND CAKE

makes 1 bundt cake

3 cups sifted flour
½ teaspoon salt
¼ teaspoon baking soda
1 cup softened sweet butter
2¾ cups sugar
6 large eggs
¾ cup canned pumpkin
¼ cup sour cream
¼ cup apricot brandy
1 teaspoon pure vanilla extract
½ teaspoon pure orange extract
½ teaspoon rum extract

Preheat the oven to 325°F. Generously butter and flour a 2½-quart bundt pan. Set aside.

In a bowl sift together the flour, salt and baking soda.

In a large bowl cream the butter. Gradually add the sugar and beat until the mixture is light and fluffy. Add the eggs, one at a time, beating well after each addition. Scrape sides of the bowl with a rubber spatula as needed.

Add the pumpkin, sour cream, apricot brandy, vanilla extract, orange extract and rum extract. Beat until blended. Add the sifted flour mixture and stir until flour is thoroughly incorporated.

Pour batter into prepared pan and bake in the oven for 1 hour 10 minutes or until a cake tester inserted near the center comes out clean.

Remove from the oven. Let cake cool in the pan on a wire rack for 1 hour. Turn cake out onto rack and cool completely.

LOAF CAKES

Carrot Maple Crumb Loaf

makes 1 loaf cake

¼ cup sweet butter
2 cups grated carrot
1½ cups fine unflavored breadcrumbs
½ cup unsweetened shredded coconut
1 teaspoon cinnamon
½ teaspoon grated nutmeg
¼ teaspoon salt
4 large eggs, separated
⅓ cup pure maple syrup
1½ teaspoons pure vanilla extract

Preheat the oven to 350°F. Butter a 9 × 5-inch loaf pan. Set aside.

In a skillet, melt the butter over a moderate heat. Add the carrots and sauté until soft, approximately 5 minutes. Remove from the heat.

In a medium-sized bowl combine the breadcrumbs, coconut, cinnamon, nutmeg and salt. Add the carrot mixture and stir until well mixed.

In a small bowl beat the egg yolks together with the syrup and vanilla extract. Add to the carrot mixture and blend well.

In another small bowl, beat the egg whites until stiff but not dry. Fold whites into the carrot mixture. Gently turn batter into prepared pan. Bake for 35 to 40 minutes or until cake tester inserted into the center of the cake comes out clean.

Remove from the oven. Cool in pan on rack for 5 minutes. Turn cake out onto rack and cool completely.

Lemon-Walnut Loaf

makes 1 loaf cake

1½ cups flour
1½ teaspoons baking powder
½ teaspoon salt
½ cup sweet butter, softened
1 cup sugar
2 large eggs
½ cup milk
½ cup coarsely chopped walnuts
3 tablespoons grated lemon rind

Preheat the oven to 350°F. Butter and flour an 8 × 4-inch loaf pan.

Into a bowl sift together the flour, baking powder and salt.

In a large bowl cream together the butter and sugar. And the eggs, one at a time, beating well after each addition.

Add the flour mixture and beat until smooth. Add the ·milk and mix just until blended. Gently stir in the walnuts and lemon rind. Turn batter into the prepared pan and bake for 1 hour or until a cake tester inserted into the center of the cake comes out clean.

Remove from the oven. Cool in pan on wire rack for 10 minutes. Turn cake out onto rack and cool completely.

LEMON-GINGER SWIRL CAKE

makes 1 loaf cake

LEMON BATTER:
¾ cup flour
½ teaspoon baking powder
⅛ teaspoon salt
½ cup softened sweet butter
¾ cup sugar
2 large eggs
1 tablespoon grated lemon rind
¼ cup milk

GINGER BATTER:
⅔ cup flour
1 teaspoon ground cinnamon
1 teaspoon ground ginger
½ teaspoon grated nutmeg
¼ teaspoon ground cardamom
¼ teaspoon baking soda
¼ cup softened sweet butter
¼ cup firmly packed light brown sugar
1 large egg
½ cup molasses
3 tablespoons finely chopped crystalized ginger

Preheat the oven to 325°F. Generously butter and lightly flour an 8 × 4-inch loaf pan. Set aside.

Sift together the flour, baking powder and salt. In a medium-sized bowl cream the butter until light and fluffy. Add the sugar, a little at a time, and beat until well blended. Add the eggs and the lemon rind and mix.

Add the flour mixture alternately with the milk. Stir gently until just mixed. Do not over-blend. Set aside.

For the ginger batter, into a bowl sift together the flour, cinnamon, ginger, nutmeg, cardamom and baking soda. Set aside.

In a medium-sized bowl cream the butter until light and fluffy. Add the brown sugar and egg and beat until blended. Add the molasses (treacle) and mix until well blended.

Add the flour mixture, stirring until just blended. Do not overmix. Gently fold in chopped ginger.

Place alternate spoonfuls of the lemon and ginger batter into the prepared pan. Swirl through with a knife two to three times in each direction. Bake for 1½ hours or until a cake tester inserted into the center of the cake comes out clean.

Remove from oven. Cool in pan on wire rack. Wrap in aluminum foil and store.

MAPLE LOAF CAKE

makes 1 9-inch loaf cake

⅓ cup softened sweet butter
½ cup sugar
¾ cup pure maple syrup
2¼ cups flour
1 tablespoon baking powder
½ teaspoon salt
⅓ cup milk
3 egg whites
1 teaspoon vanilla extract
Maple Nut Frosting (see page 171)

Preheat the oven to 350°F.
In a mixing bowl cream the butter and sugar until light and fluffy. Add the maple

syrup and mix well.

Combine the flour, baking powder, and salt. Add this to the butter mixture alternately with the milk.

In a separate bowl beat the egg whites until they are stiff but not dry. Fold into the batter. Add vanilla and mix.

Pour into a greased 9 × 5 × 3-inch loaf pan and bake for 35 minutes or until a cake tester inserted in the center comes out clean. Remove cake to a cooling rack. Cool in the pan for 15 minutes, then turnout onto rack and continue cooling.

When cake is cool, frost with maple nut frosting.

ORANGE-RAISIN LOAF CAKE

makes 1 8-inch loaf cake

½ cup golden raisins
1 tablespoon sifted flour
3 tablespoons sweet butter, softened
1 tablespoon solid vegetable shortening
½ cup sugar
1 large egg, lightly beaten
½ teaspoon pure orange extract
grated rind of ½ orange
½ teaspoon baking soda
6 tablespoons buttermilk
1 cup flour

Preheat the oven to 350°F. Generously butter an 8 × 4 × 2-inch loaf pan.

In a food processor or blender, blend the raisins with the 1 tablespoon flour until well minced.

In a large bowl cream together the butter and solid shortening. Gradually add the sugar, beating well until the mixture is light and fluffy.

Add the raisin mixture, the egg and the orange extract. Beat until well blended. Add the orange rind and stir to blend.

In a small bowl combine the baking soda and the buttermilk.

Add the buttermilk mixture, alternately with the remaining 1 cup flour to the raisin mixture.

Stir until well mixed. Turn the batter into the prepared pan and bake for 35 to 40 minutes or until a cake tester inserted into the center of the cake comes out clean.

Remove from the pan. Cool in the pan on a wire rack for 5 minutes. Invert cake onto the rack and cool completely.

WALNUT HONEY CAKE

makes 1 loaf cake

½ cup sweet butter
⅓ cup sugar
⅔ cup honey
1 tablespoon crushed anise seeds
2 cups flour
2 teaspoons baking soda
⅔ cup finely chopped walnuts
½ cup boiling water

Preheat the oven to 350°F.

In a saucepan combine the butter, sugar and honey. Cook over low heat until melted. Add the crushed anise seeds and stir. Remove from heat and set aside.

Combine the flour and baking soda in a bowl. Add the chopped walnuts and stir.

Add the flour and nut mixture to the honey mixture. Stir until well blended. Stir in the boiling water.

Butter a 9 × 5 × 3-inch loaf pan. Line it with waxed paper and butter again. Pour in the batter.

Bake for 30 minutes or until a cake tester inserted into the middle of the loaf comes out clean.

Remove cake from oven and cool in the pan. When completely cool, turn loaf out and peel off waxed paper.

WALNUT CAKE WITH CHOCOLATE-NUT FROSTING

makes 2 loaf cakes

3 cups sifted cake flour
1 tablespoon baking powder
¼ teaspoon salt
1 cup sweet butter, cut into pieces
2 cups sugar
2 cups coarsely chopped walnuts
1 tablespoon flour
4 large eggs
1 cup milk
1 teaspoon pure vanilla extract
½ teaspoon pure almond extract
Chocolate-Nut Frosting (see page 170)

Preheat the oven to 350°F. Butter two 9 × 5 × 3-inch loaf pans.

Sift together cake flour, baking powder and salt. Set aside.

Place the butter into a mixing bowl. Add the sugar, a little at a time, beating for 10 minutes.

Combine the chopped walnuts with the 1 tablespoon flour. Toss well.

Add the eggs, one at a time, to the butter mixture, beating well after each addition.

Add the vanilla extract and almond extract to the milk. Add the flour mixture and milk mixture alternately to the butter mixture.

Beat well after each addition. Add the walnut mixture and mix until well blended.

Evenly distribute the batter between the two prepared pans. Bake for 50 minutes or until a cake tester inserted into the center comes out clean.

Remove pans from the oven. Cool in pans on wire racks for 10 minutes. Turn cakes out onto racks and cool completely.

Spread equal amounts of frosting on the top of each cake. Let frosting set before serving.

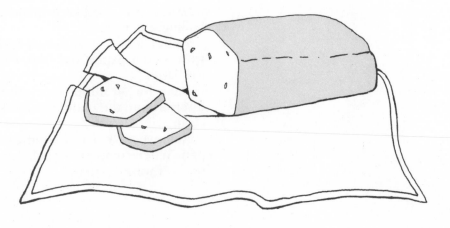

—SHORTCAKES—

APPLE, BLACKBERRY AND NUT SHORTCAKE

makes 1 large shortcake

4 medium-sized cooking apples
½ cup unsweetened apple juice
2 cups fresh blackberries
1 cup water
2 tablespoons blackberry preserves
1 cup sugar
4 teaspoons arrowroot
2¼ cups flour
1½ teaspoons baking powder
10 tablespoons sweet butter, softened
⅓ cup confectioners' sugar
1 large egg
½ teaspoon pure vanilla extract
1 cup walnut halves
whipped cream for garnish

Peel, core and cut the apples into slices ½-inch thick. In a saucepan combine the apples and juice. Cook, covered, over a moderate heat for 5 minutes or until the apples are just tender. Measure out 2 cups of the apple slices and drain. Reserve the syrup and remaining fruit for another use.

In a saucepan combine the blackberries, water, and preserves. Combine the sugar and arrowroot and add to the berry mixture. Stir well to blend. Cook over a moderate heat for 5 minutes or until the mixture has thickened. Remove from the heat and cool.

Preheat the oven to 325°F.

Into a bowl sift together the flour and baking powder. Set aside.

In a large bowl cream together the butter and confectioners' sugar until light and fluffy. Add the egg and vanilla extract and beat to blend. Add the flour mixture and combine until a dough forms. Divide the dough into two parts, one slightly larger than the other.

On a piece of waxed paper, roll the larger part out to form a 12-inch circle. Fit the circle into a 9-inch pie pan. Top layer with the apples. Then sprinkle walnut halves on top and finish with the blackberry mixture.

On a piece of waxed paper roll out the remaining dough to form a 9-inch circle. Fit over the filling and press the edges together to seal. With a fork, prick the top layer all over.

Place the pan on a baking sheet and bake for 1 hour or until golden. Remove from the oven and serve warm with cream.

PEACH GINGER SHORTCAKE

makes 4 shortcakes

3 ripe peaches
1½ cups water
⅓ cup honey
¼ cup sugar
peel of ½ orange, cut into very thin strips

SHORTCAKES:
¼ cup cake flour
2 teaspoons baking powder
¼ teaspoon salt
1 teaspoon grated fresh ginger
1½ teaspoons flour
1 tablespoon sugar
5 tablespoons cold sweet butter, cut into small bits
⅓ cup milk

Peel the peaches. Cut in half, remove the pits and quarter.

In a saucepan combine the water, honey and sugar. Bring the mixture to a boil and then reduce the heat. Add the orange peel and simmer gently for 5 minutes.

Add the peaches and cook gently, stirring to cover peaches, for 15 minutes or until fruit is tender. Remove from the heat and cool peaches in the pan.

Preheat the oven to 375°F.

Into a bowl sift together the ¼ cup cake flour, baking powder and salt. Sift again and set aside.

In a small bowl combine the ginger, remaining flour and sugar and stir. Set aside.

Transfer the sifted dry ingredients to a large bowl. Add the butter bits and cut in using a fork, two knives or a pastry blender until the mixture resembles a coarse meal. Add ginger mixture and toss to combine.

Make a well in the center of the dough. Add 3 tablespoons of the milk and mix only until the dough is moist enough to hold together. Add more milk if necessary.

On a lightly floured surface, knead the dough for 10 to 15 minutes. Pat or roll the dough into a ¾-inch thick round. Using a 2-inch floured biscuit cutter, cut out 4 biscuits. Put them on an unbuttered baking sheet and bake for 12 to 15 minutes or until golden.

While the shortcakes are baking, remove the peaches and orange peel from the syrup. Cut each peach piece into 3 parts. Set aside.

Over medium-high heat, cook the syrup for 7 to 10 minutes, or until it is reduced to 1½ cups.

Remove the shortcakes from the oven and transfer to four individual plates. Carefully cut each cake in half horizontally and remove the tops. Cover each bottom evenly with half the syrup and then evenly with half of the peaches. Replace the tops and cover with remaining syrup and peaches. Serve immediately.

STRAWBERRY SHORTCAKE

makes 4 shortcakes

¾ cup flour
¼ cup cake flour
2 teaspoons baking powder
¼ teaspoon salt
1 tablespoon sugar
5 tablespoons cold sweet butter, cut into bits
⅓ cup milk

TOPPING:
4 cups fresh strawberries
⅓ cup sugar
3 tablespoons sweet butter, softened
½ cup heavy cream
2 teaspoons sugar

Preheat the oven to 375°F.

Onto a piece of waxed paper sift together the flour, cake flour, baking powder, salt and sugar. Sift again into a large bowl.

Add the butter to the flour mixture. Cut in using a fork, two knives or a pastry blender until the mixture resembles a coarse meal.

Form a well in the center of the dough. Add 3 tablespoons of the milk. Mix only until the dough is moist enough to hold together. Add more milk if necessary.

On a lightly floured surface, knead the dough for 10 to 15 minutes. Roll the dough into a ¾-inch thick round. Using a 2-inch floured biscuit cutter, cut out 4 biscuits. Do not twist cutter. Transfer biscuits to an unbuttered baking sheet and refrigerate.

Clean, hull and quarter the strawberries. If berries are very large, slice them. Combine the berries and sugar together in a bowl. Adjust sugar to taste. Mix and let stand for 15 minutes.

In a bowl beat the cream with the 2 teaspoons sugar until it is fluffy and soft mounds form.

Remove biscuits from the refrigerator and bake for 12 to 15 minutes or until golden. Remove from the oven. Carefully slice the hot shortcakes in half horizontally and spread evenly with the 3 tablespoons butter.

Transfer the bottom halves, cut-side up, to 4 plates. Spoon half of the strawberry mixture evenly over each half. Replace tops. Spoon on remaining strawberry mixture and finish with a generous spoon of whipped cream. Serve at once.

COFFEE CAKES

APPLE COFFEE CAKE

makes 1 9-inch cake

2 cups sugar
1 cup softened sweet butter
2 cups apples, unpeeled and diced
1 cup cold strong coffee
1 cup coarsely chopped walnuts
1 cup raisins
2 cups flour
2 teaspoons baking soda
1 teaspoon baking powder
½ teaspoon salt
1 teaspoon grated nutmeg
1 teaspoon cinnamon
2 eggs
confectioners' sugar

Preheat the oven to 375°F.

In a large bowl cream together the sugar and butter until light and fluffy. Add the apples and coffee. Mix well.

In a small bowl mix together the walnuts and raisins.

In another bowl combine the flour, baking soda, baking powder, salt, nutmeg and cinnamon. Mix well. Add ¼ cup of the flour mixture to the raisins and nuts. Stir to coat well. Add the remaining flour mixture to the butter mixture and beat well. Add the eggs, 1 at a time, beating well after each addition. Beat in the raisin and nut mixture.

Turn the batter into a buttered 9 × 13-inch baking pan. Bake for 45 minutes. Remove from oven and cool slightly. Cut into squares, dust with confectioners' sugar, and serve.

PECAN COFFEE CAKE

makes 1 9-inch cake

1 cup softened sweet butter
2 cups sugar
2 eggs
1 cup sour cream
2 teaspoons pure vanilla extract
2 cups flour
1 teaspoon baking powder
¼ teaspoon salt

FILLING:
2 cups chopped pecans
2 tablespoons sugar
2 teaspoons cinnamon

Preheat the oven to 350°F.

Place the pecans in a shallow metal baking pan. Toast in the oven for 5 minutes or until lightly browned. Remove from the oven and cool slightly.

In a small bowl combine the pecans, 2 tablespoons sugar, and 2 teaspoons cinnamon. Mix well and set aside.

In a large mixing bowl cream the butter and sugar together until light and fluffy. Add the eggs, 1 at a time, beating well after each addition. Stir in the sour cream and the vanilla. Combine the flour, baking powder, and salt. Add to the butter mixture and fold in gently.

Spread one-third of the batter into a well-buttered 9-inch tube or bundt pan. Sprinkle batter with half the filling. Spread one-third more of the batter into the pan. Sprinkle with remaining filling. Spread with remaining batter.

Bake for 1 to 1¼ hours or until a cake tester inserted into the center comes out clean.

Remove from oven to a cooling rack. Cool in the pan for 5 minutes. Turn out onto the rack and cool for 30 minutes. Serve cake warm or let it cool completely.

SCANDINAVIAN RAISIN RING

makes 1 ring

1 package active dry yeast
¼ cup very warm water
3 cups flour
¾ cup sugar
1 teaspoon salt
¾ cup sweet butter
¼ cup melted sweet butter
1 cup light cream
3 egg yolks
grated rind of 1 small lemon
2 tablespoons cinnamon
½ cup golden raisins
½ cup diced citron
1 egg white, slightly beaten
chopped almonds
Confectioner's Icing (see page 170)

Sprinkle the yeast into a bowl with the warm water. Set aside for 2 minutes and then stir to dissolve.

In a large bowl combine the flour, ¼ cup sugar, and salt. Cut in ¾ cup butter with a pastry blender or two knives until the mixture resembles a coarse meal. Add the yeast, cream, egg yolks and lemon rind. Beat well. Wrap dough in plastic wrap and refrigerate overnight.

Remove dough from refrigerator and turn out onto a lightly floured surface. Roll out into a 16 × 12-inch rectangle. Brush with ¼ cup melted butter and sprinkle with ½ cup sugar and the cinnamon. Sprinkle with the raisins and citron.

Roll up the dough and place it on a buttered baking sheet. Join the ends to form a ring. With sharp scissors, cut all the way through the ring from the edge three-quarters of the way to the center. Make cuts at 1½-inch intervals. As pieces are cut, lift each up slightly and place on its side, turning every other piece in the opposite direction. Press the ring to flatten the dough pieces and make them all the same height. Cover and let rise until doubled in size, about 1 to 2 hours.

Preheat the oven to 350°F.

Brush the ring with the egg white and sprinkle with almonds. Bake for 30 minutes.

Remove from oven and cool completely. Frost with Confectioners' Icing.

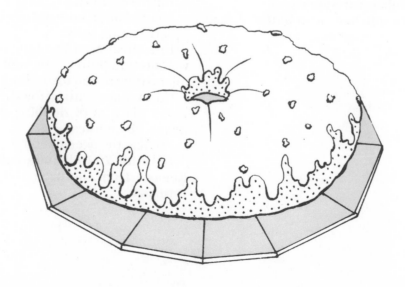

STREUSEL

makes 1 cake

1½ cups flour
3 teaspoons baking powder
¼ teaspoon salt
¾ cup sugar
¼ cup sweet butter
1 egg
⅓ cup milk
1 teaspoon pure vanilla extract

FILLING:
½ cup firmly packed light brown sugar
2 teaspoons flour
2 teaspoons cinnamon
2 teaspoons melted butter
½ cup chopped walnuts

Preheat the oven to 350°F.

Combine the flour with the baking powder, salt and sugar in a large bowl. Cut in the butter with a pastry blender or two knives until the mixture resembles a fine meal. Add the egg, milk and vanilla. Stir until well mixed.

To make the filling, combine the brown sugar, flour, cinnamon, melted butter and chopped nuts in a bowl. Mix well.

Butter an 8-inch square baking pan. Pour half the batter into the pan and sprinkle with half the filling. Add the remaining batter and top with the remaining filling.

Bake for 20 to 30 minutes.

Remove from oven and cool before serving.

YEAST COFFEE CAKE

makes 2 8-inch cakes

1 cup milk
⅔ cup sugar
1½ teaspoons salt
6 tablespoons softened sweet butter
½ cup warm water
2 packages dry or cake yeast
2 large eggs, beaten
4 cups sifted flour
½ cup firmly packed light brown sugar
¼ cup chopped walnuts
2 tablespoons softened sweet butter

In a small saucepan scald the milk. Add the sugar, salt and 6 tablespoons butter. Stir until butter melts and sugar dissolves. Cool mixture to lukewarm.

Into a large bowl pour the warm water. Sprinkle in the yeast and stir until it dissolves. Add the cooled milk mixture and stir to mix. Add the eggs and stir until well mixed. Gradually stir in the flour, mixing only enough to dampen the flour.

Spoon batter into two well-buttered 8-inch square baking pans.

In a small bowl combine the brown sugar, walnuts and butter. Mix well. Sprinkle crumb mixture evenly on top of both cakes

Cover pans with a towel and let rise in a warm place until doubled in bulk, approximately 50 minutes.

Preheat the oven to 400°F.

Bake for 20 to 25 minutes or until golden. Remove from the oven and cool in pans on wire rack.

—CHEESECAKE—

AMARETTI-AMARETTO CHEESECAKE
makes 1 10-inch cake

¾ cup ground amaretti cookies
(approximately 20 cookies)
1 tablespoon sweet butter, melted
24 ounces cream cheese, softened
¾ cup and 2 tablespoons sugar
4 large eggs
3 tablespoons amaretto or almond-flavored
liqueur
½ teaspoon pure vanilla extract
1¼ cups sour cream

In a bowl combine the amaretti cookie crumbs and butter. Mix until blended. Remove 1 tablespoon of the mixture and set aside. Press the remaining crumbs in a buttered 10-inch springform pan, covering the bottom and ½ inch up the sides. Refrigerate until needed.

Preheat the oven to 350°F.

In a large bowl beat the cream cheese until smooth and light. Scrape down sides of the bowl with a rubber spatula occasionally. Gradually add the ¾ cup sugar, beating well after each addition. Add the eggs, one at a time, beating only until blended after each addition. Add the amaretto and vanilla extract and beat to blend.

Transfer the mixture to the prepared pan and bake for 25 to 30 minutes, or until the center is not quite set. Carefully remove cake from the oven to a wire rack; cool for 20 minutes. Do not turn the oven off.

In a bowl combine the sour cream and remaining 2 tablespoons of the sugar. Allow mixture to stand until sugar dissolves. Stir well.

Gently spread the mixture over the top of the cake, being sure not to touch the sides of the pan. Bake for 10 minutes longer. Remove from the oven. Cool cake in pan on wire rack. When cake has reached room temperature, sprinkle the remaining amaretti crumbs in a border around the cake.

Refrigerate the cake, lightly covered with plastic wrap, for 3 hours or more. Carefully remove the sides of the pan and let cake stand at room temperature for 15 minutes before serving.

CHEESECAKE WITH RASPBERRY SAUCE

makes 1 9-inch cake

4 eggs
1½ cups light brown sugar
2 pounds softened cream cheese
¼ cup crème de cassis or raspberry-flavored liqueur
¼ cup heavy cream
⅛ teaspoon salt
9 ounces ground almonds or pecans
1 tablespoon sweet butter
½ cup graham cracker crumbs

SAUCE:
4 cups fresh raspberries
2 tablespoons sugar
¼ cup crème de cassis or raspberry-flavored liqueur

Preheat the oven to 350°F. Generously butter the bottom and sides of a 9-inch round layer cake pan (do not use a springform pan). Sprinkle the inside of the pan with the graham cracker crumbs. Rotate the pan until the sides and bottom are evenly coated. Shake out the excess crumbs. Set the pan aside.

In the large bowl of an electric mixer, beat the eggs until foamy. Add the brown sugar, a little at a time, and beat for 2 minutes. Add the cream cheese, liqueur, cream, and salt. Beat until the mixture is well blended and very smooth. Add the ground almonds and beat until they are evenly distributed.

Turn the batter into the prepared pan. Level off the top with a rubber spatula. Bake until firm, about 1¾ to 2 hours.

Remove the cheesecake from the oven and cool in the pan on a wire rack for 20 minutes. Put a serving plate over the top of the pan and carefully invert the pan to unmold the cheesecake. Set aside.

To make the sauce, combine the raspberries, sugar and liqueur in a bowl. Mix well and let stand at room temperature for 30 minutes.

Carefully spoon all of the sauce over the cheesecake. Refrigerate for at least 3 hours before serving.

CHOCOLATE CHIP CHEESECAKE

makes 1 9-inch cake

1¼ cups chocolate cookie crumbs
¼ cup sweet butter, melted
1 tablespoon sugar
2½ pounds cream cheese, softened
1¾ cups sugar
¼ cup flour
1 teaspoon pure vanilla extract
5 large eggs
2 egg yolks
¼ cup heavy cream
½ cup very small semisweet chocolate pieces

In a bowl combine the cookie crumbs, butter and 1 tablespoon sugar. Mix well. Press mixture in the bottom of a buttered 9 × 3-inch springform pan. Refrigerate until needed.

Preheat the oven to 475°F.

In a large bowl beat together the cream cheese and sugar until light and fluffy. Add the whole eggs and egg yolks, one at a time beating well after each addition. Add the flour and vanilla extract and continue beating until mixture is smooth. Scrape down the sides of the bowl with a rubber spatula. Add the cream and stir until smooth. Stir in the chocolate pieces. Turn batter into the prepared pan. Place pan on a baking sheet. Bake for 10 minutes. Lower the temperature to 250°F and bake for 1 hour. Turn off the oven; let cake cool in the oven for 1 hour. Open the oven door part way and let cake cool for 30 minutes longer. Remove from the oven and cool on a wire rack to room temperature.

Refrigerate 8 hours or overnight before serving.

CHOCOLATE YOGURT CHEESECAKE

makes 1 8-inch cake

**1 cup chocolate wafer crumbs
(about 16 wafers)
¼ cup melted sweet butter
16 ounces cream cheese
1 cup sugar
3 eggs, at room temperature
1½ teaspoons pure vanilla extract
6 ounces semisweet chocolate, melted and
cooled
1 cup plain yogurt**

**GLAZE:
3 ounces semisweet chocolate
2 tablespoons sweet butter
1 tablespoon corn syrup
½ teaspoon pure vanilla extract**

Preheat the oven to 300°F.

In a small bowl combine the wafer crumbs with the melted butter until well blended. Press crumbs firmly into the bottom of a heavily buttered 8-inch springform cake pan. Refrigerate until ready to use.

In a large mixing bowl combine the cream cheese and the sugar. Beat until smooth. Beat in the eggs and vanilla. Stir in the cooled chocolate and the yogurt. Mix until well blended. Turn the batter into the prepared crust.

Place a pan of hot water on the oven floor. Place the cheesecake in the middle of the oven and bake for 50 to 60 minutes or until the cake pulls away slightly from the sides of the pan. Turn off the oven. Let the cake sit in the oven with the door slightly ajar for 1 hour.

Remove cake from oven. Separate the cake from the sides of the pan with a thin knife; remove the sides. Transfer the cake to a serving plate.

To make the glaze, combine the 3 ounces chocolate, butter, corn syrup and vanilla in a small saucepan. Cook over low heat until the butter melts and the mixture is smooth. Remove from the heat and cool slightly.

With a knife spread the glaze only on the top of the cake. Swirl with the back of a spoon. Chill 5 to 6 hours or overnight before serving.

CREAMY WHITE CHOCOLATE CHEESECAKE

makes 1 9-inch cake

1½ cups graham cracker crumbs
5 tablespoons sweet butter, melted
1 to 2 tablespoons sugar
2 pounds cream cheese, softened
½ cup sweet butter, softened
4 large eggs
10 ounces white chocolate, melted
4½ teaspoons pure vanilla extract
⅛ teaspoon salt

In a bowl combine the graham cracker crumbs, sugar and melted butter. Mix well. Carefully press crumbs into the bottom and sides of a buttered 9-inch springform pan. Refrigerate for 2 hours.

Preheat the oven to 300°F.

In a large bowl beat together the cream cheese and the butter until smooth. Add the eggs, one at a time, beating well after each addition. Scrape down the sides of the bowl as necessary.

Add the melted chocolate, vanilla extract and salt. Beat together for 2 minutes. Pour mixture into the prepared pan and bake for 1 hour.

Remove from the oven and cool at room temperature for 2 hours. Refrigerate for 10 to 12 hours before removing the sides of the pan and serve.

CHOCOLATE MARBLE CHEESECAKE

makes 1 9-inch cake

2 cups vanilla wafer cookie crumbs
(approximately 50 cookies)
¼ cup sugar
¼ teaspoon ground cinnamon
¼ cup sweet butter, melted
1 ounce unsweetened baking chocolate
16 ounces cream cheese, softened
1 cup sugar
6 large eggs, separated
2 teaspoons pure vanilla extract
1 tablespoon dark rum
1 cup whipped cream

Preheat the oven to 300°F.

In a small bowl combine the cookie crumbs, sugar, cinnamon and butter. Mix well. Press mixture evenly over the sides and bottom of a buttered 9-inch springform pan.

Place the chocolate in the top of a double boiler and melt it over hot but not boiling water. Set aside.

In a large bowl beat the cream cheese until smooth. Add ½ cup of the sugar and the egg yolks. Beat until mixture is light. Add the vanilla extract and the rum; stir to blend. Add the whipped cream and fold in gently.

In a bowl beat the egg whites until frothy. Add the remaining sugar, a little at a time, and beat until soft peaks form. Gently fold egg whites into the batter.

Transfer ⅓ of the batter into the prepared pan. Drizzle a little of the melted chocolate over the batter and swirl lightly. Repeat with remaining batter and chocolate in two layers.

Bake for 1½ hours. Turn off the oven and let cake cool in the oven for 1 hour with the door open. Remove from the oven and cool completely on a wire rack. Refrigerate for at least 2 hours before serving. When ready to serve, unmold carefully.

HAZELNUT CHEESECAKE

makes 1 8-inch cake

¼ cup whole hazelnuts
2½ cups graham cracker crumbs
2 tablespoons sweet butter, melted
8 ounces cream cheese, softened
⅓ cup sour cream
⅓ cup sugar
2 teaspoons flour
2 tablespoons lemon juice
¾ teaspoon pure vanilla extract
2 large eggs, separated
⅛ teaspoon cream of tartar

Preheat the oven to 350°F. In a shallow pan toast the hazelnuts in the oven for 10 minutes. Remove from the oven and spread nuts on a clean towel. Rub gently to remove most of the skins. Allow nuts to cool. When nuts have cooled transfer to blender or food processor and process until finely ground. Measure out 2 tablespoons and set aside. Reserve the remaining ground nuts for another use. Reduce the oven temperature to 275°F.

In a small bowl combine the graham cracker crumbs and melted butter. Mix well. Press the mixture gently into the bottom of an 8-inch springform pan that is 3 inches deep.

In a large bowl beat the cream cheese together with the sour cream until mixture is light and smooth. Add the sugar and flour and beat until well mixed. Add the lemon juice and vanilla extract and beat to blend. Add the egg yolks, one at a time, beating well after each addition. Scrape down the sides of the bowl with a rubber spatula. Stir in the ground hazelnuts.

In a separate bowl, beat the egg whites with the cream of tartar until stiff but not dry. Gently fold egg whites into the batter.

Pour batter into the prepared pan and bake for 1 hour 15 minutes, or until cake is firm. Remove from the oven. Cool cake in pan on wire rack. Cover loosely and chill for at least 6 hours before serving. Carefully unmold when ready to serve.

LEMONY CHEESECAKE

makes 1 10-inch cake

4 cups graham cracker crumbs
1 cup sweet butter, melted
¼ cup cold water
2 tablespoons unflavored gelatin
¾ cup sugar
5 large eggs, separated
dash of salt
⅓ cup milk, scalded
24 ounces cream cheese, softened
⅓ cup lemon juice
¼ cup orange-flavored liqueur
½ teaspoon pure vanilla extract
½ cup sugar
finely grated rind of 2 lemons

Preheat the oven to 350°F.

In a large bowl combine the graham cracker crumbs and melted butter. Mix well. Remove ⅓ cup of the crumbs and set aside. Press the remaining crumbs into the bottom and up the sides of a buttered 10-inch springform pan. Bake crust for 12 to 15 minutes or until firm. Remove from the oven and cool on a wire rack. Turn the oven off.

In a small cup, soften the gelatin in the cold water for 4 to 5 minutes.

In the top part of a double boiler, combine the ¾ cup sugar, egg yolks and salt. Beat well. Place over slowly simmering water. Add the scalded milk, a little at a time, beating constantly until thick and smooth, approximately 5 minutes. Add the gelatin mixture and stir until totally dissolved. Remove from the heat and cool.

In a large bowl beat the cream cheese until smooth. Add a small amount of the egg yolk mixture and beat well. Fold in the remaining egg yolks. Add the lemon juice, orange liqueur and vanilla extract. Fold in until well blended.
orange liqueur and vanilla extract. Fold in until well blended.

In a large bowl beat the egg whites until soft peaks begin to form. Add the ½ cup sugar, a little at a time, beating until stiff but not dry. Gently fold egg whites in cheese mixture.

Turn mixture into prepared pan. Smooth the top with a rubber spatula and sprinkle with the reserved crumbs and the grated lemon rind. Refrigerate for 8 hours or overnight.

PECAN BRITTLE CHEESECAKE

makes 1 8-inch cake

¾ cup and 2 tablespoons pecans
2¼ cups sugar
⅓ cup water
2 pounds cream cheese, softened
4 large eggs
1 teaspoon almond extract
whipped cream for garnish (optional)

Preheat the oven to 375°F. In a shallow pan toast the pecans for 10 minutes or until lightly browned. Remove from the oven and cool nuts. Turn oven off. Coarsely chop the pecans and set aside.

Cover a baking sheet with foil and butter the foil lightly. Set aside.

In a saucepan combine ¾ cup of the sugar with the water. Cook over medium heat, stirring occasionally, until the mixture is golden; approximately 10 minutes. Add ¾ cup of the chopped pecans and cook for 30 seconds longer.

Pour the mixture, at once, onto the prepared baking sheet in a thin layer. Allow the mixture to harden and cool for 1 to 1½ hours. When cool crack the brittle and chop it coarsely with a knife. Do not grind.

Preheat the oven to 325°F.

In a blender or food processor, process the remaining pecans until they form a powder. Generously butter an 8-inch springform pan. Sprinkle the pan with the ground pecans; distribute evenly and tap out any excess.

In a bowl beat the cream cheese until smooth and light. Add the remaining 1½ cups sugar, a little at a time, beating well. Add the eggs, one at a time, beating well after each addition. Add the almond extract and the chopped brittle. Fold until well blended.

Transfer the batter to the prepared pan. Place the pan into a larger pan. Fill larger pan with enough water to reach halfway up the sides of the cake pan. Bake for 1½ hours or until top is golden. Turn off the oven and let cake cool in oven for 1 hour with the door partially open. Remove from the oven.

Unmold the cake onto a serving plate. Serve at room temperature or chilled. Accompany with whipped cream if desired.

Pumpkin-Spice Cheesecake

makes 1 10-inch cake

1¼ cups graham cracker crumbs
2 lb 3 oz cream cheese, softened
1½ cups sugar
5 large eggs
½ tablespoon grated orange rind
½ tablespoon grated lemon rind
2⅓ cups pumpkin purée
¼ teaspoon ground cinnamon
½ teaspoon ground nutmeg
2 teaspoons ground coriander
⅓ cup heavy cream
½ cup sour cream
2 tablespoons whiskey
½ cup coarsely chopped walnuts
whipped cream for garnish

Preheat the oven to 375°F. Generously butter a 10-inch springform pan. Sprinkle pan evenly with the graham cracker crumbs. Set aside.

In a large bowl beat together the cream cheese and sugar until smooth. Add the eggs, one at a time, beating well after each addition. Scrape down the sides of the bowl occasionally. Add the orange rind, lemon rind, pumpkin, cinnamon, nutmeg, coriander, cream, sour cream and whiskey. Beat very well until thoroughly mixed.

Transfer mixture to the prepared pan and sprinkle the top with the walnuts.

Place pan in a larger pan with enough water to reach 1 inch up the sides of the pan. Bake for 35 minutes.

Remove cake from the oven and cool in pan on wire rack. When cooled to room temperature, refrigerate for at least 3 hours before serving. When ready to serve, carefully unmold the cake and serve with whipped cream if desired.

Triple Ginger Cheesecake

makes 1 9-inch cake

2 cups whole pecans
2 tablespoons light brown sugar
1 large egg white, beaten until foamy
1 teaspoon ground ginger
1 teaspoon finely grated lemon peel
2 pounds cream cheese, softened
¾ cup sugar
4 large eggs, lightly beaten
½ cup heavy cream
1 teaspoon pure vanilla extract
⅔ cup ginger preserves
2 teaspoons ground ginger
1 tablespoon finely grated ginger
¼ cup chopped crystalized ginger

In a blender or food processor finely grind the pecans. In a large bowl combine the ground pecans, light brown sugar, egg white, ground ginger and lemon peel. Mix just to combine. With slightly wet fingers, press the crust mixture into the bottom and 2 inches up the side of a buttered 9-inch springform pan. Set aside.

Preheat the oven to 300°F.

In a large bowl beat the cream cheese together with the sugar until very smooth and light. Add the eggs, cream, vanilla extract, ginger preserves, ground ginger and grated ginger. Beat until very well combined. Turn batter into the prepared pan.

Bake for 1 hour and 40 minutes. Turn off the oven and let the cake cool in the closed oven for 1½ hours. Remove from the oven; cool on wire rack to room temperature. Refrigerate overnight. Remove sides of the pan. Sprinkle top of the cake with the chopped crystalized ginger and serve.

FRUITCAKES

DOUBLE-CHOCOLATE RUM FRUITCAKE

makes 2 8-inch cakes

2 cups coarsely chopped pecans
1 cup coarsely chopped dates
1 cup raisins
⅔ cup dark rum
2 cups flour
1 tablespoon ground cinnamon
1 teaspoon salt
1 cup sweet butter, softened
1⅓ cups sugar
3 ounces semisweet chocolate, melted and cooled
4 large eggs
1½ teaspoons pure vanilla extract
1 cup semisweet chocolate pieces

TOPPING:
5 tablespoons sweet butter, softened
1 cup confectioners' sugar
3 tablespoons dark rum

In a large bowl combine the pecans, dates, raisins and rum. Mix well. Cover the bowl and marinate 6 hours or overnight.

Preheat the oven to 300°F. Butter two 8-inch round pans. Line the pans with foil and butter again.

Into a bowl sift the flour, cinnamon and salt together.

In a large bowl cream together the butter and sugar until light and fluffy. Add the melted chocolate and mix well. Add the eggs, one at a time, beating well after each addition. Scrape down the sides of the bowl with a rubber spatula when necessary. Blend in the vanilla extract.

Add the flour mixture and beat until just combined. Add the marinated fruit and nut mixture and the chocolate pieces. Mix well.

Turn the batter into the prepared pans; divide evenly. Bake for 1 hour 10 minutes or until a cake tester inserted into the center comes out clean. Remove from the oven. Cool in pans for 20 minutes. Turn cakes out onto racks and remove the foil. Serve warm or at room temperature.

While the cakes cool, prepare the topping. In a bowl cream the butter until soft. Gradually beat in the sugar. Stir in the rum. Cover the bowl and chill until firm. Serve cake with topping.

GOLDEN FRUITCAKE

makes 3 9-inch loaf cakes

16 ounces golden raisins
8 ounces coarsely chopped dried figs
8 ounces coarsely chopped candied cherries
8 ounces coarsely chopped candied fruit peel
8 ounces canned pineapple chunks, drained
6 ounces dried apple chunks
6 ounces coarsely chopped dried apricots
6 ounces currants
2 cups skinned Brazil nuts
1½ cups blanched slivered almonds
1¼ cups brandy
¼ cup apricot jam
3½ cups flour
1 teaspoon ground cinnamon
1 teaspoon grated nutmeg
½ teaspoon salt
1½ cups sweet butter, softened
1 cup firmly packed light brown sugar
1 cup sugar
8 large eggs
2 teaspoons grated lemon peel
2 teaspoons grated orange peel

In a large bowl combine the raisins, figs, candied cherries, candied fruit peel, pineapple, dried apple, dried apricots, currants, Brazil nuts and almonds. Mix together the brandy and the jam. Pour the mixture over the fruit mixture and mix well. Cover the bowl and marinate 6 hours or overnight.

Preheat the oven to 275°F. Butter three 9 × 5-inch loaf pans. Line each pan evenly with foil. Butter the foil and set aside.

Into a large bowl sift together the flour, cinnamon, nutmeg and salt. Set aside.

In a large bowl cream together the butter with both sugars until light and fluffy. Add the eggs, one at a time, beating well after each addition. Scrape down the sides of a bowl with a rubber spatula as needed.

Add the flour mixture to the creamed mixture and beat until well blended. Gently fold in the marinated fruit mixture and any liquid. Add the lemon peel and orange peel. Mix well.

Turn batter into prepared pans; divide evenly. Bake for 2½ to 3 hours or until a cake tester inserted into the center comes out clean. Remove from the oven. Cool in pans on wire racks for 30 minutes. Turn cakes out onto racks. Drizzle the cakes with warm brandy, if desired. Wrap each cake in brandy-soaked cheese cloth and then in foil. Age at least two weeks before serving.

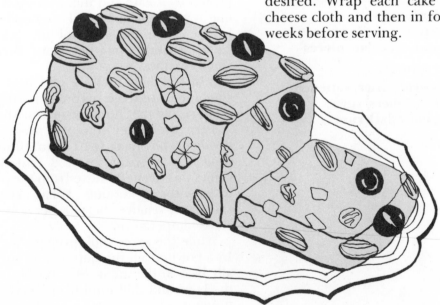

HOLIDAY FRUITCAKE

makes 1 9-inch cake

1 pound seedless dark raisins
1 pound seedless light raisins
1 pound currants
1 cup almonds
1 cup pecans
2 tablespoons flour
2 tablespoons sweet butter, softened
1 cup sweet butter
1½ cups sugar
6 eggs, separated
2 tablespoons maple syrup
2 cups flour
1 tablespoon brandy
⅛ teaspoon cinnamon
¼ teaspoon ground cloves
¼ teaspoon ground ginger
¼ teaspoon grated nutmeg
3 tablespoons orange juice
grated rind of ½ orange

Chop the dark raisins, light raisins, currants, almonds and pecans finely and mix together in a bowl. Dredge with 2 tablespoons flour. Set aside.

Line a 9-inch ring-mold cake pan with wax paper. Butter the paper and sprinkle it with flour. Set aside.

Preheat the oven to 250°F.

In a mixing bowl beat the butter until creamy. Add the sugar and beat until light, about 2 minutes. Add the egg yolks and beat until fluffy.

In a separate bowl, beat the egg whites until they are stiff but not dry. Fold the egg whites into the butter yolk. Add the syrup.

Little by little, add the flour to the mixture. Beat well after each addition. Add the brandy and beat well. Next add the cinnamon, cloves, ginger, nutmeg, orange juice, grated orange rind and fruit and nut mixture. Mix well. Pour into the cake mold.

Place the mold in a pan of water in the oven. Cover until the last 30 minutes of baking, then uncover. Bake 4 hours or until a cake tester comes out clean. Remove cake and cool completely. Wrap closely and put in a cool place until ready to use. Every 3 to 4 weeks, pour 2 ounces of whisky onto the cake to mellow it. This cake will keep for 9 months to 1 year, getting better all the time. Serve cut very thin.

NUTTY FRUITCAKE

makes 1 10-inch cake

1½ cups coarsely chopped pecans
1½ cups coarsely chopped walnuts
1 cup coarsely chopped Brazil nuts
1 cup coarsely chopped blanched almonds
1 cup golden raisins
1 cup dark raisins
⅓ cup apple brandy
melted butter
3 cups sifted flour
1½ teaspoons baking powder
1 teaspoon grated nutmeg
½ teaspoon salt
¼ teaspoon baking soda
1½ cups sweet butter, softened
1½ cups sugar
5 large eggs
2 teaspoons pure vanilla extract
⅓ cup shredded unpeeled apple
Apricot Glaze (see page 000)

In a large bowl combine the pecans, walnuts, Brazil nuts, almonds, golden raisins and dark raisins. Mix well. Pour the brandy over the mixture and cover the bowl. Allow the mixture to marinate overnight or up to 24 hours.

Preheat the oven to 325°F. Brush a 10-inch tube pan with melted butter. Carefully line the pan with parchment paper or foil. Brush the paper or foil with melted butter. Set aside.

Into a bowl sift together the flour, baking powder, nutmeg, salt and baking soda. Set aside.

In a large bowl beat the butter until light and fluffy. Add the sugar in two parts, beating for 2 minutes after each addition. Scrape down the sides of the bowl with a rubber spatula when necessary.

Add the eggs, one at a time, beating well after each addition.

Blend in the vanilla extract. Add the sifted flour mixture, blending until just mixed. This will be a stiff batter. Add the apple and marinated fruits with any liquid; stir until well combined.

Transfer batter to the prepared pan and smooth the top. Bake for 1½ hours or until a cake tester inserted into the center comes out clean.

Remove from the oven. Cool in pan on wire rack for 15 minutes. Run a knife around the edge of the pan to loosen the cake. Turn cake out onto another rack; remove pan and paper or foil. Invert right-side up. Wrap cooled cake in two layers of foil and refrigerate for 1 to 2 weeks.

Remove the cake from the refrigerator about 2 hours before glazing. Prepare the apricot glaze.

When the glaze is ready brush a thin layer over the top and sides of the cake. Let cake stand for 10 minutes; then reglaze. Allow glaze to set for 2 to 3 hours before serving.

TRADITIONAL DARK FRUITCAKE

makes 2 8-inch loaf cakes

1 cup raisins
1 cup chopped dates
1 cup diced candied fruit
1 cup slivered almonds
1 cup coarsely chopped walnuts
1½ cups coarsely chopped mixed dried fruit
2 tablespoons grated lemon rind
¾ cup brandy
½ cup sweet butter, softened
¾ cup firmly packed dark brown sugar
3 tablespoons molasses
¼ cup blackberry jam
5 large eggs
2½ cups flour
1 teaspoon baking soda
1 teaspoon ground cinnamon
1 teaspoon grated nutmeg
½ teaspoon salt

In a large bowl, combine the raisins, dates, candied fruit, slivered almonds, walnuts, dried fruit and lemon rind. Mix well. Pour the brandy over the fruits and let them marinate for at least 2 hours.

Preheat the oven to 300°F. Butter two 8 × 4-inch pans. Line the pans with wax paper and butter again. Set aside.

In a large bowl beat together the butter and brown sugar until light. Add the molasses and beat to blend. Beat in the blackberry jam until the mixture is smooth.

Add the eggs, one at a time, beating well after each addition. Scrape down the sides of the bowl with a rubber spatula when necessary.

Onto a piece of waxed paper sift together the flour, baking soda, cinnamon, nutmeg and salt. Add to the first mixture and blend well.

Fold the marinated fruit and liquid into the batter. Turn batter into the prepared pans; divide evenly. Bake for 3 hours or until a cake tester inserted into the center of the cake comes out clean.

Remove from the oven. Cool cakes in pans on wire racks.

When cool invert cakes onto another rack and remove pan and wax paper. Wrap cakes in foil and store at least 2 to 3 days before serving.

—UNUSUAL CAKES—

ANGEL CAKE

makes 1 10-inch cake

1½ cups sugar
6 eggs, separated
¾ teaspoon cream of tartar
1½ cups flour
1 teaspoon salt
¼ teaspoon almond extract
½ cup water

Preheat the oven to 350°F.

Divide the sugar into two ¾-cup portions.

In a medium-sized bowl beat the egg whites until foamy. Add the cream of tartar and beat until the egg whites hold a soft peak. Add ¾ cup of the sugar and continue beating until whites are stiff but not dry.

In a large bowl beat the egg yolks until lemon-yellow in color, approximately 3 minutes. Add the remaining sugar and continue beating until the yolks have thickened.

Add the flour, salt and almond extract to the egg yolk mixture alternately with the water, beating until smooth after each addition.

Carefully fold the egg whites into the egg yolk mixture alternately with the water, beating until smooth after each addition.

Carefully fold the egg whites into the egg yolk mixture. Gently pour batter into an unbuttered 10-inch tube pan. Bake for 1 hour or until the cake tests done.

Remove from the oven and place the pan on a wire rack. Allow the cake to cool completely in the pan. Turn cake out onto plate and serve plain or with fresh fruit, ice cream or frost with a favorite frosting.

ANGEL FOOD CAKE WITH
CHOCOLATE SAUCE

makes 1 10-inch cake

1 cup sifted cake flour
1¼ cup sugar
9 large egg whites
1 tablespoon lemon juice
½ teaspoon salt
½ teaspoon cream of tartar
1 tablespoon pure vanilla extract

CHOCOLATE SAUCE:
3 ounces bittersweet chocolate, cut into pieces
1½ ounces unsweetened chocolate, cut into pieces
2 tablespoons water
⅔ cup heavy cream

Preheat the oven to 350°F.

Into a bowl sift the flour together with ¼ cup of the sugar.

In the large bowl of an electric mixer, beat the egg whites together with the lemon juice and the salt until they are frothy. Add the cream of tartar and continue beating until the whites hold a soft peak.

Beat in the remaining 1 cup sugar, a little at a time, and the vanilla extract, beating until the egg whites are stiff but not dry.

Sift the flour mixture over the egg white mixture, one-fourth at a time, and gently fold it in.

Gently transfer the batter to an ungreased 10-inch tube pan that has a removable bottom. Bake in the oven for 40 to 45 minutes or until a cake tester inserted near the center comes out clean.

Remove from the oven and place pan on a wire rack. Cool in the pan.

While the cake cools prepare the sauce. In a saucepan, combine the bittersweet chocolate, the unsweetened chocolate and the water. Melt the mixture over low heat. Stir until smooth. Scald the cream and add it to the chocolate mixture. Heat until sauce is warm and smooth. Stir constantly.

When ready to serve invert the cake on a plate and serve each slice with sauce spooned over or serve the sauce on the side.

BLUEBERRY-NUT CRUMB CAKE

makes 1 cake

1¾ cups flour
1 teaspoon baking powder
1 teaspoon baking soda
¼ teaspoon salt
¼ cup softened sweet butter
¼ cup solid vegetable shortening
1 cup sugar
3 large eggs
1 cup sour cream
3 teaspoons grated lemon rind
3 cups blueberries, cleaned and gently tossed
with 1 tablespoon flour

TOPPING:
1 cup firmly packed light brown sugar
¼ cup flour
½ cup finely chopped pecans
¼ cup cold sweet butter, cut into pieces

Preheat the oven to 350°F. Butter and flour a 13 × 9-inch baking pan. Set aside.

Sift together the flour, baking powder, baking soda and salt. Set aside.

In a large bowl cream together the butter and vegetable shortening. Gradually beat in the sugar, beating until the mixture is light and fluffy. Beat in the eggs, one at a time, beating well after each addition. Scrape sides of bowl with a rubber spatula when necessary.

Stir in the sour cream alternately with the flour. Stir only until the mixture is just combined. Add the lemon rind and blueberries and fold gently into the batter. Turn the batter into the prepared pan and smooth the top.

In a bowl combine the brown sugar, flour and pecans. Add the butter and stir until the mixture resembles a coarse meal.

Crumble the topping evenly over the cake and bake for 50 minutes or until a cake tester inserted into the center of the cake comes out clean.

Remove from the oven and cool in pan on wire rack for 10 to 15 minutes. Cut cake into squares while still warm. Serve warm or cool completely.

SPONGE CAKE

makes 1 10-inch cake

4 large eggs, separated
½ cup boiling water
1½ cups superfine sugar
1½ cups sifted cake flour
1 teaspoon pure vanilla extract
½ teaspoon pure almond extract
⅛ teaspoon salt

Preheat the oven to 350°F.

In the large bowl of an electric mixer, beat the egg yolks for 1 minute on the highest speed. Add the boiling water and continue beating for 5 minutes longer.

Gradually add the sugar and beat until blended.

With the mixer set on the lowest speed, add the flour, vanilla extract, almond extract and salt. Blend in as quickly as possible.

In a clean bowl beat the egg whites until stiff but not dry. Using a rubber spatula, carefully fold the egg whites into the egg yolk mixture.

Pour batter into an unbuttered 10-inch tube pan and bake for 40 to 50 minutes or until cake springs back when touched lightly.

Remove from the oven. Invert the pan on a wire rack and cool cake in pan.

LEMON CHIFFON CAKE

makes 1 9-inch cake

2 cups sifted flour
1 teaspoon baking powder
¼ teaspoon salt
1 cup sweet butter, softened
1 cup sugar
5 teaspoons grated lemon rind
1 tablespoon lemon juice
1 cup sour cream
1 cup finely ground blanched almonds
8 large egg whites
cream of tartar

Preheat the oven to 350°F. Butter a 9-inch tube pan and line the bottom with waxed paper. Butter the paper and set aside.

Into a large bowl sift together the flour, baking powder and salt. Sift again.

In a large bowl cream the butter until light and fluffy. Add ¼ cup of the sugar, the lemon rind and lemon juice. Beat until well mixed.

Add the flour mixture alternately with the sour cream to the lemon mixture. Fold in each thoroughly before making the next addition. Add the almonds and fold in until well blended.

In a small bowl beat the egg whites with a pinch of cream of tartar until the whites hold soft peaks. Gradually add the remaining ¾ cup of sugar and beat until the whites hold stiff peaks.

Add 4 tablespoons of the egg whites to the batter and fold in gently. Add the remaining egg whites, mixing gently but thoroughly.

Turn the batter into the prepared pan and smooth the top. Bake for 1 hour or until the cake begins to pull away from the sides of the pan.

Remove from the oven. Let the cake cool in pan on a wire rack for 10 minutes. Turn cake out onto rack and remove the paper. Turn cake right-side up and cool completely.

Wrap cake in foil and age for 1 day before serving.

REFRIGERATOR RUM CAKE

makes 1 8-inch square cake

¾ cup raisins
¾ cup boiling water
2 tablespoons dark rum
5 ounces unsweetened chocolate
¼ cup evaporated milk
½ cup sweet butter, softened
⅔ cup superfine sugar
2 large eggs, separated
1¼ cups vanilla wafer crumbs
½ teaspoon pure vanilla extract
1 cup heavy cream
2 tablespoons sugar
2 tablespoons dark rum

Butter an 8 × 8 × 2-inch baking pan. Line the pan with aluminum foil, and butter again.

Place the raisins in a small bowl. Pour the boiling water over the raisins and let them soak for 10 minutes. Drain the raisins through a strainer set over a bowl. Measure out 3 tablespoons of the liquid and set aside. Return the raisins to the liquid. Pour the rum over the raisins and reserve.

In the top part of a double boiler, melt the chocolate together with the evaporated milk and reserved raisin liquid, over hot but not boiling water. Stir until well combined and smooth. Remove from the heat.

In a bowl beat together the butter and ⅓ cup sugar until very light and fluffy. Add the egg yolks, one at a time, beating well after each addition. Add the cooled chocolate mixture, the cookie crumbs, vanilla extract and raisins. Beat until well combined.

In a separate bowl beat the egg whites with the remaining sugar, adding a little at a time. Beat until stiff but not dry. Gently fold the whites into the chocolate mixture. Combine thoroughly.

Gently transfer the mixture to prepared pan. Cover pan and refrigerate overnight.

In a bowl beat together the cream, sugar and rum until cream is stiff. Remove the cake from the refrigerator and turn out onto a plate. Remove the pan and foil. Serve with the whipped cream on the side.

TOPPINGS

APRICOT GLAZE

makes 1¼ cups

1¼ cups apricot jam
1 tablespoon water
1 tablespoon lemon juice

In a saucepan heat the jam together with the water over low heat. Stir constantly until dissolved; approximately 5 minutes. Then bring mixture to a boil; lower the heat slightly and simmer for 2 to 3 minutes. Remove from the heat. If pulp is still visible strain jam through a sieve. Stir in the lemon juice and use at once.

CARAMEL TOPPING

1 cup sugar
½ cup buttermilk
¼ cup sweet butter
1 tablespoon light corn syrup
½ teaspoon baking soda
½ teaspoon pure vanilla extract

In a medium-sized saucepan combine the sugar, buttermilk, butter, corn syrup, baking soda and vanilla extract. Stirring constantly, bring mixture to a boil over high heat. When the sugar is totally dissolved reduce the heat to moderate. Cook, stirring constantly, until mixture registers 225 to 230°F on a thermometer (soft ball stage), approximately 6 to 8 minutes. Remove from the heat. Cool 1 minute before using.

CHOCOLATE FROSTING

6 ounces unsweetened chocolate
3 cups confectioners' sugar
6 egg yolks
½ cup sweet butter, softened
5 tablespoons hot water

In a saucepan melt the chocolate. Add 1½ cups confectioners' sugar and the hot water. Beat until well blended. Add the remaining sugar and beat well. Slowly beat in the egg yolks, one at a time. Continue beating until smooth and well blended. Beat in the softened butter. Beat only until frosting is smooth and well blended.

To frost the cake, place one layer top-side down on a serving plate. Surround the layer with strips of waxed paper to keep the plate clean. Place about one-quarter of the frosting on top of the layer and spread evenly. Place the second layer on top, top-side down. Spread about one-quarter of the icing on top. Place the last layer on top, top-side up. Frost the sides together and then frost the top. Swirl frosting with a knife or the back of a spoon. Let cake sit for a few hours before serving.

CHOCOLATE GLAZE

3 ounces semisweet chocolate, cut into pieces
¼ cup sifted confectioners' sugar
2 tablespoons sweet butter
2 tablespoons water
⅛ teaspoon salt
1 tablespoon dark rum

In the top part of a double boiler, cook the chocolate, sugar, butter, water and salt together over hot but not boiling water. Stir constantly until chocolate is melted and the mixture is smooth.

Remove from the heat. Add the rum and stir. Refrigerate, uncovered, for 20 minutes or until the glaze has thickened.

CHOCOLATE-NUT FROSTING

4 ounces unsweetened chocolate
2 tablespoons strong coffee
4 large egg yolks
¼ teaspoon salt
½ cup sugar
1 cup sweet butter, cut into pieces
1 cup coarsely chopped walnuts

Place a mixing bowl into a larger bowl of simmering water. Add the chocolate and the coffee to the mixing bowl and stir over the simmering water until the chocolate is melted and mixture is well blended.

In another bowl combine the egg yolks, salt and sugar. Place the bowl into a larger bowl of simmering water and beat with a wire whisk until it is thickened and forms a ribbon when the whisk is held up.

Add the chocolate mixture to the yolk mixture. Return the bowl into the larger bowl of simmering water and continue to beat. Beat in the butter, piece by piece.

Remove the bowl from the water and continue beating until the mixture thickens somewhat and becomes spreadable. Add the walnuts and beat. Continue beating with a wooden spoon until the chocolate becomes somewhat lighter. Let frosting cool until it is a spreadable consistency.

CONFECTIONERS' ICING

1 tablespoon boiling water
½ teaspoon lemon juice
¾ cup confectioners' sugar

Mix the boiling water and lemon juice in a bowl. Add the confectioners' sugar and mix well. Drizzle or spread on completely cooled cake.

CREAMY CHOCOLATE FROSTING

1 cup sugar
4 tablespoons cake flour
4 ounces unsweetened chocolate, cut into pieces
1½ cups milk
2 tablespoons sweet butter

In a medium-sized saucepan combine the sugar, cake flour and chocolate. Add the milk and mix well.

Cook over moderate heat, stirring constantly, until the mixture boils and is thick and smooth. Remove from the heat. Add the butter and stir to blend. Cool before using.

FRUIT FROSTING

½ cup pitted dates
1½ cups raisins
1 orange, peeled
1 lemon, peeled
⅓ cup sugar

Grind the dates and raisins together and place in a saucepan.

Peel the orange and lemon. Cut into pieces and remove all seeds. Grind the pieces together and add to the saucepan.

Add the sugar to the saucepan and cook over medium heat until mixture thickens. Stir constantly. Spread over cake while still warm.

To frost the jam cake, place one cake layer top-side down on a serving plate. Brush off any crumbs. Spread with about one-third the frosting mixture. Place the second layer, top-side up, on top. Frost the sides of both layers and then frost the top. Smooth the frosting. Allow the frosting to set for a few hours before cutting the cake.

FUDGE FROSTING

4 ounces unsweetened chocolate
1½ cups milk
4 cups sugar
⅛ teaspoon salt
4 teaspoons light corn syrup
¼ cup sweet butter
2 teaspoons pure vanilla extract

Place the chocolate and milk in a heavy saucepan. Cook over low heat, stirring constantly, until well blended.

Add the sugar, salt, and corn syrup. Stir until the sugar is dissolved. Boil the mixture over very low heat, stirring occasionally, until small amounts dropped into cold water form

soft balls. This will be when the mixture is approximately 234°F to 240°F on a candy thermometer.

Remove the saucepan from heat. Add the butter and vanilla and mix well. Cool to lukewarm and then beat until creamy.

To frost the Wellesley Fudge Cake, place one layer top-side down on a cake plate. Spread with approximately one-third of the frosting. Place the second layer on top, right-side up, and frost the sides with approximately one-third the frosting. Then frost the top of the cake with the remaining frosting. Smooth frosting and swirl with a knife. Let frosting set before cutting cake.

MAPLE ICING

2 cups pure maple syrup
2 egg whites
⅛ teaspoon salt

In a bowl beat the egg whites and salt until stiff but not dry.

Boil the syrup in a saucepan until it registers

232°F on a candy thermometer or spins a soft thread.

Pour the syrup slowly over the egg whites and beat with a whisk or electric mixer until the mixture forms soft peaks.

Spread the sides and top of the cooled cake with icing.

MAPLE NUT FROSTING

1 cup sugar
1 cup pure maple syrup
⅓ cup water
¼ teaspoon cream of tartar
1 egg white
½ cup chopped nuts

Place the sugar, maple syrup, water and cream of tartar in a saucepan. Cook, stirring

constantly, until mixture spins a thread when dropped from spoon.

Beat the egg white in a mixing bowl until it is stiff but not dry. Pour the sugar mixture slowly over the egg white, beating constantly. Continue to beat mixture until it is of spreading consistency.

Fold in nuts and spread frosting on cake.

COOKIES

— DROP COOKIES —

ALMOND CHIP COOKIES

makes approximately 50 cookies

¾ cup sweet butter, softened
1 cup sugar
1 large egg
1 teaspoon pure almond extract
½ teaspoon pure vanilla extract
2 cups sifted flour
1 cup coarsely chopped almonds
1 cup semisweet chocolate pieces
27 whole almonds, cut in half lengthwise

Preheat the oven to 375°F.

In a large bowl combine the butter and sugar. Beat together until light and fluffy. Add the egg and beat to mix well. Add the almond extract and vanilla extract. Mix to blend.

Add the flour and stir until well blended. Fold in the chopped almonds and chocolate pieces and mix until evenly distributed.

Drop the batter by teaspoonfuls onto ungreased baking sheets. Press an almond half into each cookie.

Bake for 12 to 14 minutes or until golden. Remove from the oven and transfer cookies to wire racks. Cool on racks.

ANISEED DROPS

makes approximately 30 cookies

½ cup flour
½ cup sugar
⅛ teaspoon salt
1 teaspoon aniseed
¾ teaspoon grated lemon rind
1 large egg, beaten
½ teaspoon anise extract or 2 drops oil of anise

Into a large mixing bowl, sift the flour, sugar and salt together. Add the aniseed and lemon rind and stir. Add the egg and anise extract and stir until well blended.

Drop the dough by half-teaspoonfuls onto well-buttered baking sheets, allowing 1 inch between cookies. Allow the cookies to stand, uncovered, at room temperature for at least 12 hours. The dough will have appeared to form a top layer; this is correct.

Preheat the oven to 300°F.

Bake the cookies for 20 to 25 minutes or until the entire cookie begins to 'tan'. Remove from the oven. Transfer cookies to wire racks and cool.

BROWN SUGAR OATMEAL COOKIES

makes approximately 30 cookies

1 cup flour
1 cup sweet butter, softened
¾ cup firmly packed light brown sugar
½ cup sugar
1 large egg
3 tablespoons water
¾ teaspoon salt
½ teaspoon baking soda
¾ teaspoon pure vanilla extract
3½ cups quick-cooking rolled oats
(not instant)

Preheat the oven to 375°F.

In a large bowl combine the flour, butter, brown sugar, sugar, egg, water, salt, baking soda and vanilla extract. Beat the mixture with an electric mixer at a low speed until well blended. Scrape the bowl with a rubber spatula when necessary. Add the oats to the mixture and, using a spoon, stir until thoroughly combined.

Drop the dough by heaping tablespoons onto a well-buttered baking sheet. Space cookies about 2 inches apart.

Bake for 10 to 12 minutes or until golden. Remove from the oven and carefully transfer cookies to wire racks. Cool on wire racks. Store cookies in tightly covered containers.

CARROT LEMON-NUT COOKIES

makes 40 cookies

1½ cups sifted flour
½ cup whole wheat flour
2 teaspoons baking powder
¼ teaspoon baking soda
½ teaspoon ground cinnamon
¼ teaspoon ground nutmeg
¼ teaspoon salt
½ cup sweet butter, softened
½ cup firmly packed dark brown sugar
½ cup sugar
1 large egg
½ teaspoon pure lemon extract
½ teaspoon pure vanilla extract
2 teaspoons grated lemon rind
1 cup coarsely grated carrot
1 cup coarsely chopped pecans

Preheat the oven to 375°F.

Into a large bowl sift the flour, whole wheat flour, baking powder, baking soda, cinnamon, nutmeg and salt together. Stir with a spoon to mix well.

In a large bowl combine the butter, brown sugar, sugar, egg, lemon extract, vanilla extract and lemon rind. Beat the mixture together until well blended and fluffy.

Add the sifted flour mixture and stir until well blended. Add the grated carrots and chopped nuts. Stir until distributed evenly.

Drop the batter by heaping teaspoonfuls approximately 2 inches apart onto lightly buttered baking sheets. Bake for 12 to 15 minutes or until the tops of the cookies are golden and spring back when touched lightly. Remove from oven and transfer to wire racks. Cool on racks.

CHOCOLATE-WALNUT-RAISIN DROPS

makes 48 cookies

1¾ cups flour
½ teaspoon baking soda
½ teaspoon baking powder
¼ teaspoon salt
½ cup sweet butter, softened
1 cup sugar
1 egg
1 egg yolk
3 ounces unsweetened chocolate, melted
1 teaspoon pure vanilla extract
½ cup milk
1 cup raisins
1 cup coarsely chopped walnuts

Preheat the oven to 350°F.

Combine the flour with the baking soda, baking powder and salt in a bowl.

In a mixing bowl cream the butter until light and fluffy. Beat in the sugar gradually. Add the egg and egg yolk. Beat well. Add the melted chocolate and vanilla. Stir until well blended. Add the flour alternately with the milk. Stir in the raisins and nuts.

Drop the batter by teaspoons onto a buttered baking sheet. Bake for 12 to 14 minutes.

Remove from oven and transfer to cooling racks. Store in an airtight container.

COCONUT JUMBLES

makes approximately 36 cookies

⅔ cup sweet butter, softened
1 cup sugar
1 egg, beaten
1 cup flour
1 cup grated coconut

Preheat the oven to 375°F.

Heavily grease two baking sheets and set aside.

Cream the butter in a large mixing bowl. Add the sugar and continue creaming until mixture is light and fluffy. Add the egg and mix well. Stir in the flour and mix well. Gradually add the coconut and mix until the batter is stiff.

Drop batter by well-rounded teaspoons onto the baking sheets. Bake 5 to 7 minutes or until lightly browned.

Cool for 30 seconds on the cookie sheets and then remove to cooling racks. Continue cooling.

CURRANT COOKIES

makes approximately 30 cookies

1 cup flour
1 teaspoon baking powder
6 tablespoons sweet butter, softened
½ cup firmly packed brown sugar
1 large egg
½ teaspoon grated lemon rind
¼ cup currants

Preheat the oven to 350°F.

Into a large bowl sift together the flour and baking powder. Set aside.

In the medium-sized bowl of an electric mixer, beat the butter until it is light and fluffy. This will take approximately 2 minutes. Add the brown sugar, a little at a time, and beat thoroughly after each addition. Scrape the sides of the bowl with a rubber spatula when necessary.

Add the egg and beat well. Add the lemon rind and the currants. Stir until well mixed.

Gradually add the sifted flour mixture to the butter-sugar mixture. Stir until well blended.

Drop the dough by teaspoonfuls onto a lightly oiled baking sheet. Space cookies approximately 1½ inches apart. Bake for 10 minutes or until lightly browned.

Remove from the oven. Transfer cookies to wire racks and cool thoroughly.

DROP BUTTER COOKIES

makes 24 cookies

½ cup sweet butter, softened
⅓ cup sugar
½ teaspoon pure vanilla extract
1 large egg
¾ cup sifted flour
⅛ teaspoon salt

Preheat the oven to 350°F.

In a medium-sized bowl, cream the butter, sugar, vanilla and egg together until the mixture is fluffy and light in color.

Add the flour and salt and beat until well blended.

Drop the dough by well-rounded half teaspoons onto ungreased baking sheets. Bake 10 minutes or until the edges of the cookies turn golden brown. Remove from the oven and transfer cookies to wire racks using a wide spatula. Cool on wire racks.

FRUIT AND WALNUT COOKIES

makes approximately 50 cookies

½ cup finely chopped dried apricots
1 cup boiling water
2 cups sifted flour
1 teaspoon baking powder
½ teaspoon baking soda
⅔ cup sweet butter, softened
1 cup sugar
1 teaspoon grated orange rind
1 teaspoon grated lemon rind
2 large eggs
1 tablespoon lemon juice
½ cup sour cream
¼ cup finely chopped candied orange peel
¾ cup finely chopped candied pineapple
⅔ cup coarsely chopped walnuts

Place the chopped apricots in a small bowl. Cover with the 1 cup boiling water and allow apricots to soak for 10 minutes. Drain apricots. Discard liquid and set fruit aside.

Preheat the oven to 350°F.

Into a large bowl sift the flour, baking powder and baking soda together. Set aside.

In a large bowl combine the butter, sugar, orange rind, lemon rind, eggs and lemon juice. Beat the mixture at high speed until it is light and fluffy.

Add the sifted flour mixture and the sour cream. Stir until well blended. Add the apricots, orange peel, pineapple and walnuts. Fold in the batter until thoroughly incorporated.

Drop the mixture by tablespoons onto well-buttered baking sheets. Space the cookies 1½ inches apart. Bake for 15 minutes or until the edges of the cookies are golden.

Remove from the oven. Transfer cookies to wire racks and cool.

HERMITS

makes 72 cookies

½ cup sugar
⅓ cup sweet butter, softened
1 egg
3 cups flour
½ teaspoon salt
1 teaspoon cinnamon
½ teaspoon grated nutmeg
½ cup molasses
½ cup buttermilk
1 cup raisins

Preheat the oven to 350°F.

In a mixing bowl cream together the sugar and butter until light and fluffy. Beat in the egg.

Combine the flour, salt, cinnamon and nutmeg. Mix the molasses with the buttermilk. Add the molasses mixture alternately with the flour to the creamed sugar and butter. Stir in the raisins.

Drop by teaspoons approximately 1 inch apart onto a greased baking sheet. Bake for 8 to 10 minutes, or until lightly browned. Cool on a rack.

JUMBO CHOCOLATE CHIP COOKIES

makes 24 cookies

2 cups flour
1 teaspoon baking soda
½ teaspoon salt
1 cup sweet butter, softened
1 cup dark brown sugar
½ cup sugar
1 teaspoon pure vanilla extract
2 large eggs, lightly beaten
1½ cups semisweet chocolate pieces or 1
8-ounce chocolate bar cut into small bits
1 cup coarsely chopped pecans

Preheat the oven to 375°F.

Into a large bowl sift the flour, baking soda and salt together. Set aside.

In the large bowl of an electric mixer, combine the butter, brown sugar, sugar and vanilla. Cream the mixture together until well blended.

Add the eggs and beat until well mixed.

Gradually add the flour mixture to the creamed mixture, beating well after each addition. Scrape the sides of the bowl with a rubber spatula when necessary.

Add the chocolate pieces and chopped nuts and stir to distribute evenly.

For each cookie drop 2 tablespoons of the dough onto a lightly buttered baking sheet. Space cookies 2 inches apart. Flatten the top of the dough slightly.

Bake for 12 minutes or until lightly golden. Remove from the oven and transfer cookies to wire racks. Cool on racks.

JUMBO PEANUT DROPS

makes 24 cookies

2 cups sifted flour
½ teaspoon salt
1½ teaspoons baking powder
¾ cup sweet butter, softened
1 cup light brown sugar
½ cup peanut butter
2 tablespoons milk
2 large eggs, lightly beaten
1 cup slightly toasted unsalted peanuts

Preheat the oven to 350°F.

In a large bowl sift the flour, salt and baking powder together. Set aside.

In the large bowl of an electric mixer, combine the butter and sugar. Beat together until light and fluffy. Add the peanut butter and beat until well blended.

Add the milk, eggs and flour mixture. Beat until well combined. Fold in the nuts until evenly distributed.

Drop 2 tablespoons of the dough onto a buttered baking sheet for each cookie. Space cookies 2 inches apart.

Bake for 15 to 20 minutes or until lightly browned. Remove from the oven and transfer cookies to wire racks. Cool completely.

LACE COOKIES

makes 72 cookies

¼ cup solid vegetable shortening
¼ cup sweet butter
½ cup light corn syrup
⅔ cup firmly packed light brown sugar
1 cup sifted flour
1 cup finely chopped walnuts
6 ounces semisweet chocolate, broken into pieces

Preheat the oven to 325°F. Prepare baking sheets by buttering them lightly and then covering them with foil. Set aside.

In the top of a double boiler, combine the shortening, butter, corn syrup and brown sugar. Bring the mixture to a boil over direct heat. Remove from the heat as soon as the mixture begins to boil.

Add the flour and the nuts and mix well.

Drop the mixture by well-rounded teaspoonfuls, 3 inches apart onto the prepared sheets. Keep the remaining batter warm by placing the top of the double boiler over boiling water between batches.

Bake for 8 to 10 minutes. Remove from the oven and cool cookies on sheets before transferring to wire racks. Cool on racks.

Place the chocolate in the top of a double boiler. Soften over hot but not boiling water. Remove when the chocolate is only partially melted. Stir until melted completely.

Brush the melted chocolate on the cooled cookies. Allow chocolate to set before serving.

MELT-AWAYS

makes approximately 76 cookies

½ cup sweet butter, softened
1 cup firmly packed light brown sugar
1 teaspoon pure vanilla extract
1 large egg
¾ cup sifted flour
1 teaspoon baking powder
½ teaspoon salt
½ cup finely chopped walnuts

Preheat the oven to 400°F.

In a medium-sized bowl combine the butter, brown sugar, vanilla and egg. Beat the mixture until well blended and light and fluffy.

Add the flour, baking powder and salt and beat until a smooth dough forms. Add the nuts and stir to blend well.

Drop the dough by well-rounded teaspoons onto ungreased baking sheets. Bake for 5 minutes or until cookies are evenly browned. Remove from the oven and cool on the sheets for 1 minute before transferring to wire racks. Cool on racks.

MOCHA CHIP COOKIES

makes approximately 80 cookies

1½ cups semisweet chocolate pieces
½ cup sweet butter
4 ounces unsweetened chocolate
½ cup flour
½ teaspoon baking powder
½ teaspoon salt
4 large eggs
1½ cups sugar
1½ tablespoons instant espresso powder
2 teaspoons pure vanilla extract
1½ cups semisweet chocolate pieces

In the top of a double boiler combine the chocolate pieces, butter and unsweetened chocolate. Set the top over hot but not boiling water and allow the mixture to melt. Stir mixture until smooth. Remove and set aside.

Preheat the oven to 350°F. Prepare baking sheets by buttering them lightly and then lining them with waxed paper or parchment. Set aside.

In a small bowl combine the flour, baking powder and salt. Set aside.

In the large bowl of an electric mixer, combine the eggs, sugar, espresso powder and vanilla. Beat at high speed for 2 minutes. Add the chocolate mixture and stir until well blended.

Stir in the flour mixture. Mix well. Add the chocolate pieces and stir to distribute evenly.

Drop the batter by teaspoonfuls onto the prepared sheets. Space 1 inch apart. Bake for 8 minutes or until the cookies are shiny and cracked outside but soft inside.

Remove from the oven. Allow cookies to cool completely on sheets. Store in airtight containers.

OATMEAL-CRANBERRY COOKIES

makes approximately 60 cookies

1½ cups flour
1 teaspoon baking soda
1 teaspoon baking powder
1 teaspoon salt
1½ teaspoons cinnamon
¼ teaspoon grated nutmeg
1 cup solid vegetable shortening
1½ cups firmly packed dark brown sugar
2 large eggs
½ cup buttermilk
3 cups quick-cooking rolled oats (not instant)
1½ cups coarsely chopped cranberries

Preheat the oven to 400°F.

In a large bowl sift together the flour, baking soda, baking powder, salt, cinnamon and nutmeg. Set aside.

In a large bowl combine the shortening and brown sugar. Cream together until light and fluffy. Add the eggs, one at a time, beating well after each addition. Add the buttermilk and stir to blend.

Add the sifted flour mixture to the butter-sugar mixture. Stir until well blended. Add the oats and cranberries (currants). Mix well.

Drop the mixture by heaping tablespoons onto well-buttered baking sheets. Space cookies 2 inches apart.

Bake for 10 minutes or until the cookies begin to brown on the edges.

Remove from the oven and transfer cookies to wire racks to cool. Cool completely.

OATMEAL LACE COOKIES

makes approximately 84 cookies

1 cup sweet butter, melted
1½ cups firmly packed dark brown sugar
2¼ cups quick-cooking rolled oats
(not instant)
3 tablespoons flour
1 tablespoon molasses
1 teaspoon pure vanilla extract
1 large egg, slightly beaten
½ teaspoon salt

In a large bowl combine the butter, sugar and oats. Stir until well blended. Allow the mixture to stand overnight or long enough for the oats to absorb all the butter.

Preheat the oven to 375°F.

Add the flour, molasses, vanilla extract, egg and salt to the bowl with the oats. Stir until well mixed.

Drop the batter by half-teaspoons, 2 inches apart onto well buttered baking sheets.

Bake one sheet at a time in the center of the oven for 6 to 8 minutes or until the cookies are golden brown. Remove from the oven and allow the cookies to cool for 30 seconds before removing. Then, working quickly, either remove the cookies to wire racks to cool or roll the cookies around the handle of a wooden spoon and then cool on racks.

OATMEAL RAISIN-NUT COOKIES

makes 36 cookies

1 egg, beaten
½ cup sugar
¼ cup melted sweet butter
¼ cup melted lard
2 teaspoons molasses
2 teaspoons milk
1 cup quick-cooking rolled oats
(not instant)
¼ cup raisins
¼ cup coarsely chopped walnuts
¾ cup flour
½ teaspoon cinnamon
¼ teaspoon baking soda
¼ teaspoon salt

Preheat the oven to 325°F.

In a large mixing bowl combine the egg, sugar, melted butter, melted lard, molasses and milk. Mix well.

In another bowl combine the oats, flour, cinnamon, baking soda and salt. Stir in the raisins and the nuts. Add to first mixture and combine until well blended.

Drop by heaping teaspoons about 2 inches apart onto greased baking sheets. Bake for 10 to 12 minutes or until browned. Cool cookies on racks.

SNICKERDOODLES

makes 36 cookies

2 eggs
2 cups sugar
½ cup sweet butter, softened
1 teaspoon pure vanilla extract
4 cups flour
4 teaspoons baking powder
1 teaspoon salt
1 cup milk
1 cup chopped raisins
1 tablespoon sugar
1 teaspoon cinnamon

Preheat the oven to 350°F.

Beat the eggs in a mixing bowl, gradually adding the sugar. Stir in the butter and add the vanilla extract.

Combine the flour, baking powder and salt. Add the flour mixture to the egg mixture alternately with the milk. Beat well after each addition. Stir in the raisins.

Drop by teaspoons about 1 inch apart onto greased baking sheets. Combine 1 tablespoon sugar and the cinnamon. Sprinkle generously over the cookies. Bake for 20 minutes or until cookies are golden. Cool on racks.

TOASTED HAZELNUT DROPS

makes approximately 72 cookies

1½ cups hazelnuts
1 teaspoon sweet butter, melted
3 egg whites, at room temperature
⅛ teaspoon salt
1 cup sugar
1 teaspoon grated lemon rind
½ teaspoon ground cinnamon

Preheat the oven to 400°F. Place the hazelnuts in a shallow pan with the 1 teaspoon of melted butter. Toast in the oven for 10 to 15 minutes or until brown. Stir nuts every 3 to 5 minutes. Remove from the oven and turn nuts out onto a piece of brown paper to cool. When nuts are cool, grind them and measure out 1 cup. If there are extra ground nuts, reserve them for another use. Set the ground nuts aside.

Reduce the oven temperature to 275°F.

In a medium-sized bowl beat the egg whites until foamy. Add the salt and continue beating until the egg whites begin to hold their shape.

Add the sugar, a little at a time, beating constantly until the whites are stiff but not dry.

Add the lemon rind, cinnamon and ground nuts. Fold gently until well blended. Drop the meringue by teaspoonfuls onto well-buttered baking sheets. Space cookies 1 inch apart. Bake for 20 to 25 minutes or until cookies are firm and dry to the touch.

Remove from the oven and cool on sheets for 1 minute before transferring to wire racks. Cool completely on racks before storing in airtight containers.

TOLL HOUSE COOKIES

makes 48 cookies

½ cup sweet butter, softened
½ cup sugar
¼ cup firmly packed light brown sugar
1 egg, beaten
1 teaspoon pure vanilla extract
1 cup flour
½ teaspoon baking soda
½ cup chopped walnuts or pecans
6 ounces semisweet chocolate pieces

Preheat the oven to 375°F.

In a large mixing bowl cream the butter until soft. Gradually beat in the sugar and brown sugar, beating well after each addition. Beat in the egg and vanilla extract.

Add the flour and baking soda to the mixture. Stir until smooth. Stir in the nuts and chocolate bits, making sure they are evenly distributed throughout the batter.

Drop by scant teaspoons 2 inches apart onto lightly greased baking sheets. Bake for 8 to 10 minutes or until edges are beginning to brown. Transfer to racks and cool.

WASPS' NESTS

makes approximately 120 cookies

1 cup sugar
½ cup water
5 cups slivered almonds
5 egg whites
⅛ teaspoon salt
1 teaspoon pure vanilla extract
3½ ounces confectioners' sugar
4 ounces unsweetened chocolate, melted

Preheat the oven to 300°F.

Combine the sugar and water in a saucepan. Cook over medium-low heat until the mixture registers 234°F on a candy thermometer or spins a thread. Remove from heat. Gradually add the nuts to the syrup. Stir constantly until all the syrup is absorbed.

In a mixing bowl beat the egg whites until foamy. Add the salt and vanilla. Continue beating until egg whites are very stiff but not dry. Slowly beat in the confectioners' sugar. Fold in the nut mixture and the chocolate.

Drop the batter by rounded teaspoons onto heavily buttered baking sheets. Bake for 20 to 25 minutes.

Remove from oven and transfer to cooling racks with a wide spatula.

BALL COOKIES

COUNTRY-STYLE GINGER MOLASSES COOKIES

makes 30 cookies

6½ cups flour
1 tablespoon baking soda
1 tablespoon ground cinnamon
2¼ teaspoons ground ginger
1 teaspoon grated nutmeg
2 cups sweet butter, softened
¾ cup packed light brown sugar
¾ cup molasses
¼ cup water
1½ teaspoons salt
3 large eggs, at room temperature
sugar

Into a large bowl sift together the flour, baking soda, cinnamon, ginger and nutmeg. Set aside.

In another large bowl, beat the butter until soft and smooth. Add the brown sugar, molasses, water and salt. Beat together until the mixture is light and fluffy. Add the eggs, one at a time, beating well after each addition. Scrape sides of bowl with a rubber spatula as needed. Gradually add the flour mixture and beat until well mixed. Cover bowl and refrigerate dough for at least 20 hours.

Preheat the oven to 350°F.

Remove the dough from the refrigerator. Shape dough into 2-inch balls and roll each ball in the sugar. Space the cookies 3 inches apart on an ungreased baking sheet. Bake for 15 to 18 minutes or until cookies are lightly browned and set.

Remove cookies from the oven and transfer to wire racks to cool.

FROSTED LEMON BUTTER BALLS

makes approximately 40 cookies

1 cup sweet butter, softened
½ cup confectioners' sugar
1½ cups flour
¾ cup cornstarch
¼ teaspoon salt
2 teaspoons grated lemon rind
1 cup finely chopped blanched almonds

FROSTING:
1 cup confectioners' sugar
2 tablespoons sweet butter, melted
1 tablespoon lemon juice

Preheat the oven to 350°F.

In a large bowl cream together the butter and sugar until light and fluffy.

Sift in the flour, cornstarch and salt together. Mix well. Add the lemon rind and mix well.

Shape the dough into 1-inch balls and roll in the chopped almonds. Press nuts in gently. Place cookies 1 inch apart on buttered baking sheets. Bake for 15 minutes. Remove from the oven and transfer to wire racks to cool.

To make the frosting, in a small bowl combine the confectioners' sugar, melted butter and lemon juice. Stir until smooth. Drizzle frosting over cooled cookies. Allow frosting to harden before storing cookies in an air-tight container.

HAZELNUT BUTTER BALLS

makes 42 cookies

½ cup sweet butter, softened
¼ cup sugar
1 medium-sized egg, separated
1 tablespoon white rum
½ teaspoon pure vanilla extract
1 cup flour
½ cup finely chopped hazelnuts

In a medium-sized bowl cream together the butter and sugar until light and fluffy. Add the egg yolk, white rum and vanilla extract. Beat until well blended. Add the flour and mix well. Cover the bowl and refrigerate 4 hours or overnight.

Preheat the oven to 325°F.

Remove the dough from the refrigerator. Form the dough into ¾-inch balls. Arrange the chopped hazelnuts in one bowl and the egg white in another bowl. Slightly beat the egg white.

Dip the top of each ball into the egg white and then into the hazelnuts. Place cookies, nut-side up, 1 inch apart on a lightly buttered baking sheet. Bake for 12 to 14 minutes or until golden brown.

Remove from the oven and transfer to wire racks to cool. Cool completely and store in airtight containers.

HAZELNUT COOKIES

makes 30 cookies

¾ cup hazelnuts
⅔ cup sugar
2 large egg yolks
1 teaspoon pure vanilla extract
½ teaspoon grated lemon peel
⅛ teaspoon salt
sugar

Remove 15 whole hazelnuts and carefully cut them in half. Set aside.

Finely grind the remaining nuts in a blender or food processor. Empty ground nuts into a large bowl. Add the sugar and mix well. Then add the egg yolks, vanilla, lemon peel and salt. Beat until well blended and mixture begins to form a ball. Add ice water if necessary to help dough adhere. Wrap dough in plastic wrap and refrigerate for 2 hours.

Preheat the oven to 350°F.

Remove dough from refrigerator. Shape dough into ¾-inch balls. Arrange the balls 3 inches apart on well-buttered cookie sheets. Flatten the cookies by using the bottom of a glass that has been dipped in sugar. Be sure to twist the glass when removing it to prevent it from sticking to the dough. Press a hazelnut half firmly in the center of each cookie.

Bake for 10 minutes or until cookies are slightly golden and dry.

Remove from the oven. Immediately transfer cookies to wire racks. Cool completely and store in airtight containers.

LEMONY GINGER COOKIES

makes 48 cookies

**2½ cups sifted flour
3 teaspoons ground ginger
2 teaspoons baking soda
1 teaspoon ground cinnamon
½ teaspoon salt
¾ cup sweet butter, softened
1 cup firmly packed dark brown sugar
1 large egg
¼ cup molasses
1 tablespoon grated lemon rind
¼ cup sugar**

Preheat the oven to 350°F.

Into a large bowl sift together the flour, ginger, baking soda, cinnamon and salt. Set aside.

In a large bowl beat the butter together with the brown sugar and egg until mixture is light and fluffy.

Add the molasses and lemon rind and beat until smooth and well mixed. Add the flour mixture in two additions. Stir well after each addition and continue mixing until flour is thoroughly mixed.

Shape the dough into balls using level tablespoons. Roll balls in sugar and space 2 inches apart on ungreased cookie sheets. Bake for 10 minutes. Centers will be soft.

Remove from the oven and cool on sheets for 1 minute. Transfer cookies to wire racks and cool completely. Store cookies in tins.

MEXICAN WEDDING COOKIES

makes 48 cookies

**1 cup sweet butter, softened
½ cup confectioners' sugar
1 teaspoon pure vanilla extract
¼ teaspoon salt
2 cups flour
confectioners' sugar**

In a large bowl cream the butter until light and fluffy. Add the sugar, vanilla extract and salt. Beat until well blended. Add the flour and stir until thoroughly mixed. Cover bowl and refrigerate for 30 minutes or until dough is firm enough to be handled.

Preheat the oven to 375°F.

Remove dough from the refrigerator and shape into 1-inch balls. Space 1 inch apart on unbuttered baking sheets. Bake for 12 to 15 minutes or until light golden in color.

Remove from the oven and transfer cookies to a wire rack. Place cookies close together. While cookies are still warm dust heavily with confectioners' sugar. Cool completely and store in airtight containers.

MOCHA BUTTER BALLS

makes 72 cookies

1¾ cups sifted flour
¼ cup Dutch-process cocoa
2 teaspoons instant espresso powder
½ teaspoon salt
1 cup sweet butter, softened
½ cup sugar
2 teaspoons pure vanilla extract
2 cups finely chopped walnuts
confectioners' sugar

Preheat the oven to 325°F.
Into a large bowl sift the flour, cocoa, instant espresso and salt together. Set aside.

In a medium-sized bowl cream together the butter, sugar and vanilla until fluffy and light in color.

Add the sifted dry ingredients and mix well. Stir in the nuts.

Shape the dough into 1-inch balls and space 1-inch apart on unbuttered baking sheets. Bake for 15 minutes.

Remove from the oven and transfer cookies to wire racks to cool. When cookies are cool, roll them in the confectioners' sugar. Store in airtight containers.

NO-BAKE WHISKEY BALLS

makes 48 balls

1 cup semisweet chocolate pieces or 6 ounces semisweet chocolate broken into pieces
½ cup sugar
3 tablespoons light corn syrup
⅓ cup whiskey
2½ cups vanilla wafer crumbs
(approximately 60 wafers)
1 cup pecans, finely chopped
confectioners' sugar

In the top part of a double boiler, melt the chocolate over hot but not boiling water. Remove from the heat.

Add the sugar and corn syrup to the chocolate and stir until smooth. Add the whiskey and mix until well blended. Stir in the wafer crumbs and the chopped pecans and mix well.

Shape the dough into 1-inch balls. Roll each ball in confectioners' sugar and store in airtight containers. Allow ball to age for 1 to 2 days before serving.

PECAN BUTTER BALLS

makes approximately 36 cookies

½ cup sweet butter, softened
2 tablespoons sugar
1 teaspoon vanilla extract
1 cup flour
⅛ teaspoon salt
1 cup finely chopped pecans
confectioners' sugar

Preheat the oven to 375°F.

In a large bowl cream the butter and sugar together until light and fluffy. Add the vanilla and mix well.

Combine the flour and salt. Add to the creamed mixture and mix well. Add the nuts and stir until thoroughly combined.

Place batter by well-rounded teaspoons on ungreased baking sheets. Bake for 20 minutes.

Remove from oven and cool for 1 minute on the sheets. Roll each ball in confectioners' sugar and continue cooling.

PIGNOLI ROUNDS

makes 48 cookies

4 cups flour
1 cup sugar
1 tablespoon baking powder
¼ teaspoon salt
1 cup sweet butter, softened
2 large eggs
½ cup cold strong coffee
1 teaspoon pure vanilla extract
1 teaspoon pure almond extract
warm honey
2 cups pignoli nuts (pine nuts)

Preheat the oven to 375°F.

In a large bowl combine the flour, sugar, baking powder and salt. Cut the butter into the flour mixture using a pastry blender or two knives. Mixture will resemble a coarse meal when it is sufficiently blended.

Add the eggs, coffee, vanilla extract and almond extract to the flour and butter mixture. Stir until well mixed.

Shape the dough into 1-inch balls and place on ungreased baking sheets approximately 1 inch apart. Bake for 12 to 15 minutes or until cookies are lightly browned.

Remove from the oven and transfer cookies to wire racks to cool. When cookies are completely cool brush the tops with the warm honey and then dip them into the pignoli. Allow cookies to dry.

TRIPLE CHOCOLATE COOKIES

makes 20 to 30 cookies

3 ounces semisweet chocolate
1 ounce unsweetened chocolate
1 tablespoon sweet butter
1 egg
⅓ cup packed dark brown sugar
1 tablespoon water
1 teaspoon pure vanilla extract
2 tablespoons sifted flour
⅛ teaspoon baking powder
6 ounces semisweet chocolate bits
1 cup coarsely chopped walnuts

Melt the semisweet chocolate, unsweetened chocolate and butter together in the top of double boiler over hot but not boiling water. Pour the melted chocolate into a mixing bowl and let cool slightly.

Add the egg, brown sugar, water and vanilla extract to the chocolate mixture. Mix until well blended. Add the flour and baking powder. Stir well. Add the chocolate bits and walnuts and stir until evenly distributed. Cover the bowl with plastic wrap and refrigerate until the dough is firm and easy to handle, about 1 hour.

Preheat the oven to 350°F. Line two baking sheets with aluminum foil.

Shape the dough into 1-inch balls and put them 1 inch apart on the cookie sheets. Bake the cookies until they are slightly firm to the touch, about 13 to 15 minutes.

Remove the cookies from the oven. Slide the foil from the baking sheets and let the cookies cool completely on the sheets before removing. Store in an airtight container.

RUM BALLS

makes 72 balls

1 pound vanilla wafers
1 tablespoon Dutch-process unsweetened
cocoa
½ cup light corn syrup
½ cup dark rum
½ cup finely chopped hazelnuts
confectioners' sugar

Crush the wafers and place the crumbs in a large bowl. Add the cocoa, corn syrup, rum and chopped hazelnuts. Mix until well blended.

Shape the dough into a large ball and divide it into four equal parts. Shape each part into a roll, 1 inch in diameter. Place rolls parallel to each other on a board. Cut crosswise through all four rolls, forming ¾-inch slices. Shape the slices into 1-inch balls. Place balls in an airtight container and store for 1½ days.

Preheat the oven to 325°F.

Place the rum balls on lightly buttered baking sheets and let stand for 30 minutes. Bake for 10 minutes or until lightly browned.

Remove from the oven and transfer rum balls to wire racks. While cookies are still warm, sift confectioners' sugar over them. Cool completely and store.

SHORTBREAD-CHIP COOKIES

makes approximately 90 cookies

2 cups sweet butter, softened
2 cups plus 3 tablespoons confectioners'
sugar
2 teaspoons pure vanilla extract
½ teaspoon salt
4½ cups flour
2 cups semisweet chocolate pieces

Preheat the oven to 350°F.

In a large bowl, cream the butter and 2 cups of the confectioners' sugar together until light and fluffy. Add the vanilla and salt and beat until blended.

Add the flour, a little at a time, and stir until well blended. Add the chocolate pieces and stir until evenly distributed. The dough will be stiff, so use your hands if necessary.

Shape the dough into 1-inch balls and place them 2 inches apart on ungreased baking sheets. Flatten dough with a fork to form 1½-inch rounds.

Bake for 15 minutes or until lightly golden. Remove from oven and transfer to wire racks. While the cookies are still warm, dust them with the remaining 3 tablespoons confectioners' sugar. Cool cookies completely.

SUGARY BUTTER COOKIES

makes 48 cookies

1 cup butter, softened
½ cup sifted confectioners' sugar
2¼ cups sifted flour
1 teaspoon pure vanilla extract
¼ teaspoon salt
¾ cup finely chopped walnuts
confectioners' sugar

In a medium-sized bowl, cream together the butter and confectioners' sugar until light in color. Add the flour, vanilla extract, salt and chopped walnuts. Stir until well mixed. Cover the bowl and refrigerate for 2 to 3 hours.

Preheat the oven to 400°F.

Remove dough from the refrigerator and shape into 1-inch balls. Space 1 inch apart on unbuttered baking sheets. Bake for 10 to 12 minutes.

Remove from the oven and immediately roll cookies in confectioners' sugar. Cool completely on wire racks. If desired roll again in sugar once cookies have cooled. Store in airtight containers.

BAR COOKIES

APRICOT WALNUT BARS

makes 24 bars

½ cup sweet butter, softened
¼ cup sugar
1 cup flour

FILLING:
⅓ cup flour
½ teaspoon baking powder
¼ teaspoon salt
1 cup firmly packed light brown sugar
2 eggs, beaten
1 cup chopped dried apricots
1½ cups chopped walnuts
1 teaspoon pure vanilla extract

Preheat the oven to 350°F.

Make the crust for the bars by combining the butter and sugar in a small bowl. Cream together until well blended. Add 1 cup flour and mix well. Spread the mixture over the bottom and partway up the sides of an ungreased 8-inch square baking pan. Bake for 15 to 20 minutes or until crust is lightly browned.

To make the filling, in a bowl mix together ⅓ cup flour, the baking powder, salt and brown sugar. Beat in the eggs. Add the apricots and walnuts; mix well. Stir in the vanilla.

Spread the walnut and apricot mixture in the crust. Return the pan to the oven and bake for 30 minutes or until set.

Remove from oven to a cooling rack. Cool in the pan. When completely cooled, cut into 24 bars or squares.

BRAZIL NUT LAYER BARS

makes approximately 12 bars

¼ cup sweet butter, softened
1 cup flour
½ teaspoon salt
¾ cup firmly packed dark brown sugar
2 large eggs, slightly beaten
1½ cups finely chopped Brazil nuts
½ cup flaked coconut
1 teaspoon pure vanilla extract
1 cup semisweet chocolate pieces
¼ cup light corn syrup
1 tablespoon water

Preheat the oven to 375°F.

In a small bowl combine the butter, flour and ¼ teaspoon salt. Mix until well blended. Transfer dough to a buttered and floured 9-inch square baking pan. Press dough firmly into the bottom and bake for 15 minutes.

Meanwhile beat the brown sugar and eggs until smooth. Add the remaining salt, 1 cup nuts, coconut and vanilla. Mix well.

Remove the pan from the oven and spread the topping evenly over the base. Return to the oven and bake for 15 minutes longer. Remove from the oven and cool in the pan on a wire rack.

In the top of a double boiler melt the chocolate over hot but not boiling water. Stir in the corn syrup and the water. Remove from the heat.

Spread the chocolate mixture evenly on baked base and sprinkle with the remaining nuts. Let stand until the topping is firm. Cut into bars.

BUTTERSCOTCH BARS

makes 16 large bars

1 cup sifted flour
½ cup firmly packed light brown sugar
⅓ cup sweet butter, softened
2 tablespoons flour
½ teaspoon baking powder
¼ teaspoon salt
1 cup firmly packed light brown sugar
2 large eggs
1 teaspoon pure vanilla extract
1½ cups chopped walnuts

Preheat the oven to 350°F.

Combine the 1 cup flour and ½ cup brown sugar in a bowl. Add the butter and blend with fingers until the mixture forms a coarse meal.

Press the mixture into a buttered 7 × 11 × 2-inch baking pan. Bake for 15 minutes.

Meanwhile, sift together the 2 tablespoons of the flour, the baking powder and the salt. Set aside. Sift the brown sugar and set aside.

Beat the eggs in a mixing bowl until very light, approximately 5 minutes. Add the brown sugar and beat well. Add the vanilla and the flour mixture. Mix well. Add the nuts and stir.

Remove the pan from the oven. Pour the topping over the base and spread evenly. Return to the oven and bake for 30 to 35 minutes.

Remove from the oven and cool briefly on a wire rack. Cut into bars while still warm and continue to cool in pan.

CHOCOLATE-ALMOND OATMEAL BARS

makes 36 bars

½ cup flour
½ teaspoon salt
½ teaspoon baking soda
½ cup butter, softened
¾ cup firmly packed light brown sugar
1 large egg
1 teaspoon vanilla
1½ cups quick-cooking rolled oats
(not instant)
½ cup finely chopped almonds
¾ cup semisweet chocolate pieces
¼ cup finely chopped almonds

Preheat the oven to 375°F.

In a small bowl combine the flour, salt and baking soda. Set aside.

In a large bowl cream together the butter and brown sugar until light and fluffy. Add the egg and vanilla extract and beat to blend.

Add the flour mixture and stir until well blended. Add the oatmeal and the ½ cup chopped almonds. Stir well. Transfer dough to a well-buttered 13 × 9 × 2-inch baking pan. With lightly floured hands pat dough evenly into pan. Bake for 12 minutes or until golden brown.

Remove from the oven and place pan on a wire rack. Sprinkle with the chocolate pieces. Let chocolate stand until it melts, approximately 3 minutes, and then spread evenly. Sprinkle the remaining almonds on top of the chocolate. Cool until chocolate hardens, then cut into bars.

CHOCOLATE CHEESE SQUARES

makes 36 squares

½ cup sweet butter
1½ cups chocolate wafer crumbs
(about 30 wafers)
½ cup finely chopped almonds
6 ounces cream cheese, at room temperature
½ cup sugar
⅓ cup Dutch-process cocoa
1 large egg
1 teaspoon pure vanilla extract
¼ cup finely chopped almonds

Preheat the oven to 350°F.

Place the butter into a 9-inch square baking pan and place in the oven to melt. Remove the pan from the oven. Carefully add the cookie crumbs and ½ cup chopped nuts. Stir until the mixture absorbs the butter. Pat mixture evenly to cover the bottom of the pan. Set aside.

In a small bowl beat the cream cheese until fluffy. Add the sugar, cocoa, egg and vanilla and beat until smooth and well blended. Pour mixture over the crust and sprinkle the top with the remaining ¼ cup chopped nuts.

Bake for 20 minutes. Remove from the oven and cool in pan on rack. Cut into squares and refrigerate until serving.

CHOCOLATE MINT BARS

makes 32 bars

½ cup sweet butter, softened
1 cup sugar
2 large eggs
1 teaspoon pure vanilla extract
2 ounces unsweetened chocolate, melted and cooled
½ cup sifted flour
½ cup coarsely chopped walnuts
3 tablespoons sweet butter
1½ cups sifted confectioners' sugar
¼ teaspoon pure peppermint extract
1 to 2 tablespoons milk
1 ounce unsweetened chocolate
1 teaspoon sweet butter

Preheat the oven to 350°F.

In a medium-sized bowl beat together the butter and sugar until fluffy and light in color. Add the eggs and vanilla extract and beat until well mixed. Beat in the chocolate until smooth. Add the flour and walnuts and stir until well mixed.

Transfer batter to a buttered 8 × 8 × 2-inch square baking pan and spread evenly. Bake for 25 minutes or until the center springs back when lightly touched. Remove from the oven and cool in pan on wire rack.

In a small bowl combine the 3 tablespoons of butter, the confectioners' sugar and the peppermint extract. Add the milk, a little at a time, and stir until frosting is of spreading consistency. Spread evenly over the cooled layer. Refrigerate until frosting is set.

In a small bowl set over hot water, melt the 1 ounce of unsweetened chocolate. Add the butter and stir until smooth.

Drizzle the glaze over the set frosting. Refrigerate until glaze is set. Cut into bars.

Chocolate Chip Coconut Bars

makes 18 bars

2 large eggs
¾ cup firmly packed light brown sugar
½ cup flour
¼ teaspoon salt
¼ teaspoon baking soda
1 teaspoon pure vanilla extract
1 cup flaked coconut
½ cup semisweet chocolate pieces

Preheat the oven to 350°F.

In a medium-sized bowl, combine the eggs and brown sugar. Beat together until smooth. Add the flour, salt, baking soda, vanilla extract and coconut. Beat until well blended.

Transfer batter to a buttered 8 × 8 × 2-inch baking pan. Sprinkle the top with the chocolate pieces. Bake for 25 minutes or until a cake tester inserted into the center comes out clean.

Remove from the oven and cool in pan on wire rack. Cut into squares.

Coconut Pecan Squares

makes 48 small squares

½ cup sweet butter, softened
1½ cups firmly packed dark brown sugar
1 cup flour
2 eggs
½ teaspoon baking powder
½ teaspoon vanilla extract
1 cup finely chopped pecans
1 cup shredded coconut

Preheat the oven to 375°F.

In a bowl combine the butter and ½ cup brown sugar. Cream together until the mixture is light and fluffy. Beat in the flour, half at a time. Mix thoroughly.

Turn the dough into a generously buttered 13 × 9 × 2-inch pan. Pat the dough down and smooth it with the fingers. Bake for 15 minutes or until very lightly browned.

In a mixing bowl combine the eggs, baking powder and vanilla extract. Whisk together until well blended. Add the remaining brown sugar and whisk. Stir in the pecans and coconut.

Pour the pecan and coconut mixture over the cooked dough and smooth lightly. Return to oven and bake 15 minutes longer or until the top is golden and firm.

Remove from the oven and cool completely in the pan. Cut into 1½-inch squares.

Date-Nutmeg Bars

makes approximately 18 bars

8 ounces pitted dates
1 cup pecans
1 cup sifted confectioners' sugar
2 large eggs, lightly beaten
½ teaspoon salt
1 tablespoon vegetable oil
1 tablespoon lemon juice
¼ cup sifted flour
¾ teaspoon finely grated nutmeg
confectioners' sugar

Preheat the oven to 350°F.

Chop the dates and nuts together in a food processor or through a food mill with a medium blade. Place the dates and nuts in a large bowl.

Add to the date and nut mixture the confectioners' sugar, eggs and salt. Mix well. Add the oil, lemon juice, flour and nutmeg. Mix until well blended. Turn batter into a 9-inch square pan. Spread evenly and bake for 30 minutes.

Remove from the oven and cool partially in pan on wire rack. Cut into bars. Roll each bar in confectioners' sugar. Return to racks to cool completely.

Coconut Walnut Squares

makes 24 squares

½ cup sweet butter, softened
1½ cups light brown sugar
1¼ cups sifted flour
2 large eggs, lightly beaten
½ teaspoon salt
1 teaspoon pure vanilla extract
1 cup flaked coconut
1 cup coarsely chopped walnuts

Preheat the oven to 375°F.

In a medium-sized bowl cream the butter together with ½ cup of the brown sugar until fluffy and light in color. Add 1 cup of the flour and stir until well blended. Transfer the dough to a 13 × 9 × 2-inch buttered baking pan and pat down evenly.

Bake for 12 minutes.

While the layer is baking combine the remaining brown sugar, the remaining flour, the eggs, salt, vanilla extract, coconut and chopped walnuts. Mix until well blended. Remove pan from the oven and spread mixture evenly over layer. Return the pan to the oven and bake 20 minutes longer.

Remove from the oven and cool in pan on wire rack. Cut into squares.

Dried Fruit and Pecan Bars

makes 24 bars

1¾ cups flour
½ teaspoon baking powder
½ teaspoon salt
¼ teaspoon ground cinnamon
⅛ teaspoon grated nutmeg
⅓ cup coarsely chopped golden raisins
⅓ cup finely chopped dried apricots
⅓ cup coarsely chopped dried prunes
½ cup sweet butter, softened
1 cup firmly packed light brown sugar
1 large egg
1 teaspoon pure vanilla extract
1 cup coarsely chopped pecans

Preheat the oven to 350°F.

Into a large bowl combine the raisins, apricots and prunes. Sprinkle 1 tablespoon of the flour mixture over the fruits and toss until fruits are coated evenly. Set aside.

In a large bowl beat the butter together with the brown sugar until fluffy and light in color. Add the egg and vanilla and beat until well blended.

Add the flour mixture and stir until well mixed. The dough will be very stiff. Add the dried fruits and pecans and stir until they are distributed evenly in the batter.

Transfer the batter to a well-buttered 13 × 9 × 2-inch baking pan. Spread evenly. Bake for 18 to 20 minutes or until the edges of the dough begin to brown slightly. Remove from the oven and cool in pan on wire rack. Cut into bars. Store at least one day in an airtight container before using.

FIG AND NUT SQUARES

makes 48 small squares

¾ cup flour
1 teaspoon baking powder
¼ teaspoon grated nutmeg
¼ teaspoon cinnamon
¼ teaspoon salt
3 eggs
1 cup sugar
1 teaspoon pure vanilla extract
2 cups dried figs, finely chopped
1 cup finely chopped walnuts
confectioners' sugar

Preheat the oven to 325°F.

In a bowl combine the flour, baking powder, nutmeg, cinnamon and salt.

In the large bowl of an electric mixer beat the eggs until smooth. Add the sugar and the flour mixture, half at a time. Beat well after each addition. Add the vanilla, figs and nuts; stir well to combine.

Turn the batter into a generously buttered and floured 13 × 9 × 2-inch baking pan. Smooth the top with a knife or spatula.

Bake for 25 minutes or until lightly brown and firm to the touch.

Remove from oven to a cooling rack and cool in the pan. Cut the cake into 1½-inch squares. Dust lightly with confectioners' sugar and serve.

FILLED OATMEAL NUT BARS

makes 36 to 40 bars

1 cup apricot preserves
½ cup peach preserves
½ cup pineapple jam
2 tablespoons lemon juice
½ teaspoon grated nutmeg
2 cups quick-cooking rolled oats
(not instant)
1¾ cups flour
1 cup sweet butter, chilled and cut into
small pieces
1 cup firmly packed light brown sugar
½ cup finely chopped pecans
¼ cup sunflower seeds
½ teaspoon grated nutmeg

Preheat the oven to 375°F.

In a saucepan combine the apricot preserves, peach preserves and pineapple jam. Cook, stirring constantly, over low heat until warm and thin. Add lemon juice and nutmeg. Stir. Remove from heat but keep warm.

In a large bowl combine the oats, flour, butter and brown sugar. Using a pastry blender or two knives, cut the butter in until a crumbly dough forms.

Grind the pecans and sunflower seeds together in a blender or nut grinder. Add ground nuts to the dough and mix until well blended.

Spread half of the dough into a lightly buttered 15 × 10-inch jelly roll pan. Pat down evenly. Spread the preserve mixture over the layer. Top with the remaining dough. Pat gently. Bake for 25 to 30 minutes or until golden. Remove from the oven and cool in pan on wire rack. Cut into bars.

Lemon Squares

makes approximately 46 squares

2¼ cups flour
½ cup confectioners' sugar
1 cup sweet butter, softened
1 teaspoon baking powder
4 large eggs
2 cups sugar
1 tablespoon grated lemon peel
4 tablespoons lemon juice

Preheat the oven to 350°F.

In a large bowl combine 2 cups of the flour and the confectioners' sugar. Add the butter and using a pastry blender or two knives, cut it in until the mixture resembles a coarse meal. Using your hands, gently knead the mixture into a smooth dough.

Press the dough into the bottom and up the sides of a lightly buttered 13 × 9 × 2-inch baking pan. Bake for 15 minutes or until dough is firm to the touch.

While the base bakes combine the remaining ¼ cup flour and the baking powder. Set aside.

In a medium-sized bowl beat the eggs until foamy. Add the sugar and stir. Add the lemon peel, lemon juice and flour mixture. Stir until just blended.

Remove pan from oven. Pour mixture over hot base and return to the oven for 25 minutes or until filling is set and top is golden.

Remove from the oven. Cool in pan on wire rack. Cut into squares.

Mellow Walnut Squares

makes 16 squares

6 tablespoons flour
½ teaspoon baking powder
½ cup sweet butter, softened
¾ cup firmly packed light brown sugar
1 large egg
½ teaspoon pure vanilla extract
2 tablespoons milk
2 tablespoons port wine
½ cup finely chopped walnuts
2 tablespoons port wine

Preheat the oven to 350°F.

In a small bowl combine the flour and baking powder. Set aside.

In a medium-sized bowl, cream the butter and brown sugar together until fluffy. Add the egg and beat until well blended. Add the vanilla extract, milk and the first 2 tablespoons of port. Stir to blend.

Stir in the flour mixture and the chopped walnuts. Mix only until blended. Transfer mixture to buttered and floured 9-inch square baking pan. Bake for 15 to 20 minutes or until a cake tester inserted in the center comes out clean.

Remove from the oven and immediately brush with the remaining port. Allow cookie to cool in pan on wire rack. Cut into squares when cool.

MERINGUE NUT BARS

makes 36 bars

1¼ cups flour
1 teaspoon baking powder
2 large eggs, separated
1½ cups firmly packed light brown sugar
½ cup chopped walnuts
1 teaspoon pure vanilla extract
½ cup sweet butter, softened

Preheat the oven to 325°F.

In a small bowl combine the flour and baking powder. Set aside.

In a small bowl beat the egg whites until foamy. Gradually add 1 cup of the brown sugar to the egg whites and beat until whites are stiff but not dry. Add the nuts and vanilla extract and fold gently. Set aside.

In a large bowl combine the butter, egg yolks and remaining brown sugar. Beat until fluffy. Add the flour mixture and stir until well blended.

Turn dough into a buttered 13 × 9 × 2-inch baking pan. Spread evenly. Spread the reserved meringue evenly over the top. Bake for 25 minutes or until the top is light brown and firm.

Remove from the oven and cool in pan on wire rack. Cut into bars when cool.

MOCHA PECAN BARS

makes approximately 32 bars

1 cup flour
1 teaspoon baking powder
½ teaspoon ground nutmeg
¼ teaspoon salt
¼ cup butter, softened
⅔ cup firmly packed light brown sugar
1 large egg
1 teaspoon pure vanilla extract
⅓ cup strong coffee
½ cup coarsely chopped pecans
1 cup confectioners' sugar
4 teaspoons strong cold coffee

Preheat the oven to 350°F.

In a small bowl combine the flour, baking powder, nutmeg and salt. Set aside.

In a large bowl cream the butter and brown sugar together until fluffy and light in color. Add the egg and vanilla extract and beat until well blended.

Alternately add the flour mixture and ⅓ cup coffee. Stir well after each addition. Add the pecans and stir.

Transfer batter to a 9-inch square buttered baking pan. Bake for 25 minutes or until a cake tester inserted into the center comes out clean. Remove from the oven and cool in pan on wire rack.

Combine the confectioners' sugar and cold coffee. Stir until smooth. Spread icing evenly on cooled cookie base. Cut into bars.

OLD-FASHIONED WALNUT MOLASSES BARS

makes 50 to 60 bars

¼ cup boiling water
¼ cup sweet butter
¼ cup lard
½ cup firmly packed brown sugar
½ cup molasses
1 teaspoon baking soda
3 cups flour
1 teaspoon salt
½ tablespoon ground ginger
⅓ teaspoon grated nutmeg
1 cup chopped walnuts

Preheat the oven to 350°F. Grease two cookie sheets and set aside.

Place the butter and lard in a large bowl. Pour the boiling water over them. Add the sugar, molasses, baking soda, flour, salt, ginger and nutmeg. Mix until well blended. Place dough in refrigerator and chill for 2 to 3 hours.

Roll the dough out on a lightly floured surface to ¼-inch thickness. With a pastry wheel or sharp knife, cut the dough into strips 3½ × 1½ inches wide. Sprinkle strips with chopped walnuts and carefully place on cookie sheets.

Bake 10 minutes or until done. Remove from sheets to racks. Cool completely.

PEACH SQUARES

makes 12 squares

2 cups flour
¾ cup sweet butter
1 cup sugar
1 egg yolk
3 tablespoons milk
½ teaspoon grated lemon rind
1 quart fresh peaches, sliced
¼ teaspoon ground cinnamon
¼ cup currants
1 egg white, lightly beaten
confectioners' sugar

Preheat the oven to 375°F.

Place the flour in a large bowl. Cut in the butter with a pastry blender or two knives until the mixture resembles a coarse meal. Stir in ¼ cup sugar, the egg yolk, milk and lemon rind. Mix well and shape the dough into a ball. Divide dough in half and reshape into two balls. Wrap each ball in plastic wrap and refrigerate for 12 to 15 minutes.

Knead each half for 2 minutes. Roll each out onto a lightly floured surface to form two 9 × 13-inch rectangles.

Combine the peach slices, ¾ cup sugar, cinnamon and currants in a bowl.

Transfer one dough rectangle to a 9 × 13-inch baking pan. Top with the peach mixture. Cover with the second dough rectangle. Prick with a fork and brush with egg white. Bake for 35 minutes or until golden.

Remove from oven and cool in the pan. When completely cooled, cut into 3-inch squares and dust with confectioners' sugar.

Raspberry Crumb Bars

makes 30 bars

1¾ cups flour
½ teaspoon baking soda
1 cup sweet butter, softened
1 cup firmly packed light brown sugar
1½ cups quick-cooking rolled oats
(not instant)
1 cup raspberry jam

Preheat the oven to 400°F.

In a small bowl combine the flour and the baking soda. Set aside.

In a medium-sized bowl cream together the butter and brown sugar until fluffy and light in color. Add the flour mixture and stir until well blended. Add the oats and mix well. This may be easiest to do with your hands.

Press half of the dough into a well-buttered 13 × 9 × 2-inch baking pan. Spread the layer evenly with the jam. Crumble the remaining dough over the top. Pat gently.

Bake for 20 to 25 minutes or until lightly browned. Remove from the oven and cool in pan on wire rack. Cut into bars while still warm. Serve warm or cool. Store airtight in a cool place.

Toffee Squares

makes 24 bars

1 cup flour
½ teaspoon ground cinnamon
½ cup sweet butter, softened
½ cup firmly packed light brown sugar
1 egg, separated
1 cup semisweet chocolate pieces
½ cup coarsely chopped walnuts

Preheat the oven to 275°F.

In a small bowl combine the flour and the cinnamon. Set aside.

Beat together the butter, brown sugar and egg until fluffy. Add the flour mixture and stir just until well mixed. Transfer the batter to a 9-inch square buttered baking pan. Bake for 35 minutes or until lightly browned.

While the base bakes, melt the chocolate in the top of a double boiler over hot but not boiling water. Remove from the heat and cool.

Remove pan from the oven. Cool the base in the pan on a wire rack.

Spread the chocolate evenly over the cookie base. Sprinkle with the chopped nuts. Chill for 5 to 10 minutes or until chocolate is firm. Cut into squares.

——SLICED COOKIES——

ALMOND GINGER ROUNDS

makes approximately 100 cookies

3½ cups flour
1 cup sliced toasted almonds
1 cup sugar
1 tablespoon ground ginger
2 teaspoons cinnamon
2 teaspoons grated nutmeg
1 teaspoon baking soda
1 cup sweet butter, cut into pieces and softened
½ cup molasses
ice water, as needed

In a large bowl combine the flour, almonds, sugar, ginger, cinnamon, nutmeg and baking soda. Add the butter and molasses and mix with a wooden spoon. If dough does not hold together when pinched, add ice water and knead until blended.

Form the dough into a ball and divide in thirds. Shape each third into a bar that is 1 × 3 × 6 inches. Wrap each bar in plastic wrap and refrigerate for 5 hours or until firm.

Preheat the oven to 325°F.

Remove the dough from the refrigerator and slice into cookies ⅛-inch thick. Place cookies ½ inch apart on lightly buttered cookie sheets. Bake for 10 to 12 minutes or until cookies begin to darken. Remove from the oven and transfer to wire racks to cool. Store in airtight containers.

BUTTERCOOKIE SANDWICHES

makes 36 cookies

2 cups cake flour
¼ cup sugar
¼ teaspoon grated lemon rind
½ cup sweet butter, cut into pieces
2 tablespoons ice water, if needed

FILLING:
½ cup sweet butter, softened
½ cup sifted confectioners' sugar
grated rind of 1 large lemon
1 tablespoon lemon juice

In a large bowl combine the flour, sugar and lemon rind.

Using a pastry blender or two knives, cut in the butter until the mixture forms a coarse meal. Knead the dough until it is firm and holds together. Add the ice water if necessary.

Form the dough into a long roll, approximately 2 inches thick. Wrap in plastic wrap and refrigerate for 2 hours.

Preheat the oven to 350°F.

Remove dough from the refrigerator. Slice the roll into ¼-inch cookies and place 1 inch apart on buttered baking sheets. Bake for 10 minutes or until lightly golden.

Remove from the oven and transfer to wire racks to cool. While cookies cool, make the filling.

In a small bowl combine the butter, confectioners' sugar, lemon rind and lemon juice. Mix until very well combined.

Assemble cooled cookies by spreading the bottom of each with about 1 tablespoon of the filling. Gently place the bottoms together. Store cookies in refrigerator.

CARDAMOM COOKIES

makes 120 small cookies

4 cups sifted flour
1 tablespoon ground cardamom
¼ teaspoon salt
¼ teaspoon baking soda
1 cup sweet butter, softened
1 cup sugar
½ cup sour cream

In a large bowl combine the flour, cardamom, salt and baking soda. Mix until evenly combined. Set aside.

In another large bowl cream together the butter and sugar until light and fluffy. Add the sour cream and mix well. Stir in the flour mixture and blend until it is thoroughly combined.

Shape the dough into a ball and then divide in half. Shape each half into a long roll approximately 2 inches wide. Cover rolls with plastic wrap or waxed paper and refrigerate 8 hours or overnight.

Preheat the oven to 375°F.

Remove the dough from the refrigerator. Slice rolls into cookies ⅛-inch thick and place 1 inch apart on unbuttered baking sheets. Bake for 8 to 10 minutes.

Remove from the oven. Transfer cookies to wire racks and cool.

CRYSTALIZED GINGER COOKIES

makes 72 cookies

2½ cups sifted flour
1 teaspoon baking soda
1 teaspoon ground ginger
½ teaspoon grated nutmeg
¼ teaspoon salt
⅔ cup sweet butter, melted
1 cup sugar
¼ cup molasses
1 large egg
½ cup finely chopped crystalized ginger
¼ cup finely chopped candied orange peel
¼ cup finely chopped walnuts
1 egg white, slightly beaten
1 cup finely chopped almonds

Preheat the oven to 325°F.

Into a large bowl sift together the flour, baking soda, ginger, nutmeg and salt. Set aside.

Place the melted butter in a large bowl. When the butter is cool, add the sugar, molasses and egg. Stir vigorously until well mixed. Add the crystalized ginger, candied orange peel and the nuts and mix well.

Gradually add the flour mixture and stir until well blended. It will probably be easier to mix with your hands.

Divide the dough into 8 equal pieces. Using floured hands, shape each piece into a roll approximately ½ inch wide. Place the rolls side by side. Brush the rolls with the beaten egg white and cut rolls into slices 2 inches thick. Dip cookies in chopped almonds and place on lightly buttered baking sheets approximately 1½ inches apart.

Bake for 12 to 14 minutes. Remove from the oven and cool cookies on sheets before transferring to wire racks to cool completely.

GINGERSNAPS

makes 60 cookies

4 cups flour
½ cup sugar
½ teaspoon salt
1 teaspoon ground ginger
½ cup sweet butter
½ cup lard or solid vegetable shortening
1 teaspoon baking soda
1 tablespoon hot water
1 cup molasses

Preheat the oven to 350°F.

Combine the flour, sugar, salt and ginger in a large mixing bowl. Cut in the butter and lard with a pastry blender, two knives or your fingers. Blend until particles are like coarse crumbs.

Dissolve the baking soda in the water. Make a well in the center of the flour mixture and pour in the hot water and molasses. Mix well.

Form dough into a narrow cylinder and wrap in aluminum foil. Chill thoroughly in refrigerator. Cut dough into slices ½ inch thick.

Place the slices 2 inches apart on a greased baking sheet. Bake for 5 to 7 minutes. Cool on a rack.

NUT LOGS

makes approximately 48 cookies

3¾ cups sifted flour
1 cup plus 6 tablespoons sugar
1½ teaspoons baking powder
3 tablespoons fresh unflavored breadcrumbs
4 whole eggs
1 egg yolk
1 teaspoon pure almond extract
1 teaspoon pure vanilla extract
1 cup whole unblanched almonds
1 cup whole hazelnuts
1 egg white

Preheat the oven to 375°F. Line two baking sheets with brown paper and butter the paper lightly. Set aside.

Into a large bowl sift the flour, sugar and baking powder together. Add the breadcrumbs and stir well.

In a small bowl beat together the eggs, the egg yolks, almond extract and vanilla extract. Beat until frothy. Add the egg mixture to the flour mixture and beat until well blended. The dough should be moist.

Add the almonds and hazelnuts to the dough. Using your hands, work the nuts into the dough until the dough begins to hold together. Turn the dough out onto a piece of waxed paper.

Divide the dough in half. Shape each half into a log about 12 inches long and 2 inches wide. Place the logs on the prepared sheets. Gently beat the egg white and brush over each log.

Bake for 30 minutes or until golden. Remove from the oven and transfer the logs, with the bran paper, to wire racks. Cool for 1 hour.

Preheat the oven to 350°F.

Carefully slice the logs into 48 cookies. Return to unbuttered baking sheets and bake for 10 minutes.

Remove from the oven and transfer cookies to a wire rack to cool. Store in tins.

NUT-RIMMED CHOCOLATE COOKIES

makes approximately 96 cookies

3 cups sifted cake flour
½ cup Dutch-process unsweetened cocoa
¼ teaspoon salt
1¼ cups sweet butter, softened
1½ cups sifted confectioners' sugar
1 large egg
1½ cups chopped walnuts
8 ounces sweet chocolate

In a large bowl combine the sifted flour, cocoa and salt. Stir until well mixed.

In another large bowl cream together the butter and confectioners' sugar until light. Add the egg and beat until fluffy and well blended.

Add the flour mixture and beat until well mixed. Cover the bowl and refrigerate dough for 2 to 3 hours.

Divide the dough in half and shape each half into a long roll approximately 1½ inches wide. Roll each in the chopped walnuts until completely coated. Wrap rolls in plastic wrap or waxed paper and refrigerate 8 hours or overnight.

Preheat the oven to 400°F.

Remove rolls from the refrigerator. Slice the rolls into ⅛-inch cookies and place them 1 inch apart on unbuttered baking sheets. Bake for 8 to 10 minutes. Remove from the oven and transfer to wire racks to cool.

In the top half of a double boiler, melt the chocolate over hot but not boiling water. Spread chocolate in the center of each cookie. Let chocolate harden before storing cookies.

PINWHEEL COOKIES

makes 36 cookies

½ cup sweet butter, softened
¾ cup sugar
1 teaspoon pure vanilla extract
1 large egg
1½ cups sifted flour
¼ teaspoon baking powder
¼ teaspoon salt
1 ounce unsweetened chocolate, melted

In a medium-sized bowl, beat together the butter, sugar, vanilla and egg until light in color and fluffy. Add the flour, baking powder and salt and mix until well blended.

Form the dough into a ball. Divide the dough in half. Remove one half and wrap it in plastic wrap. To the other half add the melted chocolate and mix well. Wrap in plastic wrap and refrigerate both halves for 1 hour or until dough is firm enough to handle.

On a lightly floured surface, roll the white dough out to form a 16 × 6-inch rectangle. Roll the chocolate dough to the same size. Carefully invert the chocolate dough onto the white dough. Roll the dough up from the long side. Make sure that the center is rolled tight. Wrap the roll in plastic wrap and refrigerate overnight.

Preheat the oven to 350°F.

Remove the dough from the refrigerator and place the roll on a board. Cut ⅛-inch slices and place them on buttered baking sheets. Bake for 10 to 15 minutes or until just lightly browned.

Remove from the oven and transfer to wire racks to cool. Store in airtight containers.

CUT COOKIES

JOE FROGGERS

makes 48 to 60 cookies

1 cup sweet butter, softened
2 cups sugar
1 tablespoon salt
¾ cup water
¼ cup dark rum
2 teaspoons baking soda
2 cups molasses
2 cups flour
1 tablespoon ground ginger
1 teaspoon grated nutmeg
½ teaspoon ground cloves

Preheat the oven to 375°F.

Cream the butter and sugar together in a mixing bowl until light and fluffy.

In a small bowl dissolve the salt in the water and mix in the rum.

In another small bowl, add the baking soda to the molasses.

Combine the flour, ginger, cloves and nutmeg. Add alternately with liquid ingredients to creamed butter and sugar. Stir well between additions. The dough will be sticky. Chill overnight in refrigerator.

Flour a work surface and rolling pin. Roll the dough out to ½-inch thickness. Cut into circles or shapes with a large cookie cutter. Place cookies 2 inches apart on greased baking sheets. Bake for 10 to 12 minutes or until golden. Cool on racks.

NUT-TOPPED MARSALA COOKIES

makes approximately 100 cookies

1 cup sweet butter, softened
2 cups sugar
2 egg yolks
5 cups sifted flour
⅛ teaspoon salt
⅔ cup Marsala wine
1 egg white, slightly beaten
1½ cups finely chopped pignoli (pine nuts)

In a large bowl cream together the butter and sugar. Add the egg yolks and beat until light and fluffy. Add the flour and salt alternately with the Marsala. Mix well. Cover the bowl and chill for 4 hours or overnight.

Preheat the oven to 325°F.

On a floured surface, roll out the dough until it is thin. Cut the dough with 2-inch cookie cutters. Place cookies 2 inches apart on unbuttered baking sheets. Brush each cookie with the egg white and sprinkle with the nuts.

Bake for 8 to 10 minutes or until lightly golden. Remove from the oven and transfer to wire racks to cool. Store in tightly covered containers.

OLD-FASHIONED NUT COOKIES

makes 48 cookies

1½ cups sugar
1 cup sweet butter, softened
3 eggs, well beaten
½ cup molasses
1½ cups raisins
½ cup finely chopped hickory nuts
2 cups flour
1 teaspoon baking soda
½ teaspoon cinnamon
¼ teaspoon ground cloves
⅛ teaspoon salt

Preheat the oven to 350°F.

Combine 1 cup flour, the baking soda, cinnamon, cloves, and salt in a bowl. Set aside.

In a large bowl cream the butter and sugar together until light and fluffy. Add the eggs and molasses. Beat well. Stir in the raisins and nuts. Mix well. Add the flour mixture and stir. Add enough additional flour to make a soft dough, about 1 cup.

Chill the dough for 10 minutes or until it is easy to handle

Roll the dough out thinly on a lightly floured surface. Cut out cookies with a cookie cutter.

Transfer the cookies to a buttered baking sheet and bake for 10 to 12 minutes.

Remove from oven and transfer cookies with a spatula to cooling racks.

ORANGE SUGAR COOKIES

makes 36 cookies

2½ cups sifted flour
1 teaspoon baking powder
1 teaspoon salt
½ cup sweet butter, softened
2 tablespoons grated orange rind
1 cup sugar
¼ cup orange juice
2 tablespoons lemon juice
1 egg white, beaten with water
sugar

Into a bowl sift together the flour, baking powder and salt. Set aside.

In a large bowl beat together the butter, orange rind and sugar until light and fluffy. Add the orange juice and lemon juice and mix well. Add the flour mixture and stir until well blended. Cover the bowl and refrigerate 8 hours or overnight.

Preheat the oven to 375°F.

On a lightly floured surface, roll out one-third of the dough at a time to ⅛-inch thickness. Cut into desired shapes with cookie cutters and arrange 1 inch apart on an unbuttered baking sheet. Brush cookies with the egg white wash and sprinkle with sugar.

Bake in the oven for 8 minutes or until lightly golden. Remove from the oven and transfer to wire racks to cool.

ROLLED SUGAR COOKIES

makes 60 cookies

2 cups flour
¼ teaspoon salt
½ cup sweet butter, softened
½ cup sugar
1 large egg
½ teaspoon pure vanilla extract
1½ tablespoons lemon juice
1 egg white, lightly beaten with water
sugar

Into a medium-sized bowl sift together the flour and salt. Set aside.

In a large bowl cream the butter and sugar together until light and fluffy. Add the egg, vanilla extract and lemon juice; beat until blended. Add the flour mixture and stir until well blended.

Divide the dough in half. Wrap each half in plastic wrap and refrigerate for 3 to 4 hours.

Preheat the oven to 350°F.

Roll the dough out onto a lightly floured surface to ⅛-inch thickness. Cut into desired shapes with cookie cutters. Space cookies ½ inch apart on lightly buttered baking sheets. Brush each cookie with the egg white–water mixture and sprinkle with sugar.

Bake for 8 to 10 minutes or until cookies are very lightly browned. Remove from the oven and transfer to wire racks to cool. Store in loosely covered containers.

SAND COOKIES

makes approximately 130 cookies

2 cups sweet butter, softened
1 cup sugar
1 large egg
1½ teaspoons pure vanilla extract
4½ cups sifted flour
6 ounces pecans, ground
¼ cup sugar

Preheat the oven to 350°F.

In a large bowl beat the butter together with the 1 cup sugar until light. Add the egg and continue beating until fluffy. Add the vanilla and beat until blended. Add the flour and ground pecans and stir until well blended and a stiff dough forms. Form the dough into a ball.

On a lightly floured surface, roll out one-quarter of the dough at a time to ¼-inch thickness. Cut with 1½-inch round cookie cutters and place 1 inch apart on unbuttered baking sheets. Repeat the process until all the dough is used. Reroll all the trimmings.

Bake for 15 minutes or until the edges of the cookies just begin to brown. Remove from the oven. Roll the warm cookies in the remaining sugar. Transfer cookies to wire racks to cool. Store in airtight containers.

—CRESCENT COOKIES—

ALMOND CRESCENTS

makes approximately 72 cookies

5 ounces whole almonds
1 cup sweet butter, softened
½ cup sugar
1 teaspoon pure vanilla extract
1 teaspoon pure almond extract
2 cups flour
¾ cup sugar

Preheat the oven to 400°F. Place almonds in a shallow baking pan and toast in oven for 5 minutes or until golden. Turn twice. Remove from the oven and cool. When cool, grind nuts and measure out 1¼ cups. Reserve. Turn off oven.

In a bowl beat the butter until fluffy. Add the ½ cup sugar and continue beating until mixture is light in color. Add vanilla extract and almond extract and mix well. Add flour and almonds and mix until well blended. Form dough into a ball and cover with plastic wrap. Refrigerate for 1 hour.

Preheat the oven to 350°F.

Using 1 teaspoonful of dough for each cookie, shape dough into crescents about 2 inches long. Place cookies 1 inch apart on an unbuttered baking sheet.

Bake for 15 minutes or until cookies are light and golden in color. Remove from the oven. Allow cookies to cool on sheets for 5 minutes before transferring to wire racks to continue cooling.

When the cookies are cool, roll them in the ¾ cup sugar. Store in an airtight container.

HAZELNUT CRESCENTS

makes approximately 92 cookies

1 cup sweet butter, softened
1 cup sugar
1 cup finely ground hazelnuts
2 cups flour
¼ teaspoon salt
2 teaspoons pure vanilla extract
confectioners' sugar

Preheat the oven to 300°F.

In a large bowl cream together the butter and sugar until fluffy and light in color. Add the ground nuts, flour, salt and vanilla extract.

Using your fingers, work the dough until it holds together. If mixture will not hold together add ice water, 1 tablespoon at a time, until it does.

Using 1 teaspoonful of dough for each cookie, shape into small crescents. Place on unbuttered baking sheets 2 inches apart. Bake for 20 to 25 minutes or until cookies are lightly browned.

Remove from the oven and carefully transfer to wire racks to cool. While cookies are still warm dust with confectioners' sugar. Cool completely and store in an airtight container.

SOUR CREAM CRESCENTS

makes 48 cookies

1 cup sweet butter, softened
½ cup sugar
1 large egg yolk
1 teaspoon grated lemon rind
1 cup finely ground pecans
1 cup sour cream
3 cups flour
½ teaspoon grated nutmeg
1 teaspoon baking soda
confectioners' sugar

In a large bowl cream the butter until light and fluffy. Add the sugar, egg yolk, lemon rind, ground nuts, sour cream, flour, nutmeg and baking soda. Mix very well. Cover bowl and refrigerate overnight.

Preheat the oven to 325°F. Butter and lightly flour two baking sheets.

Remove dough from the refrigerator. Using level teaspoonfuls of dough, shape the dough into thin lengths and curve into crescents. Space on baking sheets 2 inches apart.

Bake for 12 minutes or until lightly browned. Remove from the oven. Carefully transfer cookies to wire racks. Dust the cookies with confectioners' sugar while they are still warm. Cool completely and store in airtight containers.

WALNUT CRESCENTS

makes 60 cookies

1 cup sweet butter, softened
½ cup confectioners' sugar
2 teaspoons pure vanilla extract
¼ teaspoon salt
1¾ cups flour
1 cup finely chopped walnuts
½ cup sugar

In a large bowl cream together the butter, confectioners' sugar, vanilla extract and salt until light and fluffy. Add the flour and walnuts and stir until well blended. Cover the bowl and chill until dough is firm enough to handle, approximately 40 minutes.

Preheat the oven to 300°F.

Remove dough from the refrigerator. Working on a lightly floured board, break off small pieces of dough and roll into finger-thick strips. Cut the strips into 2-inch lengths. Taper the ends and shape into crescents.

Place cookies 1 inch apart on an unbuttered baking sheet. Bake for 18 to 20 minutes or until cookies are firm.

Remove from the oven. While the cookies are still warm roll them in the ½ cup sugar. Cool on wire racks and store in an airtight container.

BROWNIES

BLONDIES

makes 48 blond brownies

2½ cups sweet butter
3⅓ cups firmly packed light brown sugar
3¾ cups flour
5 teaspoons baking powder
5 large eggs
5 teaspoons pure vanilla extract
2½ cups coarsely chopped walnuts
4 cups semisweet chocolate pieces

Preheat the oven to 350°F.

In a large saucepan, melt the butter over a low heat. Add the brown sugar and stir. Cook, stirring constantly, until sugar dissolves and mixture is smooth and shiny. Remove from the heat and cool.

Combine the flour and baking powder. Reserve.

Add the eggs and vanilla extract to the cooled butter and sugar mixture. Stir well. Add the flour mixture and stir just until well blended. Add the walnuts and chocolate pieces. Stir until blended.

Distribute batter evenly between two buttered 15 × 10-inch jelly-roll pans. Bake for 25 minutes or until a cake tester inserted into the center comes out clean.

Remove from the oven. Cool in pans on wire racks. Cut into 24 brownies per pan.

Note: These freeze well. Make one pan to serve and freeze the other for a later date.

BROWNIE ALMOND THINS

makes 40 to 50 pieces

3 ounces unsweetened chocolate
2 ounces semisweet chocolate
¾ cup sweet butter
1¼ cups sugar
¼ teaspoon salt
2 eggs, lightly beaten
1½ teaspoon pure vanilla extract
⅔ cup sifted flour
1⅓ cups whole blanched almonds

Preheat the oven to 325°F. Line the bottom of two 9 × 9 × 2-inch square pans with foil and set aside.

Combine the two chocolates and the butter in the top of a double boiler. Melt the mixture over hot but not boiling water. Remove from the heat and stir until well blended.

Add the sugar and salt to the chocolate mixture. Mix well. Add the eggs and vanilla extract. Stir until well blended. Gently fold the flour in until well blended.

Spread a thin layer of the batter over the bottom of each prepared pan. Sprinkle each evenly with the almonds. Spread the remaining batter evenly over the almond layer.

Bake for 20 minutes or until a cake tester inserted in the center comes out barely dry. Remove from the oven and cool in pan on wire rack. Cover the pan and let stand overnight or at least 8 hours.

Invert the brownies onto plates. Carefully remove the foil and break the brownies into irregular pieces.

CAKE BROWNIES

makes 20 brownies

2 ounces unsweetened baking chocolate
⅔ cup sifted flour
½ teaspoon baking powder
¼ teaspoon salt
¼ cup sweet butter, softened
1 cup sugar
2 large eggs, separated
¼ cup milk
1 teaspoon pure vanilla extract
½ cup coarsely chopped walnuts

Preheat the oven to 350°F.

In the top of a double boiler melt the chocolate over hot but not boiling water. Remove from the heat and cool to room temperature.

In a small bowl combine the flour, baking powder and salt. Mix well and set aside.

In a medium-sized bowl combine the butter and sugar. Beat together until light and fluffy. Add the egg yolks, one at a time, beating well after each addition. Add the milk and vanilla extract and beat well. Add the cooled chocolate and stir well. Fold in the flour mixture and mix gently but thoroughly.

In a small bowl beat the egg whites until firm but still soft. Gently fold egg whites into the chocolate mixture. Fold in nuts.

Carefully spread batter in a buttered 9 × 9 × 2-inch pan and bake for 25 to 30 minutes or until top is firm and dry. Remove from the oven and cool in pan on wire rack.

MARBLE BROWNIES

makes 20 to 25 brownies

3 tablespoons sweet butter
3 tablespoons Dutch-process cocoa
2 tablespoons sweet butter, softened
3 ounces cream cheese
¼ cup sugar
1 large egg
1 tablespoon flour
½ teaspoon pure vanilla extract
2 large eggs, beaten
¾ cup sugar
½ teaspoon baking powder
¼ teaspoon salt
½ cup flour
1 teaspoon pure vanilla extract
4 tablespoons sour cream

Preheat the oven to 350°F.

Melt the 3 tablespoons butter in a large saucepan. Add the cocoa and stir well. Remove from the heat and set aside to cool.

In a medium-sized bowl, cream together the 2 tablespoons of butter and the cream cheese. Add the ¼ cup sugar and beat until fluffy. Add the 1 egg and beat until well blended. Beat in the 1 tablespoon flour and ½ teaspoon vanilla extract. Set aside.

To the cooled chocolate mixture in the saucepan, add the ¾ cup sugar and mix until well blended. Add the baking powder, salt and flour and stir until mixed. Add the two eggs and stir to blend. Stir in the vanilla extract and sour cream.

Into a buttered 8-inch square baking pan spread half of the chocolate batter. Then spoon the cream cheese batter over this. Smooth. Place the remaining chocolate batter on top. Using a knife, swirl twice through the batter the length of the pan.

Bake for 30 to 35 minutes or until a cake tester inserted into the center comes out dry. Remove from the oven and transfer to a wire rack to cool. Cut into squares and keep refrigerated.

NUT BROWNIES

makes 16 to 20 brownies

4 ounces unsweetened chocolate
1 cup butter, cut into pieces
2 cups sugar
4 eggs
1½ cups flour
¼ teaspoon salt
1½ teaspoons vanilla extract
1½ cups coarsely chopped pecans or walnuts

Preheat the oven to 375°F.

In the top of a double boiler over hot but not boiling water, melt the chocolate. Add the butter gradually, stirring well after each addition. Add the sugar and stir until completely melted. Remove from heat.

Add the eggs, one at a time, beating after each addition. Beat in the flour, salt and vanilla extract. Add the nuts and stir.

Turn batter into a buttered and floured 9 × 9 × 2-inch square baking pan. Bake for 40 minutes or until brownies begin to shrink away from sides of pan. Do not overbake. Cool in pan, then cut into squares.

WALNUT-TOPPED BROWNIES

makes 25 brownies

3 ounces unsweetened chocolate
6 tablespoons sweet butter
1 cup sugar
¼ teaspoon salt
2 large eggs, lightly beaten
1½ teaspoons pure vanilla extract
½ cup sifted flour

TOPPING:

¼ cup sweet butter
¼ cup sugar
½ cup firmly packed dark brown sugar
2 tablespoons flour
2 large eggs, lightly beaten
1½ teaspoons pure vanilla extract
3½ cups coarsely broken walnut pieces

To prepare the brownie base, in a heavy saucepan melt the chocolate together with the butter over a very low heat. Remove from the heat and stir until well blended.

Add the sugar and salt to the chocolate mixture. Stir until smooth. Add the eggs and vanilla extract. Stir until well blended. Add the flour and fold in until thoroughly incorporated. Spread the batter evenly in a buttered 9 × 9 × 2-inch baking pan. Refrigerate for 2 hours.

Preheat the oven to 350°F.

To prepare the topping, in a heavy saucepan melt the butter over low heat. Add the sugar and brown sugar. Cook, stirring constantly, for 1 minute. Remove from the heat.

Add the flour and eggs to the butter mixture and stir to blend well. Return the mixture to the heat. Cook, stirring constantly, over a low heat for 3 minutes or until thick and light in color. Be careful not to overcook or the eggs will curdle. Remove from the heat. Add the vanilla extract and walnuts. Stir until the walnuts are evenly coated.

Remove the brownie base from the refrigerator. Spoon the topping over the base and spread evenly. Bake for 40 to 50 minutes or until top is dry and a cake tester inserted into the center comes out barely dry.

Remove from the oven. Cool in pan on wire rack. Cover pan and let set overnight. Cut into squares.

MERINGUES

ALMOND MERINGUES

makes approximately 75 cookies

¾ cup ground blanched almonds
¼ cup amaretto or almond-flavored liqueur
2 large egg whites, at room temperature
¼ teaspoon cream of tartar
½ cup sugar
½ teaspoon pure almond extract
¼ cup sliced blanched almonds

In a small bowl combine the ground almonds and the liqueur. Stir and set aside.

Place the egg whites in the medium-sized bowl of an electric mixer. Beat the whites until they are foamy. Add the cream of tartar and continue beating the egg whites until they hold a soft peak.

Gradually add the sugar and the almond extract. Continue beating until the mixture becomes stiff and holds a stiff peak. Carefully fold in the ground almond mixture.

Preheat the oven to 325°F. Prepare baking sheets by covering them with parchment or waxed paper. If necessary, attach the paper to the sheet by putting a drop of the meringue mixture on the underside of each corner.

Drop the batter by teaspoonfuls, 2 inches apart on the sheets. Smooth the tops of the cookies and press a sliced almond into the center of each cookie.

Bake for 15 to 20 minutes or until meringues are dry to the touch. If the cookies begin to brown, reduce the oven temperature to 300°F and open the oven door slightly.

Remove from the oven. Let cookies cool on the sheets for 3 minutes before transferring them to wire racks. Cool completely before storing in airtight containers.

CHIP AND NUT MERINGUES

makes approximately 48 cookies

2 egg whites, at room temperature
⅔ cup superfine sugar
1 teaspoon pure vanilla extract
⅛ teaspoon salt
1 cup semisweet chocolate pieces
1 cup coarsely chopped walnuts

Preheat the oven to 350°F. Prepare two baking sheets by covering them with foil. Set aside.

In a small bowl, beat the egg whites until foamy. Add the sugar gradually and continue beating until the whites form and hold a stiff peak. Add the vanilla extract, salt, chocolate pieces and nuts. Fold gently into the meringue until well blended.

Drop the batter by teaspoonfuls onto the prepared sheets. Place cookies 1 inch apart. Place in the oven. Close the door and turn the oven off. Do not open the oven door for at least 6 hours or overnight.

Remove from the oven. Using a wide spatula, transfer the cookies to airtight containers.

CHOCOLATE CHIP PUFFS

makes 45 cookies

½ cup egg whites, at room temperature
¼ teaspoon salt
¼ teaspoon cream of tartar
1 cup sugar
2 teaspoons orange-flavored liqueur
1 cup semisweet chocolate bits
1 tablespoon confectioners' sugar

Preheat the oven to 275°F. Line two baking sheets with aluminum foil, shiny-side down.

Beat the egg whites and salt together in a large mixing bowl. When the mixture is foamy, add the cream of tartar and continue beating until the whites form soft peaks. Gradually beat in the sugar, a little at a time. Continue to beat until the meringue is stiff and glossy but not dry. Add the liqueur and beat until just blended. Gently fold in the chocolate bits.

Place level teaspoons of the meringue mixture 2 inches apart on the prepared baking sheets. Lightly sift the confectioners' sugar over the cookies.

Bake the cookies until they are firm to the touch and very lightly colored, about 35 to 45 minutes.

Remove the cookies from the oven. Using a wide spatula, carefully transfer the cookies to wire racks and cool completely. Store in an airtight container.

CHOCOLATE MERINGUE SANDWICHES

makes approximately 48 cookies

3 large egg whites, at room temperature
¼ teaspoon cream of tartar
⅓ cup sugar
½ teaspoon pure almond extract
½ cup ground blanched almonds
4 ounces semisweet chocolate

In the medium-sized bowl of an electric mixer, beat the egg whites until they are frothy. Add the cream of tartar and continue to beat the whites until they hold a soft peak.

Gradually add the sugar and the almond extract. Continue beating until the whites are very stiff but not dry. Gently fold in the ground almonds.

Preheat the oven to 200°F. Prepare baking sheets by lining them with parchment or wax paper. If necessary, use a drop of meringue on the underside of each corner to attach the paper to the sheet.

Drop the batter by teaspoonfuls onto the prepared sheets. Space meringues 2 inches apart. Bake for 45 to 50 minutes or until cookies are firm and dry and can be loosened from the paper with the tip of a knife.

Remove from the oven and transfer cookies to wire racks to cool.

Melt the semisweet chocolate in the top part of a double boiler set over hot but not boiling water. Allow chocolate to cool before using.

Spread a thin layer of the chocolate on the bottom of each cookie and attach the cookies, bottom to bottom. Transfer cookies to wire racks and allow them to stand for 1 hour or until the chocolate is hard.

CHOCOLATE WALNUT PUFFS

makes approximately 36 puffs

1 cup semisweet chocolate pieces
2 egg whites
⅛ teaspoon salt
½ cup sugar
½ teaspoon pure vanilla extract
½ teaspoon distilled white vinegar
¾ cup chopped walnuts

Preheat the oven to 350°F.

Melt the chocolate in the top of a double boiler over hot but not boiling water. Remove from heat.

In a mixing bowl, beat the egg whites with the salt until they are foamy. Gradually add the sugar and beat until stiff but not dry. Beat in the vanilla and the vinegar. Fold in the melted chocolate and the walnuts.

Drop the batter by teaspoons onto a buttered baking sheet. Bake for 10 minutes.

Remove sheet from oven. With a wide metal spatula transfer the puffs to cooling racks. Cool completely. Store in an airtight container.

FUDGE NUT MERINGUES

makes approximately 42 cookies

1 cup semisweet chocolate pieces
3 tablespoons sweet butter
4 large eggs
2 tablespoons corn syrup
¼ teaspoon cream of tartar
½ teaspoon salt
1 cup sugar
½ teaspoon pure almond extract
½ teaspoon pure vanilla extract
1 cup finely chopped Brazil nuts

In the top part of a double boiler, melt the chocolate together with the butter over hot but not boiling water. While the chocolate is melting, separate the eggs. Beat the yolks slightly and reserve the whites for the meringues. Add the egg yolks and corn syrup to the melted chocolate. Cook, stirring constantly, for 5 minutes. Remove pot from the heat and beat chocolate until it has thickened to a spreading consistency. Set aside.

Preheat the oven to 300°F. Prepare baking sheets by covering them with waxed paper. Set aside.

In a medium-sized bowl beat the reserved egg whites until they are foamy. Add the cream of tartar and salt and beat until the whites hold a soft peak.

Add the sugar, a little at a time, and continue beating until whites are stiff but not dry. Add the almond and vanilla extracts.

Drop the cookies by teaspoonfuls onto the prepared sheets. Space cookies 1 inch apart. With a teaspoon, make a depression in the center of each cookie. Fill each with the reserved chocolate and sprinkle with the chopped nuts.

Bake for 25 minutes or until cookies are firm. Remove from the oven and transfer cookies to wire racks to cool. Store in airtight containers.

HAZELNUT MERINGUES

makes approximately 24 cookies

1½ cups hazelnuts
1 cup sugar
3 egg whites
2 tablespoons cornstarch

Preheat the oven to 350°F.

Spread the hazelnuts on a cookie sheet and place in oven for 20 minutes or until lightly roasted. Remove the nuts from the oven and place them on a clean, damp towel. Rub the nuts with another damp towel to remove the skins. Put the nuts in the container of an electric blender or food processor and pulverize until they are a finely ground powder.

Place the powdered hazelnuts in a large bowl. Add the sugar. With the back of the spoon, mix the nuts and sugar together. When they are well mixed, add the egg whites, 1 at a time. Beat well. Continue to beat until the dough is smooth and thick enough to hold its shape.

Reduce the oven temperature to 300°F. Heavily butter two baking sheets and sprinkle them with cornstarch. Drop the dough by tablespoons onto the sheets, about 1 inch apart. Bake for 30 minutes or until the cookies are golden and firm to the touch.

Remove the sheets from the oven. Using a metal spatula, transfer the cookies to a cooling rack. Cool completely. Cookies will keep well for two weeks in a tightly closed container.

PECAN MERINGUES

makes approximately 24 cookies

1 egg white
1 cup sifted light brown sugar
1½ cups pecan halves

Preheat the oven to 250°F.

In a mixing bowl beat the egg white until it is stiff enough to form a soft peak. Beat in the brown sugar, a little at a time, until the mixture is stiff and no longer glossy. Gently fold in the pecan halves.

Drop the batter by well-rounded tablespoons onto buttered baking sheets. Use a second spoon to help slide the batter off the tablespoon and onto the sheet. Space the cookies 1 inch apart.

Bake for 30 minutes or until cookies are pale brown.

Remove sheets from oven. With a wide etal spatula transfer the cookies to cooling racks. Cool completely.

WAFERS

ALMOND WAFERS

makes approximately 30 cookies

4 egg whites
⅛ teaspoon of salt
⅔ cup sugar
4 tablespoons flour
6 tablespoons sweet butter, melted and clarified
½ teaspoon pure almond extract
1 teaspoon pure vanilla extract
1 cup coarsely chopped blanched almonds

Preheat the oven to 325°F.

In the large bowl of an electric mixer, beat the egg whites with the salt until foamy. Add the sugar, 1 tablespoon at a time, beating constantly until the mixture is stiff and shiny.

Sift the flour over the egg white mixture. Fold gently.

Combine the butter, almond extract, vanilla extract and almonds. Add to the egg white mixture and fold in thoroughly but gently.

Drop the batter by teaspoonfuls, spaced 3 inches apart, onto a well-buttered baking sheet. Flatten with fingers into a 2½-inch circle.

Bake for 10 minutes. Remove from the oven. Using a wide spatula remove one cookie at a time and curve each around a rolling pin. Allow cookie to stay around pin until it has cooled. Remove when cool and store in airtight containers.

BRANDY ROLLS

makes approximately 80 cookies

½ cup molasses
½ cup sweet butter, softened
1¼ cups sifted cake flour
¼ teaspoon salt
⅔ cup sugar
1 tablespoon ground ginger
3 tablespoons brandy

Preheat the oven to 300°F.

Place the molasses in a saucepan and heat to the boiling point. Remove from the heat. Add the butter and stir until all the butter is dissolved.

Add the flour, salt, sugar and ginger. Stir until well blended. Add the brandy and mix well.

Drop the mixture by half-teaspoonfuls, approximately 3 inches apart, on well-buttered baking sheets. Do not bake more than 6 cookies at one time.

Bake for 10 minutes. Remove from the oven and cool for 1 minute on sheets. Then carefully remove with a spatula and roll immediately around the handle of a wooden spoon. Timing is important here. If the cookies are removed from the sheets too soon they will be too soft to roll. If removed too late, they will be too brittle. Allow cookies to cool completely after they are rolled.

Continue to bake the remaining cookies in the same fashion, being sure to clean the sheets with paper towels in between batches and butter them again each time.

These cookies should be stored in an airtight container or frozen to ensure freshness. Handle with care; they break easily.

BROWN SUGAR WAFERS

makes approximately 30 cookies

3 cups flour
¼ teaspoon salt
¼ teaspoon baking soda
¼ teaspoon ground cinnamon
¾ cup sweet butter, softened
1 cup firmly packed light brown sugar
1 large egg
1 egg yolk
¼ teaspoon pure vanilla extract

Into a medium-sized bowl sift together the flour, salt, baking soda and ground cinnamon. Set aside.

In a large bowl cream the butter and brown sugar together until light and fluffy. Add the egg and beat well. Scrape down the sides of the bowl with a rubber spatula. Add the egg yolk and the vanilla extract. Beat well.

Add the flour mixture and beat only to mix.

Form the dough into a ball and then divide in half. Shape each half into a long roll, approximately 2 inches wide. Place the rolls on a baking sheet and refrigerate until firm, approximately 2 hours.

Preheat the oven to 400°F.

Remove dough from the refrigerator. Cut rolls into ¼-inch thick slices. Place slices 2 inches apart on unbuttered cookie sheets and, using the bottom of a wide glass, press dough to ⅛-inch thickness.

Bake for 3 to 5 minutes or until cookies are done inside. (You may have to break one open to be sure.) Remove from the oven and loosen cookies with a wide spatula. Transfer to wire racks to cool. Store in airtight containers.

ORANGE THINS

makes approximately 96 cookies

½ cup sweet butter, softened
¾ cup sugar
1 large egg
1 tablespoon orange juice
1 teaspoon grated orange rind
1½ cups sifted flour
½ teaspoon baking powder
¼ teaspoon salt

Preheat the oven to 375°F.

In a medium-sized bowl, cream the butter and sugar together until fluffy. Add the egg and beat until the mixture is light in color.

Add the orange juice and orange rind. Stir gently. Add the flour, baking powder and salt and mix until well blended.

Drop the mixture by level teaspoonfuls onto ungreased baking sheets. Place the cookies 1½ inches apart and flatten them with the bottom of a glass that has been wrapped in cheesecloth that has been dipped in cold water and wrung out.

Bake for 7 to 8 minutes or until the edges are just lightly browned. Remove from the oven and transfer cookies to wire racks to cool.

—UNUSUAL COOKIES—

ALMOND STRIPS

makes 72 cookies

¾ cup sweet butter, softened
6 tablespoons sugar
½ teaspoon pure almond extract
2 cups sifted flour
⅛ teaspoon salt
1 egg white, lightly beaten
⅛ teaspoon ground cinnamon
⅓ cup finely chopped blanched almonds

In a medium-sized bowl cream together the butter and 4 tablespoons of the sugar. Add the almond extract and beat until light and fluffy. Add the flour and salt and mix well. Cover the bowl and chill for 2 to 3 hours or until firm.

Preheat the oven to 350°F. Mix the remaining 2 tablespoons sugar, the cinnamon and almonds in a small bowl. Set aside.

On a lightly floured board roll out the dough to ⅛-inch thickness. Using a pastry wheel, cut dough into strips 1 × 2 inches. Place cookies on unbuttered baking sheets and brush with the egg white. Sprinkle each cookie with the cinnamon, sugar and nut mixture.

Bake for 8 minutes. Remove from the oven and transfer cookies to wire racks. Store in tightly covered containers.

CHOCOLATE SPRITZ COOKIES

makes 36 cookies

1½ ounces unsweetened chocolate
½ cup sweet butter, softened
½ cup sugar
1 large egg
½ teaspoon pure vanilla extract
½ teaspoon pure almond extract
2 teaspoons milk
1½ cups sifted flour
½ teaspoon baking powder

In the top part of a double boiler melt the chocolate over hot but not boiling water.

In a bowl beat together the butter, sugar, egg, vanilla extract, almond extract, melted chocolate and milk until light and fluffy. Add the flour and baking powder and stir until smooth.

Preheat the oven to 400°F.

Fit a cookie press with the desired plate and fill the press with the dough. Press out the cookies 1 inch apart onto an unbuttered baking sheet. Repeat until all the dough is used.

Bake for 8 minutes or until set. Remove from the oven and transfer cookies to a wire rack. Cool completely. Store in airtight containers.

FINGER COOKIES

makes 42 cookies

⅔ cup sweet butter, softened
6 tablespoons sifted confectioners' sugar
1 teaspoon pure vanilla extract
½ teaspoon pure almond extract
2 cups sifted flour
¼ teaspoon salt
1 cup finely chopped pecans
sugar

Preheat the oven to 325°F.
In a medium-sized bowl cream together the butter and confectioners' sugar until light and fluffy. Add the vanilla extract, almond extract, flour, salt and chopped pecans. Mix until well blended.

Using your fingers, shape pieces of dough into fingers 2 inches long. Space cookies 2 inches apart on unbuttered baking sheets. Bake for 30 minutes or until edges are lightly browned.

Remove from the oven. Roll warm cookies in the sugar and then transfer to wire racks to cool.

GIANT CHOCOLATE THINS

makes 10 giant cookies

1 cup sweet butter, softened
1 cup sugar
1½ teaspoons pure vanilla extract
1 teaspoon salt
2 cups flour
16 ounces semisweet chocolate, cut into pieces
1 cup chopped walnuts

Preheat the oven to 350°F.
In a medium-sized bowl cream the butter until light. Gradually add the sugar, beating constantly. Add the vanilla extract and salt and beat to blend. Add the flour, chocolate pieces and chopped walnuts. Stir until well blended.

Form the cookies by measuring ½-cup portions of the dough and shaping it into 4-inch rounds. Space the cookies at least 4 inches apart on large buttered baking sheets.

Bake for 10 to 15 minutes or until the edges of the cookies begin to brown. Remove from the oven and transfer to wire racks to cool.

MOCHA STICKS

makes 72 cookies

1 cup sweet butter, softened
½ cup confectioners' sugar
2 teaspoons instant espresso powder
1½ cups flour
¼ cup ground walnuts
3 ounces semisweet chocolate
ground walnuts

Preheat the oven to 350°F. Line baking sheets with parchment paper or foil. Set aside.

In a medium-sized bowl cream together the butter and sugar until light and fluffy. Beat in the instant espresso powder. Add the flour and the ¼ cup ground walnuts. Mix until well blended.

Transfer dough to a pastry bag that has been fitted with a ½-inch tip and pipe into 2-inch lengths on unbuttered baking sheets. Bake for 10 to 15 minutes or until lightly golden brown. remove from the oven and transfer cookies to wire racks to cool.

Melt the chocolate in a heavy pan over low heat. Cool.

Dip each end of the cookie into the melted chocolate and then into the nuts. Allow chocolate to set. Store in airtight containers.

NUTTED MACAROONS

makes approximately 72 cookies

2 large egg whites
⅛ teaspoon salt
1 cup firmly packed dark brown sugar
1¼ cups firmly packed light brown sugar
2 cups coarsely chopped pecans
1 teaspoon pure vanilla extract
72 pecan halves

Preheat the oven to 350°F.

In a medium-sized bowl beat the egg whites and salt together until the whites are stiff but not dry.

Add the brown sugars slowly, beating constantly. Carefully fold in the chopped pecans and vanilla extract.

Working with floured hands, roll one teaspoon of dough at a time into a ball. Space the balls 3 inches apart on heavily buttered baking sheets. Flatten the cookie to about ½ inch thick. Press a pecan half on top of each macaroon.

Bake for 10 to 12 minutes. Remove from the oven and cool on sheets for 3 minutes before transferring to wire racks to cool. Store in airtight containers.

RICH BUTTER COOKIES

makes approximately 96 cookies

2 cups sifted flour
½ teaspoon baking powder
1 cup sweet butter, softened
8 ounces cream cheese, at room temperature
¼ cup sugar
2 tablespoons ground cinnamon
¼ cup sugar

Into a bowl sift together the flour and baking powder. Set aside.

In a medium-sized bowl cream together the butter and cream cheese. Add the sugar and beat until light and fluffy. Add the flour mix-

ture and stir until well blended. Shape the dough into a ball, wrap in foil and refrigerate 8 hours or overnight.

Preheat the oven to 375°F.

On a floured surface, roll out the dough to ⅛-inch thickness. Carefully cut the dough into 1½-inch squares. Place cookies 2 inches apart on unbuttered cookie sheets. Combine the cinnamon and the sugar and sprinkle each cookie with the cinnamon sugar.

Bake in the oven for 8 to 10 minutes or until golden. Remove from the oven and transfer to wire racks to cool.

SPRITZ COOKIES

makes 48 cookies

1 cup sweet butter, softened
1 cup sugar
2 egg yolks
1 teaspoon pure almond extract
2½ cups flour

Preheat the oven to 350°F.

In a large bowl cream the butter and sugar together until light and fluffy. Beat in the egg

yolks. When yolks are well blended, add the almond extract. Sift the flour into the mixture, a little at a time. Beat well after each addition.

Place the dough into a cookie press fitted with any shape. Press the shapes out 1 inch apart onto ungreased baking sheets.

Bake for 10 minutes or until lightly browned.

Remove from oven and transfer to cooling racks with a spatula. Cool completely. Store in tightly covered container.

SHORTBREAD

makes 24 wedges

4 cups flour
2 cups sweet butter, softened
1¼ cups confectioners' sugar
1 teaspoon baking powder
¼ teaspoon salt

Preheat the oven to 325°F.

In a large bowl combine the flour, butter, confectioners' sugar, baking powder and salt. Using your hands, mix the ingredients until well blended. The dough will be soft.

Evenly distribute dough between two 9-inch round pans. Pat down gently. Prick top of dough with fork all over.

Bake for 45 minutes or until golden. Remove from the oven. While the shortbread is warm cut it with a sharp knife into 12 equal wedges. Cool in pans on wire racks. Store shortbread in airtight containers.

WALNUT WEDGES

makes 40 cookies

2 cups flour
⅔ cup ground walnuts
1 cup softened sweet butter
½ cup confectioners' sugar
confectioners' sugar

Combine the flour and ground walnuts in a small bowl. Mix well.

In the large bowl of an electric mixer, cream the butter with the sugar until light and fluffy. Add the flour mixture, a little at a time, and mix until a firm dough forms. Cover the bowl with plastic wrap and refrigerate for 30 minutes.

Preheat the oven to 350°F. Generously butter two or more baking sheets.

Divide the dough into 10 equal pieces. Briefly knead one piece at a time until it is slightly softened. Roll the piece into a ball. Put the ball onto a prepared baking sheet and flatten it into a 4-inch round. With the back of a fork, press down the edges of the round. Prick the surface of the cookie all over with the fork. Score the round into quarters, but do not separate it. Repeat the above steps with the remaining dough.

Bake the rounds until well browned, about 20 minutes. Remove the cookies from the oven and cut them into wedges along the scored lines. Using a wide spatula, transfer the wedges to a wire rack. Sift confectioners' sugar over the cookies. Cool the cookies completely on the rack. Store in an airtight container.